CW00428014

CONTEMPORARY HISTORY IN CONTE)
Published in association with the Institute of Co

General Editor: Peter Catterall, Director, Institute of Contemporary
British History

Titles include:

Oliver Bange
THE EEC CRISIS OF 1963: Macmillan, De Gaulle, Adenauer and
Kennedy in Conflict

Christopher Brady
UNITED STATES FOREIGN POLICY TOWARDS CAMBODIA,
1977–92

Peter Catterall and Sean McDougall (*editors*)
THE NORTHERN IRELAND QUESTION IN BRITISH POLITICS

Helen Fawcett and Rodney Lowe (*editors*)
WELFARE POLICY IN BRITAIN: The Road from 1945

Harriet Jones and Michael Kandiah (*editors*)
THE MYTH OF CONSENSUS: New Views on British History,
1945–64

Wolfram Kaiser
USING EUROPE, ABUSING THE EUROPEANS: Britain and
European Integration, 1945–63

Spencer Mawby
CONTAINING GERMANY: Britain and the Arming of the Federal
Republic

Jeffrey Pickering
BRITAIN'S WITHDRAWAL FROM EAST OF SUEZ: The Politics of
Retrenchment

Len Scott
MACMILLAN, KENNEDY AND THE CUBAN MISSILE CRISIS:
Political, Military and Intelligence Aspects

Paul Sharp
THATCHER'S DIPLOMACY: The Revival of British Foreign Policy

Contemporary History in Context
Series Standing Order ISBN 0–333–71470–9
(*outside North America only*)

You can receive future titles in this series as they are published by placing a standing order.
Please contact your bookseller or, in case of difficulty, write to us at the address below with
your name and address, the title of the series and the ISBN quoted above.

Customer Services Department, Macmillan Distribution Ltd
Houndmills, Basingstoke, Hampshire RG21 6XS, England

Thatcher's Diplomacy

The Revival of British Foreign Policy

Paul Sharp
Professor of Political Science
University of Minnesota
Duluth

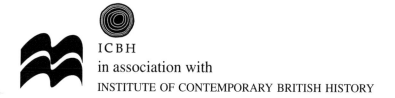

ICBH
in association with
INSTITUTE OF CONTEMPORARY BRITISH HISTORY

Published in Great Britain by
MACMILLAN PRESS LTD
Houndmills, Basingstoke, Hampshire RG21 6XS and London
Companies and representatives throughout the world

First edition 1997
Reprinted (with new preface) 1999

A catalogue record for this book is available from the British Library.

ISBN 0–333–65842–6 hardcover
ISBN 0–333–68810–4 paperback

Published in the United States of America by
ST. MARTIN'S PRESS, INC.,
Scholarly and Reference Division,
175 Fifth Avenue, New York, N.Y. 10010

ISBN 0–312–16440–8

Library of Congress Cataloging-in-Publication Data
Sharp, Paul, 1953–
Thatcher's diplomacy : the revival of British foreign policy /
Paul Sharp.
    p.   cm. — (Contemporary history in context series)
Includes bibliographical references and index.
ISBN 0–312–16440–8 (cloth)
1. Great Britain—Foreign relations—1945–   2. Conservative Party
(Great Britain)—History.   3. Thatcher, Margaret.   I. Title.
II. Series.
DA589.8.S53   1996
327.41'009'048—dc20   96–28748
                                                            CIP

This book is printed on paper suitable for recycling and made from fully managed and
sustained forest sources.

10   9   8   7   6   5   4   3   2   1
08   07   06   05   04   03   02   01   00   99

Printed and bound in Great Britain by
Antony Rowe Ltd, Chippenham, Wiltshire

For my parents

Contents

General Editor's Foreword

Mrs Thatcher came to power in 1979 with impeccable Cold War credentials, at a time when it was building towards a height, driven by the deployment of SS-20s and the West's decision to respond, both by corresponding missile deployments and increasing conventional military spending. The key decisions were taken during the preceding Labour government, although Mrs Thatcher's more robust approach to their implementation was undoubtedly welcomed in the Ministry of Defence. But this attitude reflected the continuing certainties of the Cold War in which Britain's room for manoeuvre in a divided world remained apparently strictly circumscribed. According to Paul Sharp, Thatcher, absorbed as she was by her domestic programme and difficulties, did not give much thought to appraising her foreign policy objectives and opportunities until the Falklands War in 1982. To some extent opportunities, with the exception of Rhodesia-Zimbabwe, meanwhile remained limited. Prospects for a thaw in East–West relations, for progress in South Africa or for new initiatives in Europe while the budget issue remained unsettled were not good.

By the time she fell from office, in contrast, she was arguably putting her international activities above an underestimated threat to her domestic political survival, being in Paris for the Conference on Security and Cooperation in Europe on the night of the fateful first leadership ballot. And it was on her foreign policy record that she concluded her defence of her government in the no-confidence debate that Labour then tabled. In the process she could look back, as Paul Sharp shows, on some solid achievements, as well as some significant failures. This book thus provides a valuable review of what became an important career as an international stateswoman at a time of great change.

The subject matter of that CSCE conference demonstrated that the Cold War, so palpable when she came to office, was by the close of her premiership in 1990 all but at an end. The structure of international capital and its impact upon Britain following the abolition of exchange controls in 1979, meanwhile also changed dramatically. This, perhaps as much as membership of the European Community, was to erode the scope of national sovereignty during Mrs Thatcher's years in Number Ten. But her response was rather different from her European partners. Instead of seeking to contain its effects by closer economic integration, she sought to further it by pursuing liberalization of capital and services in Europe more widely. This reflected in part quasi-Cobdenite notions of the merits of freer trade, both in economic and geopolitical terms. But it also reflected, paradoxically, calculations that Britain's interests would nevertheless be better served by such developments, certainly exemplified in the negotiation of the Single European Act.

She was able to pursue such aims in a world in which the bipolarities she inherited were of diminishing importance. Increasingly there seemed instead to be scope for pursuing an alternate vision of a liberal world economic order, in which states would have greater play for following their own particular interests. Indeed, it was the seductive promises of that liberal economic order, as much as the resolution which she from the beginning brought to the waging of the Cold War and continued to see as crucial to victory in it to the end, that helped to undermine the bipolar world order that had obtained since the 1940s. It is in this vision, founded upon her potent combination of economic liberalism and political nationalism, that Paul Sharp sees Mrs Thatcher's distinctive contribution to statecraft. In the process, though she may have started as something of an archetypal Cold Warrior, he argues persuasively that she in fact deserves a place for her role in mapping out the international politics of the post-Cold War era.

Peter Catterall
Institute of Contemporary British History
June 1996

Preface

This book is about foreign policy and diplomacy under Margaret Thatcher. These are, as Lucky Jim might have called them, 'strangely neglected topics' because of the thrust of international studies in recent years. Accordingly, I have deliberately tried to write an old-fashioned book treating countries, their policies and their interests as real, the way most people, including Thatcher, continue to think about them, while incorporating the insights of more systematic and more critical studies of foreign policy where these seem to be useful. The result, I hope, is a work which, though not uncritical in the details, makes a sympathetic assessment of what Thatcher and others were attempting to do. A more sympathetic approach to the predicaments of those to whom we give power and responsibility is long overdue in international studies and the social sciences in general, and this work may be viewed as both an attempt to help redress the balance and make a measure of personal atonement in this regard.

Many people have made this work possible. My thanks go first to several members of Thatcher's governments for their willingness to speak frankly about their role in and views of British foreign policy. Members and former members of the British Foreign Service in Ottawa, Chicago, New York, London and Ashburton were unfailingly helpful in providing me with interviews, information and perspectives. Too many colleagues to mention individually also gave great help, but I must single out two who at different times gave critical support, Professor Geoff Berridge of the Centre for the Study of Diplomacy at the University of Leicester and Professor Peter Nailor, former Provost of Gresham College. Peter provided the inspiration which led me into this field, and his death is a loss to us all. Finally, I owe a debt of thanks to the University of Minnesota for providing me with both the time and assistance to complete this project.

Paul Sharp

Preface to the 1999 Reprint

As one of the reviewers commented on the first edition, the trouble with strong personalities is that much of what they achieve passes with them when they exit the political stage. This was Bismarck's problem. No one else could operate his system. Not so with Thatcher. The future of Europe remains as uncertain as ever. Deepening, which she opposed, proceeds uncertainly, while widening, which she supported, proceeds apace. Insofar as the New Labour foreign policy of Blair and Cook has made its mark, it has not been by emphasizing human rights as its new lodestone. It has been by skilfully contributing its own voice, firm as but not identical to that of the United States, in the continuing efforts to contain Saddam Hussein.

Paul Sharp

Introduction

In undertaking this study of Margaret Thatcher's contribution to British foreign policy, I have two objectives in mind: to provide an account of her statecraft; and to make an assessment of the claim that she be regarded as an international statesman, someone who has had a decisive impact, not merely on the foreign policy of her own country, but on the conduct of international affairs in general.[1] Remarkably, given her public persona, this is not an aspect of Thatcher's political career which has received close scrutiny. Books about her are generally of two sorts: political biographies and studies of 'Thatcherism' – the set of principles about individuals, markets and the state upon which she believed modern, liberal democracies ought to be based. The biographies usually treat her international career as a source of corroborating evidence for the personal portrait, good or bad, which their authors wish to draw of her, while studies of 'Thatcherism' treat it primarily as a domestic phenomenon. Indeed, the relatively few books and articles which have been written by academics on Thatcher and British foreign policy have been at pains to emphasize both the minimal and the uninnovative character of her contribution to its substance.[2]

How is this sparse and generally unflattering treatment of her international record to be explained? Its root cause is the predisposition which exists among students of international relations to doubt that individuals can have a major impact on human affairs in general and foreign policy in particular. The latter they see as the product of complex bureaucracies functioning within increasingly dense networks of interdependent economic and political relationships between countries. At the same time, however, these same scholars see themselves as having to confront and debunk a powerful popular tradition in which world affairs are presumed to be shaped by virtuosos possessing the vision to create new orders and the guile to outwit their rivals. This 'great man (or woman)' tradition is one which politicians are quick to exploit, claiming powers they do not possess and taking responsibility for fortuitous events which they did not bring about. As a consequence, the scholars' resistance to it is often fuelled by their reluctance to gild the lilies of people who, together with their supporters, are quite capable of undertaking this process themselves.

Thatcher provides no exception to this tendency. One of the reasons why she assiduously cultivated an international reputation was to enhance her personal, political status, and she has suffered accordingly. However, in Thatcher's case, it must be added that the neglect is greater than usual because she is disliked. She is so partly because of the controversial character of her domestic agenda, one consequence of which was to alienate those who were most likely to write about her foreign policy, namely British academics, and possibly because many people found it hard to accept a woman wielding power in the way that Thatcher did. The principal reason for this hostility, however, was the impression which Thatcher often managed to convey that her political convictions, right or wrong, had been reached with insufficient agony of the soul. She either did not understand or she did not care about the full implications of, for example, closing down coal mines or confronting the Argentinians. In short, while Thatcher might have been involved in and, indeed, pivotal to some of the great events of our time, it could be claimed that she lacked the greatness and generosity of spirit, together with the real sense of history, possessed by the members of the pantheon of statesmen which it was all too clear she aspired to join.

These reasons for being reluctant to make an objective assessment of Thatcher's statesmanship no longer apply, and some of them never did. Most easily dismissed is the argument that her personality, in essence, disqualifies her from consideration as an international statesman. Public affairs and private matters should exist separately from one another. What matters, is whether or not policies are correct and not whether their author is capable of agonizing over all their consequences. Indeed, public displays of private emotion would only make difficult policies harder to undertake. As to whether Thatcher actually did agonize over the convictions to which she adhered in public, that it is nobody's business but hers and her family's. Almost as easily discounted is the claim that she used international affairs to build her own reputation. The fact that politicians exploit their international careers in this way does not preclude the possibility that they still may be international statesmen. Certainly, the possibilities realized by modern communications, together with the demands of modern democracy, have made it both easier and more necessary to create and project political images, such as the powerfully attractive one of being an international statesman. It would be a poor diplomatic historian, however, who claimed that Churchill and Roosevelt, or even Bismarck and Metternich, belonged to an era in which pure statesmanship, divorced from the sordid business of constructing a personal political image, prevailed. Indeed, image-building, inspiring confidence or deference among those with whom one worked, was always an ingredient of successful statesmanship. Now that Thatcher is out of office, therefore, the question to ask is not whether she used international affairs to gild her own lily, but, in so doing, what did she accomplish.

To ask it, of course, is to confront the original problem, the disposition against the twin ideas of the great statesman and virtuoso diplomacy. Does a study of the record of an individual, even a powerful one like Thatcher, contribute to a true understanding of international relations, an accurate explanation of why things, or some things, happen in the course of them, or a prescription for the conduct of foreign policy? When asked, in a now famous interview, what she had changed, Thatcher replied 'everything'. Her response was indicative, both of her personality and her belief in the individual or, at least, certain individuals. It was also untrue, and elaborations of the constraints under which policy is made by modern governments rightly make us highly sceptical of such claims. However, they should not be allowed to exclude the possibility a priori that particular individuals, in certain circumstances, can make critical, or even decisive, contributions to the course of events. Indeed, if the constraints on policy-makers are now greater than they used to be, then the ability of certain individuals to override them should be regarded as all the more remarkable and worthy of investigation.

Upon what, then, does Thatcher's international reputation rest? Three elements stand out: her relationship with Ronald Reagan and the strong support she gave to his Cold War policies; the successful war to recover the Falkland Islands; and her opposition to the European Community's (EC) plans for further integration. On the first, it may be said that Thatcher enabled Britain to play a long-established supporting role more effectively. By the second, she provided the country with a brief moment of modest glory. On the third, the central issue of British foreign policy, she devised a course which was both controversial and personally damaging. At best, it might be said that Thatcher pursued business as usual with a little more vim and vinegar, encouraging the country to stop exaggerating its 'impotence' and to start seeing itself as it really was:

...a middle power, given unusual influence by virtue of its historical distinction, skilled diplomacy and versatile military forces.[3]

At worst, she rallied national morale, which was valuable, but in a way which ultimately proved to be counterproductive.

This modest assessment, which uses Thatcher's own words from her memoirs, is shared by even many of the experts and professionals who are favourably disposed towards what Thatcher attempted. As it stands, it scarcely yields a record upon which to base a claim to international statesmanship. It is, however, both an inaccurate and overly modest assessment. It is inaccurate in that, in her years in office, Thatcher did not restore the confidence to reassert and exercise British influence. She did not, because she did not need to. One of the great success stories of postwar Britain was its ability, in the much-denied words of a recent foreign secretary, '...to punch above its weight' abroad no matter, by implication, how bad things got at home. In fact, this was a priority which Thatcher came to doubt, for, all too often, in her judgement, British influence was preserved at the expense of British interests.

Thatcher sought to redress this imbalance. She did so, principally, by rejecting the assumed consequences of what Wallace and Tugendhat have called the 'structural contradiction' facing all modern political communities. Most people live in and feel they belong to national political communities whose independence they value, and nearly everyone else aspires to do so. Everyone, however, increasingly depends on an international and integrated economic system to produce the things they want.[4] It is axiomatic for most foreign policy academics and professionals that the relationship between independence and prosperity possesses the qualities of a 'zero-sum' game. To maintain prosperity entails a country entering into commitments which reduce its political independence, while defending the latter has an economic cost. It is also widely assumed that the latter course of action is impractical because of the power of international capital, and undesirable because of the materialist and consumer priorities of most people.

Thatcher was able to reject this portrayal of the relationship between prosperity and independence because she was both an economic liberal and a political nationalist, a rare combination in both political and intellectual life, although as common as anything on the high street. The economic consequences of this combination are well known. At home, Thatcher sought to free the operations of the market from government intervention, while abroad she supported measures to open the international economy and resisted those designed to achieve state-managed regional integration. The political consequences, however, for British foreign policy have received far less attention. Instead of seeking to transform the British state into a modest and practical vehicle for managing the common external affairs of the bourgeoisie, Thatcher tried to restore it as a liberal great power, committed to a few vital international principles and its own, independently defined, national interests.

The combination of political nationalism and economic liberalism at the heart of Thatcher's statecraft has caused analysts a great deal of trouble. Her more virulent political opponents regarded it simply as a populist fraud. Those on the left believed Thatcher to be a flag-waver who was actually prepared to sell her country to the highest bidder. Those on the right saw her as willing to play the nationalist card and damage the country's long-term economic prospects if she believed this would help her get re-elected. Most analysts, however, simply regarded the combination as a prescription for incoherence made possible by Thatcher's inability to see the inherent tension which existed between the two. She might claim to be an economic liberal, but she was flawed by a most unliberal and emotional attachment to her own understanding of Britain's past. In the critics' view, Thatcher either hankered for, or sought to exploit, those who hankered for a world of independent states in which Britain played a leading role.

In fact, it was those who posited the irreconcilability of the tension between prosperity and independence who were soon to be exposed to the charge of living in the past. The world to which they claimed Thatcher had failed to adjust was one of increasing levels of economic integration directed and regulated by multilateral and supranational agencies. Their mistake was to see this process as almost entirely resulting from the dynamics of welfare economics and technology, seasoned by a sense among policy elites of the failures of nationalism and the desire for a better, more peaceful world. What they failed to take into account was the extent to which this order had been brought about as a matter of policy by the superpowers. The United States (US), in particular, had worked for such a system in Europe, utilizing both its material and ideological predominance, at the start of the Cold War, and the discipline of that great contest had done much to keep the system in place.

With the decline of the Cold War and ultimate collapse of the USSR, many of the constraints and incentives which kept this system in place also began to disappear, greatly expanding the opportunities for more autonomous action of many states, but most notably the European great powers.

Thatcher was the first to discover these opportunities or, more accurately, have some of them thrust upon her by the Falklands War in 1982. Until then, she had not been interested in foreign policy, but provided with confidence and status by that success, she applied her assumptions and preferences about political nationalism and economic liberalism to British foreign policy with great, if imperfect, success. It is upon this discovery and her willingness to act upon it, that Thatcher's claim to being regarded as an international statesman rests. Her vision of an international order sustained by liberal great powers acting in accordance with their national interests is sparse and disappointing to those who hope for much more. Put into practice, however, it offers a greater prospect for peace and prosperity than the present dense networks of collaboration which were established during the Cold War, which, now lacking leadership and compulsion, are increasingly lacking in direction.

The book is effectively divided into three sections. The first explores one of the central themes of postwar British foreign policy, the pursuit of influence in the face of decline, before examining the way in which Thatcher's distinctive approach to foreign policy was formed by both her convictions and her experience in office. The second section considers the two aspects of Thatcher's statecraft for which she is widely known: her American policy; and her policies on the future of Europe and Britain's place in it. The third and final section considers Thatcher's response to the end of the Cold War, focusing on her attempts to restore the Anglo-Soviet relationship and to prevent or, at least slow, the process of German unification.

1 The Pursuit of Influence

The underlying and fundamental fact which confronted those responsible for Britain's postwar foreign policy was the country's decline as a world power.[1] Between 1945 and 1979, Britain's share of the world's trade, merchant shipping, overseas investments and gross product all shrank dramatically. Over the same period, the Empire, as any sort of cohesive force in international politics, disappeared, and Britain became dependent on the US for advanced military technology, most notably the delivery systems for its nuclear warheads. It is true that this process had begun long before 1945, but until the Second World War it had been possible for British governments to act in public as if it were not happening. It is also true that, even as Britain's external decline accelerated after 1945, the country retained a highly developed industrial base and that its population of over 55 million people came to enjoy the highest standard of living in the history of the country. Even in the midst of this new prosperity, however, Britain's ability to afford the level of armed forces and military equipment commensurate with its desired status as a world power continued to shrink relative to their spiralling costs.

If the facts of Britain's international decline were quite clear, however, its significance, causes and remedy were far less so. It may be that the rise and fall of the British empire will eventually come to be seen as one episode, and plausibly an aberrant one, in a history which is much longer. Since the sixteenth century alone, for example, the country has experienced several rises and falls, together with extended periods of ordinariness. Perhaps, a willingness to view the present in terms other than the nineteenth-century ascendancy and its long drawn-out aftermath is emerging. Understandably, however, most of the people, including Thatcher, who lived through the decline assumed that something had gone wrong and that the reasons were to be found within the country. It has been argued, for example, by some political economists that Britain ultimately suffered from being the first to industrialize and making the mistakes from which others could learn, without having a model itself. Both owners and workers seemed to retain a measure of pre-capitalist hostility to the new middle–class value placed on efficiency, risk-taking and the acquisition of social status through the creation of personal wealth. Workers, for example, treated any attempt to improve productivity as a threat to their jobs. The owners of capital preferred to follow their merchant forbears in investing abroad rather than renewing Britain's industrial base, and the brightest went into finance, administration and the arts rather than the applied sciences upon which prosperity depended. As a consequence, according to this view, Britain was unable or unwilling to learn from rivals like Germany and the US and catch up with them as they had originally caught up with Britain.[2]

Others, however, have been sceptical of these social explanations and have preferred to attribute Britain's decline to the poor quality of its political and military leadership. Correlli Barnett, for example, has excoriated Britain's leaders both for what he regards as the incompetent character of their education policy and their commitment to the Empire. His argument is that the latter constituted a major drain on British power which eventually precipitated its collapse.[3] Anthony Verrier, in a similar vein, claims that Britain's postwar foreign policy has continued to be guided by the looking-glass values of its intelligence service which were moulded by the 'great game' of imperial competition on the North West Frontier and in the Arabian desert in the nineteenth century.[4] The poor quality of Britain's leadership, if such it was, could of course be explained by reference to the peculiar circumstances of Britain's industrialization outlined above. However, the implication in the work of writers such as these is that Britain's leaders had real choices to make and that the correct policy would have averted the decline and subsequent collapse of British power.

This is, of course, not so. Internal factors could only affect the rate of Britain's decline as a world power, not the fact that it was happening. Even with the most wise governments and most patriotic of investors and workers, Britain could not have hoped to maintain its dominant position in the world once its 'productive edge'[5] as the first power to industrialize had been lost. Then, declining strength made it impossible to hold on to the Empire, and when this was gone, so too were the protected markets and privileged access to raw materials which cushioned Britain from the effects of its inability to compete with larger, more modern rivals. In short, Britain declined as a world power because of the emergence of other countries such as Germany, the US, the USSR and eventually Japan, with larger and often more modern economies. Their economic size and strength gave them a potential for world power which Britain could not hope to match, let alone master. Given that Britain's relative decline was inevitable, therefore, the important question to ask is how successive British governments responded to it.

INDEPENDENCE AND INFLUENCE IN POSTWAR BRITISH FOREIGN POLICY

In 1945, those responsible for the conduct of British foreign policy faced three options. First, they could have accepted that Britain's present weaknesses were permanent and attempted to retire the country from the world stage. Secondly, they could have sought a more modest role as one of the new middle powers, no longer attempting to define and uphold the international order, but making a worthy contribution to its maintenance as a junior partner to the US or 'helpful fixer' at the United Nations (UN). Thirdly, and assuming that Britain would enjoy some sort of recovery from war time exhaustion, they could have tried to maintain a narrower version of the country's role as a great power enjoying the highest levels of international involvement and influence. There was a putative fourth and final option, acting as a world power as if nothing had changed, but although postwar British governments have often been accused of doing this, as we shall see, the charge is unfair.

The first option, retirement, was never seriously considered, even by those on the political left who opposed British imperialism. Everyone assumed that Britain would, and ought to, remain internationally involved in some sort of leadership capacity. It had to, for while Britain's means for making its way in the world had been reduced, its interests and many of its commitments remained the same. Britain was a trading power which paid for what it could not make itself by the export of goods and services. As ever, therefore, it depended on a stable, peaceful international order within which its commerce could be transacted, and, as recent history had shown, such orders neither came about nor were they maintained of their own accord. They depended on one or more countries with the power and political will to defend them from those who, rightly or wrongly, believed they did poorly from the existing state of affairs and sought to overthrow it.

This argument is not as self-evident as it seemed at the time. Many, indeed most, countries shared Britain's interest in a stable international order but this did not impel them to become leading powers with great international influence. Indeed, some, such as Sweden and the Netherlands, for example, had even enjoyed their moments in the sun like Britain, before retiring, apparently with good grace, to concentrate on becoming rich while their successors shouldered the burden of maintaining the international political order which made this possible. To make the retirement option even more attractive for Britain, it was not even being faced by a hostile takeover. The new leader, the US, was a country with which Britain was supposed to enjoy a 'special relationship' formed by ties of history, culture and kinship. Retirement was discounted, however, because these considerations paled into insignificance when compared to other factors which seemed more obvious at the time. The Second World War may have destroyed Britain's international position just as surely as it did Germany's and France's, but this is not how it seemed in 1945. Unlike them, and unlike the apparently willing retirees, Sweden and the Netherlands, Britain had not been crushed by war, but had emerged on the winning side possessing, apparently, considerable reserves of strength. In addition to being undefeated, the country was still treated as one of the Big Three by the US and the USSR. Much of the empire was still in place, and there were still hopes for the Commonwealth as a democratized but effective successor to it.

The wartime generation of British political leaders was well aware of this strength, but they were also impressed by the fact that this strength alone had not saved the international order. Britain's contribution to the defeat of the Axis powers had been vital, but not because of its power, which alone was insufficient to defeat even Germany, but because it had possessed the political will to stay in the contest and provide a rallying point for those opposed to Hitler until others, more powerful, could be drawn into the contest. By 1945, it seemed clear that the USSR would constitute the next grave threat to the international order upon which British interests were held to depend, and that the US was vacillating again about staying involved in world affairs. To help counter this threat and stiffen American resolve might not be easy and certainly would be costly to Britain, but as a great and civilized power, the country could do no less if it was to undertake its responsibilities properly.

Retirement being out of the question, the issue became on what terms Britain should remain internationally involved. The option of junior partner to the UN or US, whichever established itself as the guardian of the open, liberal international order favoured by Britain, was never seriously countenanced. The country was too strong to restrict itself to making practical contributions like peacekeepers and technical assistance to commitments determined multilaterally in New York and, besides, that opportunity never fully materialized. However, even a junior partnership of this type with the US was unattractive. The British knew that, while exercising the responsibilities of being a great power could be onerous at times, the privileges, in terms of shaping the international order in accordance with one's own preferences, were considerable for those who could afford to do so. Postwar British leaders desired neither to lose those benefits nor to see them exercised exclusively by someone else, even so friendly a country as the US.

For although the British had been extremely relieved when Roosevelt, with considerable help from the Japanese and the Germans, had finally persuaded the Americans to enter the war, this development was not without its problems for them. The American executive, at least, had expressed clear preferences about how the postwar world ought to be organized around open economies and a monetary system of freely convertible currencies, neither of which augured well for Britain. Its wealth had come to depend upon preferential relations with the Commonwealth and the empire. These served as a base for its operations in the rest of the world, in which, naturally, the British were as firm supporters as the Americans of 'openness'.[6] During the war, the US had pointed out the contradiction in this position and had imposed conditions upon its assistance to Britain during the war. It was to be used neither to build up the imperial system nor to free up Britain's own resources for this purpose. Also, Britain had given undertakings about supporting America's postwar economic aims, the content and specificity of which quickly came into dispute. The Americans had not pushed the point, but it was clear that once the war was over, their generosity was likely to be less forthcoming.[7]

Given these fears about American intentions, therefore, and Britain's own reluctance to give up the privileges of leadership, only the third option remained. Britain, its postwar leaders determined, needed to retain as much independent influence as it could in the postwar international order. To this end, it had to retain its customary high level of international involvement even if it could barely afford it, while it rebuilt the political and economic foundations of the influence it had enjoyed before the war. This decision did not betray, as some have argued, a complete failure to recognize the country's new and reduced circumstances[8]. On the contrary, it was a deliberate response to them. No doubt, most members of the first postwar government of Clement Attlee shared the sentiment expressed earlier by Churchill when he declared that he had not become prime minister to preside over the destruction of the British empire and all that this implied about the country's rightful place in the scheme of things. No one, however, who had served in the government during the war and had witnessed, during those six years, the transfer of Allied leadership from Britain to the US, could doubt that Britain's international position had been greatly changed for the worse. The questions to which they sought answers, however, were: in the long-term, how much of it could be recovered; and, in the short-term, how could the ongoing loss of influence be staunched.

FROM POSTWAR TO COLD WAR: ATTLEE AND BEVIN

The principal architects of the answers to these question were Attlee's foreign secretary, Ernest Bevin, and his senior foreign policy advisers. The country's best interests, they argued, would be served by rebuilding it as an independent centre of power in the world with its own agenda and position on the great questions of international politics. An independent Britain was not only good in itself, they reasoned. It would also be more use to America when the latter was right, and a useful counter or corrective to it when it was not. Even on the left of the party, people like Aneurin Bevan argued that the government could not neglect the country's imperial and international roles, for to do so would be to hand the 'emotional leadership of the country to the fascists'.[9] And everyone agreed that the government should seek to capitalize on both the country's success in the war and Churchill's claim that Britain alone stood at the intersection of the three great circles of Western influence: the Atlantic community with North America, Europe and the Commonwealth. These were assets too good to write off.[10]

The immediate challenge, however, was to find a way of sustaining Britain's extensive contribution to the maintenance of international order, even though the country was exhausted by the costs of the war and on the verge of bankruptcy. Commitments had to be met both for substantive reasons and, the government believed, to preserve Britain's reputation as a responsible and independent great power. The unstated premise of this concern was that, once lost, such a reputation would be almost impossible to recover. The reasoning behind this concern may have been internally consistent, but it was based upon a faulty premise which resulted in very damaging consequences for postwar British foreign policy. The premise was that scope existed for secondary hegemons independently defining the international order in what they judged to be their own regional spheres of influence. It scarcely did. During the Cold War, one could oppose a superpower or work with it, but neither of them showed much tolerance of independent thought or action on issues of general international order, once the process of decolonization was firmly under way.

One consequence, therefore, was that far from enhancing national prestige, attempts to act as an independent great power resulted in embarrassments and at least one humiliation as the country overreached its resources and had to be rescued or disciplined by the Americans. A second was that the great power priority was retained long after it became clear that no recovery on the scale hoped for was ever going to materialize. The material costs of this mistake, in terms of national resources committed to diplomatic and military policies, have been overemphasized. There is little to suggest that had Britain spent less on them then it would have developed a more competitive industrial and financial base better capable of defending the country's share of world trade. What it is hard to overestimate, however, is the extent to which this commitment prevented a clear reappraisal of the kind of country Britain was becoming during the Cold War, with the consequence that its foreign policy objectives and national interests increasingly began to diverge.

Nevertheless, the period began well. Under Attlee's government, Britain managed to shed certain major external commitments which it no longer could maintain at an acceptable price, for example, to India, Palestine and Greece, and it did so without major damage to its reputation as a great power.[11] Its role as a major and active participant in the international organizations established at the end of the war was maintained, and American pressure to open up Britain's preferential commercial system was fairly successfully resisted, although this did not prevent the continuing loss of markets to American competition. In military matters, at least, the lesson of the Second World War that Britain could stand alone for a time, but do little else, seemed particularly well learned. At Bevin's urging, Britain entered into treaty commitments with the France and the Benelux countries, aimed initially against the chance of a resurgent Germany. As perceptions of a Soviet threat to western Europe matured in 1948–9, however, these treaties were expanded into the North Atlantic Alliance, thereby satisfying the central objective of Bevin's foreign policy, to obtain an American commitment to western Europe's defence.

However, alliance building went hand-in-hand with attempts to restore an independent power base from which to exercise British influence. At home, austerity and the associated depressing of domestic consumption in favour of exports put the country on a firmer financial footing despite the unhelpful monetary policy of the US. The role of sterling as a reserve currency, the sterling area and the system of preferential trading relations with the Commonwealth were all retained and, in the absence of American assistance after 1945, Attlee's government also committed Britain to the development of its own nuclear weapons. Most tellingly in this regard, however, Indian independence did not presage a complete retreat from Britain's overseas possessions. Some of them, such as the African colonies, were regarded as not yet ready for such a step, and others, for example positions in the Mediterranean, the Middle East, the Persian Gulf and South East Asia, were regarded as militarily or commercially too valuable, whether they were ready or not. In these areas, forces and bases were retained, and even in those territories for which independence was envisaged in the near future, it was assumed that a sizeable British 'presence' in terms of political and military advisors, commercial operations and cultural links would remain.

When Churchill's Conservatives replaced the Labour government in 1951, it could be reasonably claimed that when Britain spoke, either with friends or to rivals, it did so as a modern, industrial power which was independently procuring the latest military means and was at the centre of a system of states bound by reasons of history, sentiment and practical self-interest who looked to Britain for leadership on questions of international importance. It was clear that this fortunate state of affairs had been made possible by a remarkable recovery at home, coupled with the skilful exercise of a

British diplomacy to which considerable economic and military resources had been committed. The extent to which this great mobilization of effort could realize the objectives set for it remained uncertain. However, if the Labour government had set the broad outlines of postwar foreign policy and tried to put it on a firm economic footing, then who better than Churchill and Eden to execute it? Both had experience of statecraft in far more difficult circumstances on far less substantial means, and neither shared the inhibitions of their Labour predecessors about the idea of Britain as a great power exercising international influence in pursuit of its own interests.

By all accounts, Churchill was past his best, but this did not prevent him attempting to resuscitate the old wartime intimacy of prime minister to president with Eisenhower and making an independent *démarche* towards the USSR directed at easing East–West relations.[12] Eden, as foreign secretary, gave his name to the plan by which British forces were cemented into a 'continental commitment', both completing a fundamental shift in Britain's defence policy and resolving, or *finessing*, a crisis in the organization of western European security.[13] At the same time, however, the process of withdrawal from overseas commitments became more grudging and the prime minister made clear (in a way in which he had not as leader of the opposition) his government's attitude towards European unification and Britain's place firmly outside any developments in that direction.[14] Churchill escaped the full consequences of his reluctance to disengage from the wider world and move closer to Europe. His successors, however, did not, and while Eden was prime minister, two episodes occurred which provided clear evidence that something was seriously wrong with the assumptions upon which the government was trying to conduct its foreign policy.

SUEZ AND EUROPE

The first of these was a crisis precipitated by Egypt's nationalization of the Suez Canal in July 1956, a month after the British had vacated their military base there. The origins of the crisis are complex and have been well covered elsewhere.[15] At the heart of the matter, however, was Arab nationalism's need to assert itself and the fear which this caused in Britain and its allies, both of the phenomenon itself and the threat they judged it posed to more material interests. Eden argued that Nasser, the Egyptian leader, should be made to give up the Canal, by force if necessary. Its commercial and strategic importance to the West was such that the Canal could not be left in the hands of a potentially hostile and incompetent operator. Besides, Eden added, were Nasser not stopped, he would, like Hitler before him, be encouraged to commit further aggressions, while a defeat might topple him. The Americans disagreed. They objected to the seizure, but believed that using force would harm their interests more than a compromise which left Nasser's dignity intact, or even no agreement at all. As a consequence, Eden entered into a collaboration with the French and the Israelis who, in addition to agreeing with Eden's analysis, had their own reasons for attacking Egypt. Israel, they agreed, would commence hostilities, and the other two would join in on the pretext of intervening to separate the warring parties.

The plan was put into operation in November, 1956. The Anglo-French forces landed, but after only 48 hours, in the face of severe criticism in Britain and from most of the Commonwealth and under intense American pressure, the British government called the operation off and accepted a UN ceasefire. The affair was a disaster for Eden's government, for virtually every aspect of the intervention from its anachronistic justifications to its deceptive and drawn-out execution was open to question. Of all these, perhaps the most telling is to ask what Eden proposed to do had the operation actually been allowed to succeed and British forces returned to the bases which they had vacated as being too costly and troublesome to maintain only months before.[16] With all its faults, however, a neglected fact is that, in its own narrow terms, the policy of using force at Suez was succeeding when the operation was suspended. Britain, the responsible great power, had intervened in accordance with its independent judgement of the requirements of international order. By calling the operation off, however, Eden's government accepted that those requirements were no longer for Britain to define. An attempt was made to show that Britain and France had merely led the way before handing over to the UN, but everyone knew that Britain, at least, accepted the judgement that its actions, not Nasser's, were the problem. Sound policy or not, the British government had lacked the nerve to see it through, and it was this which left a lasting impression, not least, according to her memoirs, upon Thatcher herself.

Spectacular though the Suez failure was, however, it must still be seen as a symptom, rather than a cause, of British foreign policy's problems. The government's concern to preserve Britain's good standing in the international community had a profound influence upon its response to pressure from that source. Eden might have pressed on. Some observers, certainly the French and reputedly members of the Eisenhower administration, expressed surprise when he did not, and a narrower conception of British national interests might have suggested that, once committed, pulling back would be the worst thing Britain could do. A narrower conception, however, would have kept Britain out in the first place because it was clear that such operations imposed a great strain on its means. Suez merely confirmed this in the most humiliating and confidence-sapping way. The conclusion drawn was that in future, Britain could use force in support of its political objectives only in conjunction with the Americans, as in Jordan two years later, or with their prior approval, as when it assembled a force to deter an Iraqi threat to Kuwait in 1961. This remained axiomatic for the next quarter of a century until, that is, Argentina invaded the Falkland Islands in 1982.

Far more damaging to British interests in the long run was the impact of Britain's sense of itself and its international responsibilities on the Conservative government's European policy, in particular the issue of joining the European Economic Community (EEC). In this case, the vacillations which again characterized British policy were not merely symptoms but also the causes of major problems. The enthusiastic support which postwar British governments gave to schemes for organizing western Europe's collective defence was not extended to the attempts to create an economic and, possibly, political union. The British certainly had no objection in principle to strengthening western European economic cooperation. For reasons of conviction and self-interest, however, what they wanted was a European Free Trade Area which would increase trade between European states without discriminating against outsiders. The members of the Community, in contrast, wished to establish a customs union which would place a common tariff wall around all the members. Within this a system of price supports would be established to maintain the member states' agriculture which was, by and large, small scale, inefficient and politically influential. To participate in such a system, Britain would have had to break its preferential economic ties with the rest of the Commonwealth, losing its access to their cheaper food and agricultural products, and put an end to the system by which it subsidized its own agriculture.[17]

Subsequent experience with the Community showed that once the political will existed on both sides, an applicant might haggle about the strictly economic terms of entry until agreement was reached on exemptions and derogations from the normal rules of operation. Both the British and French, however, lacked this political will to reach such an agreement. For the former, the political implications and significance of joining such a group posed apparently insurmountable problems. The predisposition towards 'pragmatism' in the outlook of Conservative politicians and the Foreign Office alike led them to suspect that any scheme for creating a political authority over the European nations was doomed to failure and disappointment. Such a union would almost certainly founder on the rocks of the national sovereignties of the members and leave them feeling more hostile towards each other than if they had never attempted such an enterprise. If, on the other hand, the scheme succeeded, then the British would like it even less, for such a success could only mean that its members' sovereignty had been lost to another centre of power, whether this was supranational or, worse, national in its character.

More important, however, than any fear of the consequences of membership, was a sense that Britain, 'with Europe, but not of it' to use Churchill's phrase, did not need to be a member of the Community.[18] Britain had not undergone the experience of conquest shared by France, Germany and Italy because it did not share their situations as vulnerable land powers. And Britain remained a force in the world precisely because it did not share their primarily European orientations. Its influence was derived from the fact that Europe was but one focus for its policy. Eden's, and then Macmillan's, government attempted to persuade the others of their view that a looser European Free Trade Area would be preferable to a customs union with aspirations to political and economic union, but were unsuccessful. The 'Europeans' completed their negotiations by the Rome treaties in 1957 and established the EEC. In 1959, Britain and several smaller European countries formed a free trade association which satisfied British preferences for protecting their own agriculture and Commonwealth food imports, and from within this they attempted to negotiate a merger of the two groups into a free trade area. The negotiations had little prospect for success and within two years the worsening condition of the British economy led the Macmillan government to reverse its policy and seek membership of the EEC.

Britain's failure to 'get in on the ground floor' of setting up the EEC is often presented as *the* great mistake of postwar British foreign policy. Supporters of membership argue that a promising future in the Community was sacrificed by Eden and Macmillan to defend relationships which were in terminal decline. Worse, by the time Britain finally did join in 1973, its position had greatly weakened, it had damaged its reputation among its friends in Europe and the best times in terms of impressive economic growth rates were over. Even many of those less convinced of the 'European idea' at the time came to believe that Britain had missed a great opportunity by not joining at the beginning. Had it done so, then it might have been able to effect the development of a Community with lower supranational ambitions for its institutions and fewer common policies of the kind which the British regarded as being harmful to their interests.

The debates about whether Britain missed a great opportunity, and what kind of opportunity it actually was, cannot be resolved. Clearly, there was a life for Britain both inside and outside the Community. Again, however, what really hurt British interests was the same sort of vacillation which had permeated the Suez adventure. Macmillan in particular has been given much credit for persuading the Conservative party to accept the difficult adjustments which had to be made to bring Britain's overseas commitments into balance with its reduced ability to maintain them. If the withdrawal from Africa and other colonial commitments signalled by the famous 'wind of change speech' represented a considered, strategic choice on his part, however, then the decision to apply for membership of the EEC in 1961 did not. By then, Britain's poor economic performance was translating into direct pressure on Macmillan's own political position, and his own aspiration to mediate East–West relations had been thwarted by both superpower summitry and the troubles to which it gave rise.[19] The decision to take Britain 'into Europe', therefore, was a dramatic initiative designed to solve (or even obscure) immediate economic and political problems. Accordingly, it was not presented as a strategic shift in the country's external orientation, but rather as a way of permitting Britain to continue doing what it had been doing, only more effectively.

Precisely for this reason, the French blocked Britain's application. To do so, de Gaulle accepted at face value the British claim that they were not like the rest of Europe and, hence, as far as France was concerned, they were not ready for membership of it. The result, to paraphrase Macmillan, was bad for Europe but worse for Britain. Just as a British government had nerved itself to take actions which implied that they no longer found sustainable the country's postwar role as an independent great power with international responsibilities, they had effectively been told that it was this or nothing for the time being. There was some comfort for Macmillan in his close relationship with President Kennedy, as a result of which a senior British diplomat was privy to American deliberations during the Cuban missile crisis. Clearly, Britain remained closer to the high political centre of gravity in world affairs than many other countries – France, for example, to the latter's perpetual chagrin.

Macmillan's other American triumph, however, the delivery of American Skybolt missiles, and when these were cancelled, the substitution of Polaris missiles and submarine technology to deliver British nuclear warheads, underlined the country's inability to stay in the front rank of military power without outside help. American sympathy and help were inadequate and, possibly, unhelpful compensations for the failure to become a member of the EEC. They did not provide an alternative to membership. The display of Anglo-Saxon intimacy provided fuel for de Gaulle's campaign against the British, and even the US was no source of comfort. It had always made it clear that Britain was more use to it in Europe than outside it. Had Britain joined at the start, it might have effectively influenced the subsequent development of the Community. Had it determined to stay out, it might eventually have secured the market access it required by arrangements short of full membership. By refusing to join, changing its mind and exposing the country to rejection, however, the Macmillan government effectively consigned British foreign policy to limbo for the next twelve years.

THE END OF BRITISH FOREIGN POLICY?

The complaint of Richard Crossman, minister in the Wilson government, that by the 1970s British foreign policy was all 'fish and Rhodesia' may have been unfair, but it does capture the sense of irrelevance pervading the enterprise. The spectacle of some of the most sophisticated anti-submarine frigates in the world escorting trawlers in Icelandic fishing grounds suggested a large gap between what Britain was good at and what it was important to be good at in the contemporary international system. The protracted negotiations started by Macmillan over Rhodesia, a place in which Britain's material interests were not nearly commensurate with the diplomatic and political time and effort invested by ultimately six different governments, seemed to underline the extent to which British foreign policy addressed and, indeed, belonged to a world which was coming to an end. The Labour government of Harold Wilson, elected in 1964, had made a great point of its predecessor's dated approach to problems both at home and abroad, juxtaposing the Conservative's allegedly 'Edwardian' priorities and sense of privilege with its own meritocratic 'modernity'. According to Wilson, Britain's problems stemmed from the antiquated process by which its future leaders were selected and educated. Therefore, educational, social and institutional reforms would be directed at creating workers, managers and administrators of a new type, enabling Britain to prosper abroad by innovation and technological leadership.[20]

To make its point, the new government identified the Foreign Office as an example of the problems it was talking about, and asked it to take a more direct interest in supporting Britain's export drive. Beyond this, however, Wilson's strategy seemed to have few implications for British foreign policy, and continuity appeared the chief priority of the government. Nuclear weapons were retained, despite commitments in opposition to the contrary, and the application for membership of the EEC was renewed with the same result. France said no, and although the application was left 'on the table', British foreign policy was powerless to remedy this state of affairs until French policy or the French leadership changed. To be sure, there was much going on besides 'fish and Rhodesia'. The declaration of independence by the white minority regime in the British colony had created a major international issue in which Britain was centrally involved, both in southern Africa and at the UN. Other Commonwealth disputes, between India and Pakistan and in Nigeria, demanded a British response which Wilson, in particular, seemed glad to make, and he also attempted a mediation to end the Vietnam war.

There were, however, few successes. In the subcontinent, British efforts were upstaged by Soviet diplomacy, and Britain's support for the government in the Nigerian civil war prompted criticism at home and abroad because of the conditions of the people in Biafra. Wilson's East–West intervention maintained his predecessors' record of declining effectiveness, succeeding mainly in annoying the Americans. And even the Rhodesian negotiations succeeded only in averting the full wrath of the Commonwealth and obtaining some good copy of Wilson meeting the rebel leader Ian Smith on British warships in the Mediterranean. To add to the sense of failure, much of the government's attention was devoted to withdrawing from external commitments which the country could no longer afford. Most notably, the decision was made to withdraw British forces from Singapore and the Persian Gulf, in spite of heavy American pressure to remain. It was so, however, not as part of any coherent strategy, but as a hasty response to the demands of an economic crisis which was confronting the government, a crisis which had been exacerbated, if not caused, by the attempt to maintain another great power commitment, the role of sterling as an international reserve currency.

Thus, no attempt was made to cover the substantive retreat by providing an acceptable version of the 'Little England' concept with which to give a new coherence to British foreign policy. Instead, the global rhetoric of the independent great power with a world role was retained. Wilson, for example, declared that Britain's frontiers rested on the Himalayas, and that it was a world power or it was nothing, such claims serving as both a compensation for Britain's failure to get into the EC and as a *quid pro quo* for membership.[21] Let us in, was the implicit argument, and we get market access together with a new power base commensurate with our global ambitions, while you get all the benefits of Britain's diplomatic connections, its experience in international leadership and the technological prowess to which Wilson attached so much importance. Indeed, to sustain the country's international position, it might now need the Community's resources, but once in, according to George Brown, the foreign secretary, Britain's job would be to lead it.[22]

Like its predecessors, the Wilson government presented the question of Britain's membership as one finely balanced. Only after 1967 did it maintain that the 'balance of the advantage' lay with joining. Edward Heath's Conservative government, elected in 1970, was far more enthusiastic. Unlike Wilson, Heath had no record of opposition to the EEC to explain. Indeed, he had conducted the negotiations at the time of the first application, and he argued that

Britain's survival as a prosperous country depended on the improved access to markets and stimulus of competition which only membership of the EEC could confer. European enthusiast though he was, however, Heath still maintained that Britain could simultaneously obtain the benefits of EEC membership and remain the independent force in world politics which it had always been. Heath too saw Britain as a leader or the leader of a European bloc in world affairs. However, the principal difference between them was that while his predecessors saw membership as a desirable component of Britain's international position, Heath saw it as the only way to retain the country's standing.[23]

Politicians, of course, are creatures of politics as well as policy, and much of what they said about British foreign policy was constrained by the expectations of the electorate. If maintaining that EEC membership would in no way diminish Britain's capacity to operate as an independent great power was what it took to convince a cautious and conservative electorate to give its assent, then so be it. Nevertheless, the fact that the claim was made reflected more than just the ambiguity in Britain's commitment to Europe which existed at all levels of society. It was also the product of a growing sense among the political, economic and intellectual elites of the country that British foreign policy, as such, did not matter much any more. There was not much future for it, because there was not much future for Britain as an independent state, nor, indeed, for foreign policy or independent states in general.

Crossman's dismissal of British foreign policy and Heath's celebration of the potential of a new European superpower under British guidance, were examples of this growing doubt about the future of states and nations, and also the degree of apparent equanimity with which many faced the prospect. Both men were of the generation which had directly experienced the consequences of nationalist passions unleashed in the service of the state during the world wars. The prevailing view was that the idea of the sovereign national state had originated in Europe, exhausted it, and eventually brought disaster upon it. Now in the age of nuclear-tipped missiles, it could cause the destruction of everything. Not even the largest countries could ignore the claim that the state had lost one of the original justifications for its existence, the ability to protect its people. It could even be claimed that the Europeans had finally taken this lesson to heart. Defence now was only to be contemplated against those to the east who had not. Between Europeans, the recent record suggested that relations involved only their shared desire to enhance their prosperity by opening their economies to each other's goods and investments and participating in an ever-increasing international division of labour. In such a world, to defend sovereignty and independence from the erosive consequences which were assumed to accompany the process of integration into the international economy was to ignore the inevitability of this process and the fact that it represented the only way to satisfy what the people really wanted, economic growth and material prosperity. Besides, the argument that states as such were *passé* was especially attractive to those who had witnessed the decline of their own state in particular and who could be accused of sharing some of the responsibility for it.

Of course, as we now know, life for Britain after 1973 as a member of the EEC was not as simple as that. For one thing, although the electorate might want prosperity, they did not like the price that had to be paid for it in terms of their ideas of Britain as a powerful, independent country. Heath's defeat in 1974 demonstrated the risks of assailing established conceptions from a position of impatience with them, and the problems associated with these expectations were worsened when joining the Community coincided with a major international recession. People began to associate membership with their experience of increased competition, rising inflation and unemployment rather than the growth which had been promised. Nor was the problem of managing expectations about the country's position purely a domestic one. Time and again, foreigners called upon British governments to act or take a position on issues to which they were connected by history but in which they had very few direct interests. For example, the Heath government reversed in a minor way the decision to withdraw from 'East of Suez', and the prime minister was forced to devote considerable attention to Britain's place in the Commonwealth, although neither issue was considered by the government to be a major foreign policy priority.

As a consequence, British foreign policy did not settle into a new orientation after 1973. Instead, under the Labour government elected in 1974, it remained largely frozen in its pre-membership state. In their election campaign, Labour challenged the terms of EEC membership obtained by Heath and promised to renegotiate them, but largely for internal party reasons. Then, on the basis of the minor concessions obtained, membership of the Community

was put to and approved by a national referendum the following year. In part, this lack of change was a consequence of the
narrow parliamentary majority enjoyed by the Wilson and Callaghan governments coupled with the deepening economic crisis
which confronted them in the late 1970s. However, it also stemmed
from a more general sense of powerlessness in both domestic and
international affairs. Nothing much could be done about
Britain's external circumstances by Britain itself, and this was a
product of not merely Britain's decline, it was widely believed, but
also changes in the way of the world. British foreign policy, therefore, was focused on satisfying domestic and foreign expectations
about what was left of its role as a responsible world power while
doing as little damage as possible to its external interests of substance.

INFLUENCE WITHOUT INTERESTS

Postwar British foreign policy, as many critics have noted, was
preoccupied with the notion of international influence. Given Britain's interest in a stable world with an open economy, its governments argued, it was important that the country's voice be heard on
the great questions of war, peace, trade and finance. It followed,
they believed, that the country should continue to commit resources
to those aspects of its international position which gave it the
influence to secure a hearing. However, the difficulty facing British
foreign policy was that this entailed committing resources to those
things which had made Britain a great power in the past, for
example maintaining armed forces and a diplomatic corps whose
competencies were global and defending sterling's role as a reserve
currency. One by one, these sinews of power were relinquished as
the country declined, and the more substantive interests they
had originally defended also disappeared. It was this process which
led many critics to argue that postwar British foreign policy pursued
international influence for its own sake or out of institutional
and bureaucratic inertia, but for no discernible British interest.
Why, for example, defend sterling when the powerful economic
base which had made its leading role possible had disappeared
along with the share of world trade which had made such a costly
policy appropriate in the past? Why struggle to maintain a military
presence East of Suez when the commercial interests and patterns

of trade which had once sustained it had been subsumed in new and far more important ones?

In fact, however, influence was never pursued for its own sake. There were always sound diplomatic reasons for doing what British foreign policy did during the period, and they usually revolved around the general argument that things would get much worse, or friends would very quickly become unhappy, if Britain relinquished its responsibilities. It may be added that both British governments and those who carried out their foreign and defence policies over the postwar period in the face of rapidly shrinking resources accomplished the task of preserving British influence and executing these responsibilities successfully. With the notable, but single, exception of the Suez crisis, Britain managed to retreat without becoming a major problem to anyone but itself. Here, however, was the problem. The successful execution of this policy permitted the begging of an important question about the changing identity of the country on behalf of which all this influence was being pursued. Was Britain a hegemonic power with enough clout, not only to make a sizeable contribution to the maintenance of international order, but to define at least some of it in accordance with its own interests? And if it had the ability, then did it possess sufficient interests in the world to make the effort worthwhile?

To these questions, those charged with responsibility for British foreign policy could only answer yes, despite the mounting evidence to the contrary. As a consequence, time and again, initiatives were launched, resources committed and positions adopted as if Britain still held a primary responsibility for defining and maintaining the international order and was capable of shaping it by its choices. And time and again, the country was forced to retreat from its original position as its resources proved inadequate or its sense of responsibility to the requirements of international order caused it to defer to those who were now in a better position to define them and had judged Britain's actions to be the problem. In short, the preoccupation with influence, insufficiently anchored in any clear sense of the identity of the state, resulted in a foreign policy which oscillated between hegemonic posturing and middle power humility. Specifically, British interests were not so much neglected by this as left undefined, with the result that foreign affairs were something that Britain was expected to do, and to do well, but to what end no one was quite sure.

In 1979, therefore, and despite the great changes which had occurred in the country's international position, British foreign policy seemed as preoccupied as ever with the pursuit of influence in Nato, the US, the UN and Europe. It was pursued without great conviction, and for no better reason than that it was expected, and there seemed little else to do. The Cold War might be reviving, the USSR going from strength to strength and the US confused, but there was little that Britain could do about any of this, for it had troubles of its own. Indeed, in the run up to the general election, a consensus existed that, for what it was worth, foreign policy was one of the few things which the Labour government of James Callaghan had not handled disastrously. Whatever was wrong with Britain, the answer did not lie in the realm of foreign policy. The most important member of this consensus, of course, was Margaret Thatcher. Take care of the economics, she maintained, and the rest, including foreign policy, will take care of itself. By 1979, British foreign policy, successful or not, had plainly ceased to matter as far as most people, including the government, were concerned.

2 Foreign Policy and the 1979 Election Campaign

Whether it mattered or not, however, if circumstances were ever to be propitious for changes in British foreign policy, then they seemed to be so in the spring of 1979. The international system was sliding towards both economic recession and the 'second Cold War'.[1] The order essentially created by American power at the end of the Second World War seemed to be in danger of disintegrating in the face of challenges from radical nationalist movements in the Third World and a newly assertive USSR whose leaders spoke of a decisive shift in the international correlation of forces. The efforts of the US to arrest the decline in its international position, either by direct intervention as in the case of Vietnam, or indirect support as in the case of Iran, had not worked. Indeed, they had further weakened both the political and economic position of the West. Yet, when the Carter administration briefly attempted to step back from competition with the USSR or the search to control developments in the Third World, the consequences were widely interpreted in terms of a crisis of American leadership.

The uncertain climate abroad had its counterpart at home with increasing pressure being mounted from both left and right on the 'postwar settlement'.[2] By this, successive British governments had sought to manage the economy with the objective of simultaneously sustaining growth, full employment, a rising standard of living and an extensive system of social welfare benefits. By the early 1970s, it had become apparent that economic growth, while constituting the basis of the postwar settlement, had occurred separately from, and some would say in spite of, government policies. Britain, along with most of the rest of the developed world, suffered as a consequence of the end of the postwar economic boom, rising inflation and the sudden increase in the price of oil. However, the consequences of the developing world recession were more severe in Britain than in other comparable countries because of its inability to compete effectively on international markets. By May of 1979, the Labour government of James Callaghan had been confronted by inflation and unemployment rising simultaneously, extensive industrial action in support of wage claims and a balance of payments problem which had necessitated an application to the IMF for a loan and the beginning of a programme of deep cuts in public expenditure.

It is a testimony to how unimportant British foreign policy had become, however, that these uncertainties at home and abroad had little impact upon either its conduct or discussion of it as a public issue. In the last months of the Callaghan government, European policy was focused on Britain's contributions to the Community budget and the Common Agricultural Policy (CAP), and Britain refused to participate in the new European Monetary System (EMS). A Defence White Paper noted Nato's commitment to a 3 per cent increase in spending per annum, signalled the need to start thinking about a replacement for Britain's Polaris nuclear force, but stressed the need for further cuts and efficiencies in equipment and personnel. Two weeks before the general election, Nato's Nuclear Planning Group (NPG) reached agreement on the need to modernize the alliance's nuclear forces in Europe, but the details of what the Labour government's representative at the talks assented to were barely considered.

In the Commonwealth, Rhodesia was becoming an issue again because of the attempt to reach a controversial internal settlement there. However, on other Commonwealth matters, for example, the execution of Bhutto in Pakistan, the commitment of British troops for a peacekeeping force in Namibia, a coup in Grenada and the removal of Uganda's Idi Amin by the Tanzanian army, the government made the appropriate statements offering modest assistance where it might help, and this seemed to be acceptable to everybody in the House of Commons. Even on the two big crises which developed during the period, consensus and routine seemed to dominate. The fall of the Shah of Iran provoked gloomy speculations in Parliament and the press about its implications for Western interests. As far as foreign policy was concerned, however, the Iranian revolution seemed only to present a series of largely practical problems regarding the evacuation of British nationals, the detention of an airliner with Britons aboard and the more vexed question of whether the Shah might spend part of his exile in Britain. The same was true of the other crisis prompted by China's incursion into Vietnam to 'punish' Hanoi for its invasion of Kampuchea. There was some consideration of the geopolitical implications of one Communist power attacking the client of another, but the only question which really sparked a measure of interest was whether the pending sale of Harrier jets to China might still go ahead. It did not, but for commercial reasons rather than political ones, and a major trade agreement was also subsequently negotiated.

There was, in other words, a lot going on. Indeed, some of the issues upon which Thatcher was subsequently to build her reputation were already becoming established, but none of it seemed to matter much. International tensions were increasing, perhaps, but they were so along the familiar lines of the Cold War. As the ambiguities of *détente* began to give way, they did so to a simpler and more familiar dynamic of competition between the superpowers in which Britain's role was clear. When, or if, what Henry Kissinger called the period of 'maximum peril' arrived, Britain would do its duty to the best of its reduced ability. Even Kissinger, however, acknowledged that it had not arrived yet and, in the meantime, Britain's own crisis certainly had with the period of industrial unrest in 1978–9 known as 'the Winter of Discontent.' In retrospect, it would appear that politicians on both the right and the left exaggerated the extent of what became known as the 'British crisis'. As academics and journalists acknowledged in their more serious moments, no 'final crisis of capitalism' was at hand. Indeed, as Peter Jenkins has pointed out, the circumstances leading up to the first election of 1974, when the miners' union had successfully challenged the government, had possibly been more dangerous in these terms.[3] However, moderation in estimating the scale of the problems which Britain confronted and the possibilities for resolving them by the application of the 'correct' policies was the first casualty of the election campaign which finally and formally began with the fall of Callaghan's government on 28 March. And in such a climate, it was to be expected that there would be even less interest in foreign policy than usual.

FOREIGN POLICY EXPECTATIONS AND THE 1979 ELECTION CAMPAIGN

Even so, general election campaigns can be important to foreign policy in that they provide one of the occasions on which the practical details of modern external relations and the high political mysteries of diplomacy and statecraft yield to a discussion of the character and identity of the political communities which both are supposed to serve. During them, the collective sense of the constraints under which policy is made may be established, reaffirmed or changed. In Britain's case, for example, public debate of the kind which occurs around elections had helped to establish the sense to be made of Britain's decline. It was to be managed, as opposed to resisted. Indeed, decline – genteel and post-material within, while responsible and disciplined (if bitter-sweet) at the shrinking margins of empire – had been presented, if not as an objective exactly, then as an honourable state of being while one waited for a purpose to turn up. In the meantime, Britain's greatness was redefined in terms of its qualities and practices which were to be protected from the onslaught of postwar, and mainly American, modernity.

In this respect, the 1979 election was important for two reasons. First, it was won by a party whose leadership, at least, rejected both the inevitability of decline and the acceptability of being content to manage it. Thatcher claimed that there was no longer anything genteel or honourable in this state of affairs. The country had reached the point of crisis and she promised that, if elected, a Conservative government would embark on a radical project of restoring Britain to its former greatness, although, as she put it, what had'...taken decades to undermine [would] take time to rebuild'.[4] Secondly, Thatcher made her case for the extent of Britain's decline primarily in terms of its international position. As she had put it in the course of a by-election at Clitheroe two months earlier:

> Twenty years ago Britain stood really high in the world, one of the richest nations in Europe and one of the most influential... Britain is now seventh out of nine nations of Europe and among the poorest after Ireland and Italy. And this is no place for Britain.[5]

In her first full campaign speech in Cardiff, Thatcher told her audience that Conservatism most of all meant 'a sense of responsibility' which seemed to be lacking in the country. She asked whether Britain remained the country which had '...stood alone in 1940 against the collapse of European civilization?' She believed it was but, if the country was to be restored, or put 'back into the international race', as Thatcher expressed it, then this would be done '...giving new life and strength to principles which made our country the great trading nation it used to be.'[6]

While she invited judgement on the basis of Britain's external performance, however, Thatcher had very little to say about what British foreign policy would actually look like under a Conservative government. Someone, either a Soviet military newspaper or a British popular journalist, had called her the 'Iron Lady' because of hawkish speeches she made on East–West relations in the mid-1970s, but beyond that there appeared to be very little to suggest what Thatcher would do or expect. During the campaign, and much to the discomfort of the Foreign Office and the Americans, she intimated that she would favour normalizing relations with Rhodesia on the basis of settlement which excluded the guerrillas of the Patriotic Front.[7] On security matters, Thatcher declared that defence policy would be restored to its rightful priority, since the 'first duty' of any government was to 'guarantee the survival of our way of life' and preserve its people from 'external aggression'.[8] Labour's response to the increase of Soviet power had amounted to 'dedicated negligence', but the Conservative's 'pledge' as she put it was only to bring the armed forces 'up to the minimum threshold for safety', and what even this entailed was not clear.[9]

For the most part, Thatcher was content to leave foreign policy pronouncements to those Conservatives who were actually charged with responsibility for it, and the principal figure in this regard was Francis Pym. His presentation was professional and orthodox, placing Europe firmly at the centre of British foreign policy under the Conservatives. In an editorial for *The Daily Telegraph*, for example, he argued that Britain had to be in the EC because, alone, it would be 'buffeted by winds' it could not control and would exert only a 'small influence' on matters affecting the national interest. Within the Community, however, Britain would play a leading role as befitted its history and have a '...significant part in fashioning the modern world'. The challenge, however, would be to move the Community beyond preoccupation with its 'internal affairs' to developing a 'world role' which would be achieved in an 'evolutionary' manner with a '...common sense and down-to-earth approach'. Collective interests would develop between the members, Pym acknowledged, but 'more often', individual states would have their own interests and be able to rely on the others for diplomatic support. None of these developments, of course, would be allowed to weaken Britain's 'strong bonds' with Canada, Australia and New Zealand. The country's 'natural and long-standing relationship' with the US would have to evolve into a 'strong link' between America and 'the whole Community'. Britain would serve as the 'linchpin' between these 'twin pillars' which safeguarded democracy in the world.[10]

Clearly, Pym belonged to the less-said-the-better school of policy presentation, and he had no intention of breaking new ground during the campaign. The practical consequence of this was that even the friendly press had no clear idea as to the part foreign policy would play in Thatcher's efforts to restore Britain. All agreed that the Conservatives would be better than Labour at foreign policy. *The Times* noted, with approval, that Thatcher could be expected to take a stronger line towards the USSR, but it urged caution because she had little experience of foreign affairs. Postwar British foreign policy, according to *The Times*, had been 'reasonably consistent' and was not to be '...lightly altered by any new government.'[11] Only Robert Conquest successfully captured what Thatcher would subsequently try to do. In an article entitled 'The Return of the British Lion', he argued that with her as prime minister, Britain would resume a pivotal role in world affairs. Thatcher had, he claimed, a clearer understanding than the Americans of threats to liberty, she was prepared to make the contributions to Nato which would earn Britain the right to lecture others, and she would reject the arguments which blamed underdevelopment in the Third World on colonialism and capitalism. With Thatcher in office he expected '...a firm and forthright Britain to replace...the jellyfish now masquerading as our country.'[12]

Surprisingly, in retrospect, the only point of substance on which most sources agreed was that, under Thatcher, there would be a tilt away from what they regarded as Callaghan's excessive atlanticism and towards Europe. No British prime minister, *The Times* maintained had been 'more firmly loyal' to the US and, indeed, Stephen Barber maintained that he was widely regarded as Carter's 'dancing bear' in Washington. Nor was this merely a matter of party affinities, Labour to the Democrats, the Conservatives to the Republicans. Callaghan was no dove, and Thatcher, while no Heath in terms of her commitment to Europe, was reported as being 'less confident' about the Atlantic relationship than Callaghan. Further, there was no strong faction within her party committed to taking Britain out of the Community. Thus, *The Times* reasoned, a Conservative government would '...put Europe higher on the country's scale of values and be less carping in its criticisms of European institutions,'[13] while *The Daily Telegraph* suggested that Britain could become 'a powerful force, *the* powerful force' especially 'in default of a clear German lead', and this would be a much more effective role for securing Britain's objectives than playing the 'awkward squad'.[14]

THATCHER'S FOREIGN POLICY EXPECTATIONS

One reason for these expectations of a European tilt, of course, was general dismay at the weakness of American leadership under the Carter administration. Once US policy was judged to be back on the right road under Reagan, criticisms of its execution or of a close Anglo-American relationship from these particular sources disappeared. Secondly, these commentators were merely reflecting what the Conservatives, principally Pym, were telling them. It was he, for example, who faulted the Labour government for having '...upset all our European partners' so much that it was no longer possible for them to negotiate with the EC '...to protect British interests'.[15] In the light of the rows which were to follow between Thatcher and her Community colleagues, Pym's complaint is not without irony. Tempting though it is, however, it would be wrong to conclude that he was already at odds with the Thatcherite agenda on foreign policy and Europe.

This is so for two reasons. First, the description of the Community and Britain's place in it which Pym gave to *The Daily Telegraph* incorporated all the key elements of what was to become known as Thatcher's position. She too regarded the Community as primarily an economic association with political implications, and sought practical cooperation among states which would 'more often' pursue their own interests with support from the others. What neither Pym nor anyone else could foresee, however, was the extent to which this position would become controversial within the Community and the intensity with which Thatcher would eventually be prepared to defend it. These developments, and not any pre-existing Thatcherite agenda, destroyed the possibility of the expected tilt towards Europe.

Secondly, and much more importantly, Thatcher had no strong foreign policy convictions at this stage. Conquest's predictions about the leadership and lecturing roles she would attempt, while subsequently accurate, were premature. To begin with, Thatcher did nothing of the sort because, as far as international affairs were concerned, she knew little and cared less. According to a senior minister with foreign policy responsibilities in her first government, when she came into office '... The Prime Minister, quite frankly, literally did not know where Calais was.' He went on to say that in so far as she thought about British foreign policy at all, she did so with 'little England instincts'. Thatcher liked Americans, but then she '... did not regard them as foreign'.[16] She had, according to a senior diplomat who worked closely with her, '... a small town hostility to Europeans and a *Daily Express* understanding of foreign affairs'.[17]

Notwithstanding the *déclassé* terms used here to account for her lack of interest, the principal reason was that Thatcher did not yet believe that international affairs were important to what she sought to accomplish. Restoring Britain, for her, was primarily a matter of pursuing the correct domestic policies: reducing the money supply, lowering taxes and cutting public expenditure. These, together with measures taken to transform the 'climate of expectations' about the respective roles of capital, labour and the government in the economy, were the keys to success with which she and her closest allies in the party were absorbed.[18] The extent of their preoccupation with 'getting the economics right', and the consequent insignificance of foreign policy, may be gauged by the fact that it was rumoured that her predecessor and rival, Edward Heath, had been offered the Foreign Office in return for a vigorous campaigning effort on his part.[19] He did not accept it, but the Cabinet announced on 7 May reflected the new prime minister's priorities. The key economic positions were dominated by her own allies, but Carrington went to the Foreign Office and Pym to the Ministry of Defence. Both departments, although powerful, were numbered among those which could be safely left in the hands of people who represented other constituencies in the Conservative party without threatening Thatcher's agenda or her own political position.[20]

3 The Thatcher-Carrington Partnership

Until Argentina invaded the Falkland Islands in the spring of 1982, Thatcher gave no sign of being anything but a very ordinary prime minister as far as foreign affairs were concerned. Certainly, she enjoyed the reputation for having some robust opinions about world affairs, but they were indistinguishable from those of many ordinary Conservative party supporters and, arguably, just as cheaply held. The economy remained Thatcher's priority, and she was content to leave foreign policy matters to the foreign secretary, Lord Carrington. This arrangement was widely judged, by herself included, to have been a great success.[1] Had not Carrington taken formal responsibility for the loss of the Falklands by resigning, it is likely that he would have continued as foreign secretary for a considerable period. After all, Geoffrey Howe held the position for a long time, even after his relationship with Thatcher had deteriorated.

There is little evidence to suggest that Carrington was a direct target of the cabinet reshuffles by which Thatcher was attempting to establish her authority during her first two years of office, although he represented a section of the party opposed to her views and disagreed with her on many matters, including important aspects of British foreign policy. Given Thatcher's poor reputation for being willing to tolerate views which differed from hers, therefore, the success their partnership enjoyed is remarkable, and given that it culminated in the débâcle of the loss of the Falkland Islands and the emergence of Thatcher as an international figure in her own right, it requires close examination.

THATCHER AND CARRINGTON

The customary view of the partnership is that Carrington, the urbane, experienced aristocrat, took care of the substance and the details of British foreign policy while Thatcher provided the broad guidelines and, on occasions, made potentially disastrous interventions on the basis of her small-town, small-business instincts. *The Times* called it a 'sweet and sour' partnership, while Denis Healey of the Labour party provided a more colourful account of it to the House of Commons in May 1981. Commenting on a recent visit by Thatcher and Carrington to the US, he said that the Prime Minister's performance had been 'half John Wayne...half Calamity Jane'. As a result, her Foreign Secretary had been forced to perform his accustomed role as her zoo keeper

> ...dragged away from the delicate diplomatic task of feeding the marmosets by the news that Rhoda the Rhino was on the rampage again.[2]

There was some substance to this. Thatcher did possess a capacity for forthrightness which sometimes bordered on rudeness and was not constrained simply by the fact that she was talking to foreigners. For example, on a visit to India in April 1981, she responded to Indian criticism of the proposed British Nationalities Act by saying that Britain was a 'small country' with a greater population density than India, which could no longer afford to let people keep 'pouring in'. Later that same year, in Kuwait on a visit to the Middle East to promote British exports, she said Britain would not recognize the Palestinian Liberation Organization (PLO) because it was a British practice to recognize only countries, not organizations. This was standard British policy. However, she then added an extempore comment about the PLO's association with terrorism, asserting that '...their real objective is to drive Israel into the sea and wipe it off the face of the globe.' She then offended the Iranian ambassador, who was in attendance, by suggesting that one of the obstacles to arranging a ceasefire in his country's war with Iraq was that '...it was not very easy to know precisely who was in command in Iran or who to deal with.'[3]

This sort of directness stayed with her throughout her career, and though it may be regarded as an admirable quality in an individual, and, indeed, a refreshing one in someone in public life, it was not always conducive to effective diplomacy. However, Thatcher herself was quite capable of playing the diplomat on occasions, covering the foreign secretary's difficulties. Several times, for example, she was able to reassure the Americans when Carrington, in his enthusiasm for a European initiative on the Middle East, seemed to disparage the significance of the US-brokered Camp David peace process. Carrington himself, certainly valued the partnership, and shared her own view that there were advantages to be gained from representing a leader with firm convictions or, as David Watt put it after the Falklands, someone who had acquired a reputation '. . . as a dangerous customer and possibly slightly mad'.[4]

However, the success of the Thatcher–Carrington partnership rested on a great deal more than their personalities and their mutual respect. It also depended upon a division of labour which reflected their respective views about what was important in foreign affairs. Beyond the formal diplomatic duties connected with her office, Thatcher was interested in those aspects of foreign and defence policy which had a direct bearing on her efforts to reduce public expenditure, and with very little else. In defence policy, for example, after initial spending increases to which the government was committed, she pressed her ministers to find ways of paying for the modernization of Britain's nuclear deterrent by saving money elsewhere. In foreign policy *per se*, Thatcher's attention remained focused upon the finances of the European Community (EC) and Britain's contribution to them.

To begin with, this resulted in heavy criticism of her foreign policy. In particular, those elements of the press which had confidently predicted a more European and less Atlanticist orientation once control had passed from Callaghan to Thatcher became alarmed at what they regarded as an exercise in mean-spiritedness which put values which were far more important than the sum of money in question at risk. Thus, in the spring of 1980, an editorial in *The Times* criticized the prime minister for rejecting a financial compromise with the EC which had been proposed by the French. It accused her of possessing a 'little England attitude' which made the country look 'ludicrously insular and chauvinist'.[5] That Thatcher should bear the brunt of these criticisms was not entirely fair, however, for they were fuelled by disappointments in areas under Carrington's purview. A plan for the neutralization of Afghanistan to which he had applied himself in the spring of 1980, for example, had gone nowhere.[6] And in March, David Spanier, commenting on a meeting of the House of Commons Select Committee, concluded that British foreign policy in the post-Afghanistan world presented 'a gloomy picture'. The only place in which it was actively promoting a policy, he maintained, was the Middle East, and here Carrington had fallen foul of the Israeli government. Elsewhere in the 'arc of crisis', Britain had '. . . not got much to say.'[7] Two months later, the government was forced by a revolt of its backbenchers to abandon the harsher elements of a package of economic sanctions against Iran for seizing the American embassy and taking its diplomats hostage. The episode was particularly damaging for not only was Britain forced to abandon a measure for helping the Americans to which it had agreed with its EC colleagues, the measure had been a Carrington and Foreign Office initiative in the first place.[8]

Within a short time, however, criticism of Thatcher's foreign policy had subsided. For example, only two months after his gloomy account of the Commons Select Committee, Spanier was praising what he identified as a new 'strong foreign policy' informed by 'a new sense of purpose'. Then, employing a foreign policy nostrum dating back to Macmillan, he asserted that Britain's strength rested not on 'real power', but on '. . . a blend of confidence and personality with a dash of bluff'. Its purpose was '. . . to rally friends and allies in times of trouble'.[9] Indeed, commenting in this vein on a 'long overdue' visit which Carrington was to make to Hungary the following autumn, *The Times* noted with approval that Britain was distinctive among western European countries in having '. . . no specific national interest in cultivating relations in eastern Europe'.[10] The principal reason for this change of heart was that it had become clear that Carrington, and not Thatcher, was to control British foreign policy during the 'dangerous decade'.[11]

The most important consequence of this development was that innovations were restricted to matters of style and process. The substance of British foreign policy would not change. Carrington, expressed this well in his address to the Conservative party conference in October 1980. People should not be surprised, he said, if they found British foreign policy becoming 'more assertive and robust'. Britain, had a 'positive role to play', and it was going to play it.[12] However, the role he had in mind was not particularly adventuresome for it involved two familiar elements: executing Britain's historic responsibilities and exploiting its membership of the EC in such a way as to maximize the country's influence on the big questions of international order. Only on the extent of Carrington's effort to use the EC in this regard, can his diplomacy be described as really innovative.

THE RHODESIAN QUESTION

However, it was the more traditional approach, exploiting Britain's historical responsibilities, which got off to a flying start with the climax of the struggle for control of Rhodesia. Rhodesia had been one of Britain's three central African colonies which prior to independence had been organized into the self-governing Central African Federation in 1953.[13] It had a more balanced and developed economy than the other two, and a significant white settler population which had tended to dominate the Federation until the latter's dissolution ten years later. Then, the white minority in Southern Rhodesia sought independence from Britain under a formula which would entrench their political and economic influence by denying the black majority most political and economic rights. The Labour government of Harold Wilson was not prepared to grant independence on such terms, and after unsuccessful negotiations, the white regime, under the leadership of Ian Smith, broke with Britain unilaterally and illegally in 1965.

From this point, British policy towards Rhodesia was based on fulfilling expectations in the international community, principally on the part of black Africa, the Commonwealth and increasingly the US, at the lowest possible cost to Britain. The Wilson government imposed economic sanctions and won United Nations support for them the following year. The resourcefulness of the Smith regime, South African sympathy and indifferent support for sanctions by major British companies ensured that the policy failed in its primary objective. Wilson attempted to break the impasse by direct talks with Smith on British warships in the Mediterranean in 1966 and 1968 but without success. Edward Heath's foreign secretary, Lord Home, managed to negotiate a settlement with Smith in the early 1970s, but this was rejected in a referendum by a large majority of the black population whose leaders increasingly looked to a guerrilla campaign to secure majority rule.

In 1976, the Rhodesian problem was a subject of Kissinger's diplomacy as the Americans decided that it increasingly posed a threat to their interests in southern Africa. However, a conference convened at Geneva merely emphasized continuing differences over how a transition to majority rule was to be affected and what white 'safeguards' would remain after independence.[14] Following this failure, Smith proceeded with his own internal settlement, accepting the principle of majority rule in 1977. The following year, he formed a transitional government in cooperation with certain black leaders, but under Smith's leadership. The Patriotic Front (PF) of Robert Mugabe and Joshua Nkomo rejected this settlement claiming that its provisions for safeguarding white influence merely disguised the continuation of white supremacy. With the support of what were termed the Front Line States (principally Zambia, Tanzania and Mozambique), Nkomo and Mugabe committed their respective political movements to the intensification of the guerrilla struggle.

Britain and America rejected the internal settlement, and called for a UN-administered transition to full democracy in which Smith would not participate.[15] By the time Thatcher was elected in May 1979, a guerrilla campaign was under way in Rhodesia, counterinsurgency operations were being conducted by the Rhodesians and South Africans against guerrilla bases in Zambia and Mozambique, and the country's first black leader, elected under the provisions of the internal settlement, was asking London and Washington for recognition.[16] To complicate matters further for the new British government, a Commonwealth conference was due to be held in the Zambian capital of Lusaka in early August.

THATCHER AND RHODESIA

Rhodesia presented a difficult foreign policy problem for any British government. Whatever ties of kith and kin that Britain had to the white minority, and whatever commercial stake it had in preserving their way of life faded into insignificance when set against the diplomatic and economic costs of alienating black Africa by doing nothing. Unfortunately, there was very little Britain could actually do. Sanctions had failed over a 15-year period and successive governments had accepted that Britain lacked the ability, let alone the inclination, to impose a solution by force of arms.[17] Yet everyone expected Britain to do something. Opinion abroad, as it was expressed at the UN, wanted Rhodesia returned to legality on the basis of majority rule. Most people at home agreed; a minority believed that Britain should do more to look after the whites. In the parliamentary debates on Rhodesia, only Enoch Powell consistently advocated that Britain lacked the will or the power to run the colony and, hence, should pull back from 'the suicidal folly' of further commitments to the 'Rhodesian morass'.[18]

These problems were compounded by Thatcher's sympathy for the idea that Britain should take the lead in recognizing the internal settlement and end sanctions. The election manifesto of the Conservative party had said that this should be done if the Rhodesian elections to be held in late April were judged to be free.[19] This was a controversial position, and Thatcher had to make it clear that, were she elected, she would do nothing before consulting Britain's allies. The reports on the elections were not a great deal of help. Lord Chitris, an observer in Rhodesia for the Rowntree Trust, denounced the elections as a 'giant confidence trick', an assessment with which most people were inclined to agree. However, Lord Boyd, who had observed them on behalf of the Conservative party, pronounced them fair enough to justify British recognition of the winner, Bishop Muzorewa.[20] This was clearly Thatcher's preference. She had been encouraged by Smith's offer of an amnesty to the PF guerrillas if they would turn in their arms and participate in the elections, and by the reportedly high levels of voting in them.[21] Indeed, on the day she announced her first cabinet, a report appeared of an interview she had given to *Time* in which Thatcher declared that the Anglo-American diplomacy on the issue had been overtaken by events. As she put it, '... There was an election; one person, one vote for four different parties. Where else would you get that in Africa?' If the Rhodesians could satisfy six conditions laid down by the Wilson government, she continued, then there would be no reason to renew sanctions after they lapsed in mid-November.[22]

CARRINGTON AND RHODESIA

Nonetheless, Britain did not act precipitously as its allies had feared. After consultations with the Americans, Carrington announced that a new British policy would be revealed once Boyd had submitted his final report.[23] Thatcher gave the details shortly afterwards. The British government, she declared, accepted that the elections were fair. Representatives would be sent to Rhodesia-Zimbabwe, as it was now to be called, the Front Line States and other Commonwealth members to maintain contacts, but there would be no early approach to Mugabe or Nkomo, the leaders of the PF. Thatcher acknowledged the possibility of a return to British control while a new constitution was worked out, and made it clear that Rhodesia's return to legality was now exclusively a British responsibility. However, she made no commitment to recognizing Muzorewa's government or ending sanctions. This was not to her liking, and it angered many of her supporters in the party. How, they asked, could Britain recognize the government of Jerry Rawlings in Ghana, who had executed previous leaders, and not recognize the new government of Zimbabwe-Rhodesia?[24]

The cautious approach was, of course, Carrington's, and events proved it to be well-advised, for the internal settlement soon came under great pressure at home and abroad. The Rhodesians intensified their counter-insurgency, launching raids into Zambia and Mozambique, and even attacked the militias of legal parties within the country. Muzorewa's party split, denying him an overall majority in the new parliament. During the same period, Lord Harlech was sent as Britain's special envoy to several African states, including Zimbabwe-Rhodesia, as a result of which speculation increased that Britain would request major constitutional changes with PF involvement as the price of accepting the internal settlement.[25] This was not the case, however, or, at least, not yet. In July, Carrington informed the House of Lords that the situation in Rhodesia had changed 'fundamentally'. Muzorewa had not been responsible for Smith's unilateral declaration of independence (UDI), and he needed Britain's 'help and encouragement' if he was to show he was in charge and committed to creating a truly multiracial society.

Muzorewa hoped for the best from these supportive remarks, declaring, on a visit to London, that Zimbabwe-Rhodesia's constitution would not be changed to please others, and claiming that Britain and the US agreed with him on this. He attributed this support to Thatcher's influence, maintaining, after requests from Conservative members of the House of Commons Foreign Affairs Committee and the party's 1922 Committee that sanctions should not be renewed in November, that she was keen to end sanctions and would lead his country '... to the promised land, so to speak'. Muzorewa, it was reported, had found Thatcher 'refreshing' in contrast to the 'old guard' at the Foreign Office. There, according to one of his aides:

> The old, petty, negative approach of waiting like Mr. Micawber for something to turn up was still very much apparent... They seem to think that the problem will go away if they sit tight and do nothing.[26]

Inactive, however, was the last thing the Foreign Office had been. Both men would have been well-advised to listen to the charge made by a right-wing Conservative backbencher, Julian Amery, that the government had, in effect, introduced a seventh and eighth principle to Wilson's six, namely that any settlement would have to be acceptable to America and the black African states. Of course, these were not additional principles but unavoidable political realities as far as Britain was concerned. Carrington had worked hard to convince Thatcher that a successful settlement would have to involve the Patriotic Front to an extent which satisfied international opinion, if not necessarily the Front itself, or Britain would be left alone with responsibility for the ensuing mess.

Seeking international support for the internal settlement had been the Foreign Office's task and, as Thatcher's own address to the Commons just before she left for the Commonwealth conference in Lusaka made clear, the results of their efforts had been disappointing. In it, Thatcher praised the progress made so far, and reiterated both the importance of the six principles and Britain's claim to exclusive responsibility for solving the problem. In a change of position, however, she also said that Britain had yet to ascertain if the recent elections had fulfilled the acceptability principle, and she recognized that Rhodesia's return to the international community depended on other governments finding a settlement acceptable.[27]

The Lusaka conference began badly. The Queen was to attend as head of the Commonwealth, and fears were expressed for her safety in the British press. According to Carrington, even Thatcher was worried about being physically attacked in Zambia.[28] Then, on the day after the British arrived, Nigeria nationalized all of British Petroleum's holdings in that country. Thatcher, however, greatly improved the general atmosphere by declaring from the start that she sought a solution which was acceptable to the Commonwealth and the international community. Her government, she said, was '. . . wholly committed to genuine black majority rule in Rhodesia' and in these terms, the present constitution was 'defective'.[29] As a consequence, agreement was quickly reached on a proposal that the Commonwealth should support Britain's effort to convene a new conference in London. Muzorewa's government and the leaders of the Patriotic Front would be invited to develop a new constitution without entrenched powers for the white minority, and to work out the details of a peaceful transition back to legality. The Lusaka meeting ended with the first images of Thatcher as a successful statesman, dancing with the Zambian President Kaunda, fêted in the local newspapers, and asking her exhausted foreign secretary to raise a smile at the press conference which announced the details of what became known as the Lusaka Accord.[30]

CARRINGTON'S TRIUMPH

The difficult part of the process, however, had barely begun. For each of those invited to attend the conference set to begin at Lancaster House in London on 10 September, whether to accept or not presented an agonizing choice. The PF leaders, Mugabe and Nkomo, had between them an estimated 45 000 guerrillas, one-third of whom were in the country.[31] They had no prospect of a quick military victory, but the longer the conflict went on, the better their chances became. However, they depended on support which the Front Line States were increasingly tired of giving. Therefore, their failure to participate might lead to a British agreement with Muzorewa alone, sanctioned by the Patriotic Front's longtime allies. On the other hand, participation in a peaceful settlement might leave their people disarmed and at the mercy of the white minority who still controlled Rhodesia's military establishment.

The dilemmas were scarcely less difficult for Muzorewa and his allies. They had already won a measure of power, and to submit to the new process would undermine their legitimacy. To reject the invitation, however, was to deny themselves the recognition which they needed to end the insurgency and the economic sanctions. While these were maintained, there was little prospect for economic development in Zimbabwe-Rhodesia, or enlarging their own independence from the whites. However, the leaders of the whites had their own problems. They too were divided on the matter of whether or not to attend the conference. Ian Smith attempted to obstruct the process. Others, notably the commander of the Rhodesian security forces, Lieutenant-General Peter Walls, advised cooperation. They were acutely aware of a deteriorating security situation in which their own forces had a barely two-to-one advantage over the guerrillas.[32] Still, they could hope that the Lusaka accord would prove impractical or impossible for the PF to accept. Participation, therefore, offered at least the possibility of success, while refusal entailed that a war which had already killed an estimated 20 000 people in seven years would continue, and that whatever the whites were seeking to protect would be destroyed.[33]

In the event, everybody turned up to be confronted by Carrington with two tasks: creating a new constitution and establishing the transitional arrangements by which a ceasefire could be affected, elections organized and the new constitution brought into force. He decided to begin with the former because, in the past, talks had always failed over the transitional arrangements.[34] In just over a month, considerable progress was made, with both Muzorewa and the PF agreeing to a British draft which effectively removed white control of the police, judiciary, civil service and armed forces, and reduced their representation in the legislature to a level below that capable of exercising a veto on constitutional reform.[35] The PF did so under protest, however, and linked its full assent to the attainment of an acceptable agreement on transitional arrangements for control of the armed forces.[36]

Carrington overcame these hesitations with a combination of incentives and coercive diplomacy. He revived Kissinger's plan for an Anglo-American or international fund which could help blacks make land purchases, while threatening to proceed to an agreement with Muzorewa only, the so-called 'second class solution'. To emphasize this possibility, PF representatives were barred from the talks while their leaders continued to hesitate about accepting the new constitution. As one Foreign Office official expressed it, success would entail '... getting Muzorewa's agreement, then putting it squarely on the table for the Front, take it or leave it.'[37] The price of PF agreement, however was that the British released the details of how the transition to legality would be managed. This was designed to shift the pressure back on Muzorewa's government, for the British plans involved a temporary return to colonial status under a colonial governor who would, perforce, become the government. Again, however, it was the PF who lodged objections once the details were released. They claimed that the governor would collaborate with Muzorewa, and that the small force of Commonwealth troops sent to oversee a ceasefire and elections would be too weak to protect their people from Rhodesian troops.

To break the deadlock this time, Carrington relied on coercive diplomacy only. In mid-November, he spoke openly about how, in his view, the new constitution had removed the cause for armed conflict. Britain's economic sanctions required their annual renewal by Parliament on 15 November and clearly, he implied, it would be hard to renew sanctions against a government which had acceded to every reasonable demand.[38] At the start of December, Carrington expressed doubts about the attainability of a 'first class solution', and on 6 December a ceasefire was declared. Even then, however, the details of the ceasefire remained to be negotiated, but it was decided to send the British governor, Lord Soames, and 400 troops to return the colony to legality whether a ceasefire was in place or not. This was a calculated risk. According to Carrington, a British presence would be necessary in Salisbury '... to make the final arrangements for bringing the ceasefire into effect'. Both sides would be asked to disengage, he continued, but whether they would or not depended on '... whether or not there is a real commitment by both sides to the ceasefire'.[39]

Soames arrived in Rhodesia the following day without the Patriotic Front's agreement to a ceasefire and with Rhodesian forces in the midst of counter-insurgency operations. After further negotiations, however, the Patriotic Front obtained an extra assembly point for their guerrillas in the centre of the country and with this, they agreed to a ceasefire to take effect in the new year. This, as Sir Ian Gilmour, the government's chief spokesman on foreign affairs in the House of Commons, expressed it, effectively marked 'the end of the war'.[40] Elections were scheduled for the latter half of February from which Mugabe's wing of the Patriotic Front emerged the victors, and the colony, under the new name of Zimbabwe, became fully and legally independent on 17 April 1980.

The Rhodesian settlement was, indeed, a triumph for Carrington aided by the Foreign Office. By a combination of persuasion, bluff and the appearance on occasions of ruthless indifference, he had managed to manipulate the fears and needs of all the parties involved to the point where he had convinced them that they dare not be left out of any agreement. As such, it was a textbook case of classical diplomacy, indeed of British diplomacy, for the very paucity of the material resources committed to the policy – a governor, his staff, a few soldiers, and a little money, in the best traditions of empire on the cheap – pointed clearly to its authorship. If an example is required of the way in which a foreign service can procure more influence for its country than its economic and military strength would seem to warrant, then it is hard to think of a better one than this.

Critics might point out that the final outcome was a defeat for, from a British point of view, 'our man'. As a black leader who could work with the whites, it was believed Muzorewa offered the best prospect for stability. That this particular ghost was kept alive right up until the elections is evidenced by Thatcher's opinion, expressed in late February, that in the absence of an outright winner, the party with the best chance of forming a coalition government should be asked to do so, even if it did not have the most votes.[41] However, this was a preference rather than an objective, for the British preferred to see Muzorewa lose fair and square than see him retain power to the exclusion of the PF from the independence process. In compensation for this disappointment, they could be glad that they had, as a *Times* editorial put it, ended an embarrassing period in British diplomacy, vindicated Britain's integrity and been as good as their word given at Lusaka and to the UN.[42] Even though Thatcher had been barely involved after her own preference in the matter had been sacrificed early on, she was quick to make this point on her first visit to the US. There, she said, that Carrington's success was evidence of Britain's active contribution to the settlement of southern Africa's problems as a whole.[43]

CARRINGTON, THATCHER AND EUROPEAN POLITICAL COOPERATION

This early success with one of Britain's historical legacies greatly helped to establish Carrington's ascendancy in foreign policy matters and confirmed that the country was still good at solving these kinds of problems. He was not so successful, however, with the other arm of his policy, taking a leading role in the construction of a European diplomatic identity. As Carrington maintained, not even the 'most important European country' could hope to speak with '... the influence of the Ten when they speak with a single voice.' Thus, their purpose was to become '... a force to be reckoned with over a wide range of international issues', and this, he claimed in 1981, they had been doing so with 'steadily increasing effectiveness'.[44] This was a generous assessment of a modest record, for the creation of a European voice in international affairs depended on two preconditions which proved very difficult to satisfy. The first was that a Western position on international affairs which was distinct from that of the Americans could be usefully articulated. The second was that an agreement which was both strong enough and timely enough to translate into practical action could be achieved.

Carrington, himself, had strong views about the former, for he was highly sceptical of the confrontational approach which he saw the Reagan administration increasingly taking on East–West relations in the 1980s. *Détente* he believed to be saveable, but it required someone to conduct a creative multilateral diplomacy to blunt the edges of the differences between the superpowers. His Afghan initiative is instructive in this regard. The USSR's intervention was to be resisted neither directly or indirectly for this would only contribute to greater levels of international tension. Instead, he believed that its conduct should be punished by a variety of small, but clear, signals of disapproval, while a proposal – the neutralization of the country – was put forward to ease the Soviet leadership out of the mess into which they had blundered.[45] While the US was pursuing a policy which was too confrontational towards the USSR, however, Carrington believed the reverse was the case when it came to the Middle East. There, Washington's efforts were hampered by its reluctance to criticize Israel or entertain proposals to which it was opposed. Accordingly, under his direction, the EC attempted to construct peace initiatives which were more critical of Israel, took more account of Palestinian concerns and which, therefore, it was believed, would strengthen both commercial and diplomatic ties with the Arab world.

However, the practical business of actually formulating and implementing a common foreign policy faced challenges which proved insurmountable. When, for example, Britain assumed the European presidency for six months in 1981, Carrington decided to revive his Afghan initiative. Over the previous year, neither the USSR nor the Non-Aligned Movement had shown much interest in the idea. It was embarrassing, but not greatly surprising, therefore, when the USSR again rejected the proposal on the eve of a visit to Moscow which Carrington was to make to advance it. He had been absorbed by the challenge of constructing a European initiative to the neglect of the question of whether much could be achieved by making it, and even this enterprise was marred when the Italians complained that they had been left out of the Anglo-French-West German deliberations which had preceded the initiative.[46]

The appearance, at least, of diplomatic action for action's sake which the effort to construct a position conveyed raised another question which membership of the EC posed for British foreign policy. Precisely what would be restored by it, British power and influence, or the power and influence of its diplomatic elite, which was not necessarily the same thing at all? What would Euro-British diplomatists do when the interests of the Community diverged from

those of Britain, for example when the construction of European
security arrangements threatened the integrity of Nato? The sceptical response was to suspect that they would become increasingly
loyal to the institutions which provided them with their new international status.

In fairness, however, it should be noted that among the professional diplomats, this distinction between British and European
interests was not nearly so harshly drawn, and not because they
had given up on the idea of British interests. For over forty years
they had been preoccupied not with the ends of policy, but with the
shrinking means available to sustain it. A frequent complaint of
theirs was that Britain's economic decline had made it increasingly
difficult for the country's diplomacy to be effective. To those outside
the profession, this sounds odd, for it implies that countries acquire
wealth and power to conduct diplomacy, when most people assume
the reverse to be the case. This formulation did not reflect a residual
mercantilism among the professionals, however, so much as a resilient confidence about what they regarded as the British approach
to international affairs.

Carrington's tenure as Britain's foreign secretary, together with
his subsequent careers in Nato and as a European diplomatist
seeking a settlement in Yugoslavia, suggest that he was a committed
and honourable, if not always successful, exponent of this view.
There was a British approach to diplomacy, combining values,
methods and a practical orientation to what is possible in a world
of states which Britain alone could no longer sustain. However, the
EC might be able to in some modified form, and if it could, then
the tradeoffs would be worth it. Britain, Europe and the world
would all benefit from a leading British role in the Community,
and Carrington, like those who worked for him, saw it as his job to
create that role. That they did so is not remarkable, for this was the
main thrust of most professional thought about postwar British
foreign policy. What does require some explanation, however, is
the extent to which Thatcher was prepared to support Carrington
in this conception of his role.

It does so, because the differences between Carrington and what
was to become the Thatcher approach to British foreign policy
were, indeed, considerable. Carrington, for example, saw the EC's
significance for Britain in primarily political terms, to the extent
that he always played down the significance of 'quarrelling', as he
called it, over the budget. This, he claimed, had never '... rubbed

off on political cooperation'. He may have been a closet integrationist, but it is much more likely that his judgement was based on the EC's past performance failing to match its ambitious rhetoric. In later years, he claimed that one of Thatcher's weaknesses was her inability to maintain a sense of proportion about internal Community issues or the way in which other members of the EC wrangled over them. In the light of subsequent events, however, this suggests that it was Carrington, and not Thatcher, who underestimated, or failed to understand, the significance of the renewed vigour with which economic and monetary integration were being pursued.

Further, Carrington's quest for a distinctive European line on major international questions often seemed to leave him in the position of merely distancing himself from the American line and carping at it. Neither activity was likely to endear him to Thatcher, but even though she was beginning to explore the potential of a prime minister-to-president relationship after Reagan's election at the end of 1980, she adhered to the broad outlines of her foreign secretary's policy. Both in the build-up to and during her visit to the US in February, for example, Thatcher emphasized the closeness of the two primarily in terms of domestic policy. This did not suit the Americans at all, for Britain was suffering the worst consequences of her monetarist policy at the time, but her views on international relations were scarcely more helpful. Her endorsement of Reagan's international position, while enthusiastic, followed Carrington's and, hence, the European line. In New York, for example, she made a rallying call to '...free people everywhere to join us', but 'the supreme task of modern diplomacy' remained 'the prevention of war' and, thus, she argued '...we seek *détente*.'[47] Indeed, when the Americans shot down two Libyan aircraft at the end of 1981, providing evidence of their own more forceful approach to dealing with challenges, Thatcher's own response was muted.[48]

Of course, differences did exist between Thatcher and Carrington on foreign policy. In addition to her preference for the 'internal settlement' in Zimbabwe, Thatcher was always uncomfortable with Carrington's Middle East initiative. At the Venice meeting which moved the Community towards supporting Palestinian self-determination and accepting the PLO, for example, she presented the Declaration as being supplemental to, rather than superseding, the American-inspired Camp David process.[49] The Israelis, especially, were upset by the Venice Declaration, and in the autumn of 1981, they used Carrington's association with it to veto British participation in an American-sponsored observer force for the Sinai. Carrington himself appears to have been reluctant for Britain to participate in a force which came under the auspices of the US, and encouraged a new Saudi initiative which gave more support to the Palestinians. The temperature was further raised when the British ambassadors to the Lebanon and Saudi Arabia both expressed the opinion that the Camp David process was about to expire. Thatcher, however, lowered the tension by claiming that support for the EC's Venice Declaration was consistent with participation in the US force for the Sinai, and that Sinai was complementary to Camp David, a point which had never been at issue, but one which allowed her to link all three, at least in a declaratory sense.[50]

These, however, were merely glimpses of differences which, while they might indicate radically different assumptions about what British foreign policy ought to be doing, where not allowed by Thatcher to prevent her deferring to her foreign secretary in most respects. Her attention remained firmly focused on domestic policy, now not only because she believed in the importance of getting the economy right, but also because she was having to manage the consequences of her indifferent success in this regard: urban riots in the spring and summer of 1981; hunger strikes in Northern Ireland; industrial action by the civil service; and sustained opposition within her own party and government over spending cuts and defence policy. In October 1981, public opinion polls reported that Margaret Thatcher had become the most unpopular prime minister ever since records had been kept.[51] She had enough to keep her busy without picking fights over an area of policy which was not her first priority with a powerful colleague whom she respected and whose support she needed.

In addition, Thatcher's own forays into foreign policy had revealed an, as yet, uncertain touch. She was forced, for example, to back down on the enthusiastic support she had given in Washington to the American plan to establish the Rapid Deployment Force in the Middle East. It was not really new, Thatcher said, when she returned home. It was merely an extension of existing commitments, and thus the British could support it. Further, she assured those who knew better than she just how embarrassed the Gulf states would be at the prospect of being rescued by Western intervention, it would have a broader mission area than just the Middle East.[52]

This uncertainty stemmed partly from Thatcher's unfamiliarity with the world of diplomacy and international affairs, but it also resulted from her own lack of confidence and certainty about what she wanted to do with foreign policy. In this regard, two episodes, one external and one domestic, are instructive. The external episode concerns differences between Thatcher and Carrington on the policy which the Contact Group of Western states were pursuing to secure the withdrawal of South African troops from their former trusteeship in what was shortly to become Namibia. The Americans were pursuing a policy known as 'constructive engagement' by which they sought to encourage, rather than force, the South African government to pursue internal reforms. Accordingly, they argued that South Africa should be given an incentive to cooperate by linking its withdrawal from Namibia with a Cuban withdrawal from Angola. The EC did not like this linkage for, according to Carrington, it would only make a Namibian settlement more difficult to achieve and, hence, a bloody civil war more likely.[53]

Thatcher did not agree, but in public she restricted herself to saying that while a Cuban withdrawal would be highly desirable, it should not be viewed as a condition of a settlement in Namibia. Her restraint is confirmed by her memoirs. In them, Thatcher recalls a discussion of the problem with Carrington while they were flying to visit the US. Carrington argued that because Namibia had become a sore point between the Americans and the Europeans, the issue of Namibia should not be raised by the British in the forthcoming discussions. Thatcher recalls agreeing with Carrington, noting in her memoirs that one should not engage '... in a conflict with a friend when you are not going to win', but where, in losing, you might jeopardize the friendship. She goes on to say, however, that she 'privately thought' the American attempt at linkage was justified.[54] Thatcher's thoughts on conflicts in relationships were clearly supposed to apply to Britain and the US. Just as clearly, however, they captured the deference she had shown, by her own account, to Carrington on an issue where she agreed with the Americans. Rarely was she to show such deference to subsequent foreign secretaries.

The domestic episode which supports the contention that Thatcher was not yet sure of herself in foreign affairs was an interview she gave on the Jimmy Young Show, a popular radio programme of friendly interviews and light music, after one year in office. According to our partners in the EC, she told the disc jockey and his listeners, she was now regarded as 'a she-de Gaulle' because of her position on the Community's finances. However, Thatcher wanted her stand to be indicative of something more. Now, she claimed, '...Britain really does count on the world scene.' When asked what this entailed, however, she proceeded to sketch out the old role claimed by every postwar British prime minister for herself as an interpreter between the Americans and the Europeans, plausible and useful like the Foreign Office briefing from which it likely came, but scarcely the stuff of a new, assertive British Gaullism with which Thatcher might make her mark on the country's foreign policy.[55] This point was developed by other commentators a year later when Thatcher's economic policies were running into severe difficulties. Enoch Powell, for example maintained that her nationalist credentials were marred because her speeches moved so quickly into '...denunciation of whole classes of British society and the economy'.[56] And David Watt argued that the urban disorders of 1981 could not be simply attributed to the diminished sense of moral responsibility of those involved. The problem was that people no longer shared a '...positive vision of what this country is and what it might be to be British', not least because Thatcher's government had failed to think in the terms of a '...valid British state which deserves the loyalty of its citizens'.[57] Of course, Powell and Watt were addressing broader issues than simply foreign policy. However, foreign policy, particularly if it was avowedly a nationalist one, had to be seen to flow from a clear sense of what the nation or political community it represents was all about.

By early 1982, Thatcher was developing her ideological and political partnership with Ronald Reagan. She was also beginning to exploit the photo-opportunities of summitry and formal diplomacy, for example standing on the Pakistan border peering at the Khyber Pass into Afghanistan. She had closed the interview with Jimmy Young in 1980 with the claim that after a year of Conservative foreign policy, the reaction to a British passport abroad was no longer 'just British', but 'Oh British! Interesting...'[58] Perhaps this was so, but as yet, Thatcher had no clear sense of what she meant by a revived British foreign policy. It took the Argentinian invasion of the Falkland Islands to transform her set of disparate, if firmly held, convictions into a coherent doctrine which gave some content to her claim to be pursuing a new, revitalized and specifically British foreign policy. Until that crisis, those convictions merely added to her curiosity value on the world stage as Britain's first woman prime minister, working in partnership with her foreign secretary, but still – as was British foreign policy as a whole – under his firm direction.

4 The Diplomacy of Disaster: Losing the Falklands

Stable and effective though the Thatcher–Carrington partnership appeared to be, it was destroyed by an unexpected event. Argentina invaded the Falkland Islands on 2 April 1982 and the dependency of South Georgia the following day. The small British garrisons offered brief resistance in both cases, causing fatalities but suffering none themselves, and then surrendered to greatly superior forces. They, together with the governor of the colony and anyone else who wished to leave, were then taken off the Islands by the Argentinians and provided with safe passage to Uruguay. After a brief hesitation, the British government demanded that the Argentinians leave the Islands and resume negotiations, and it also declared its willingness to use force should they refuse. Carrington resigned, accepting formal responsibility for the disaster, although it is clear from their respective memoirs that neither Carrington nor Thatcher thought him particularly to blame.[1] And while a response was prepared, a passionate debate developed in Britain as to what had gone wrong and who was to blame.

Of course, Argentina was primarily to blame. Whatever the merits of its claim to the Islands, its government had launched an armed and violent assault upon them, and bore the primary responsibility for what followed. Nevertheless, much of the subsequent debate in Britain focused on the extent to which the government and its diplomats had contributed to the disaster and what they might have done to avoid it. Two schools of critical thought emerged. The first consisted of those who claimed that Britain had no business still being in places as remote and useless as the Falkland Islands, and asked why they had not been abandoned long ago before they could become a reason for bloodshed. Those in the second school reserved their position on whether or not Britain should still have been on the Islands, but since it was, asked how Argentina had been allowed to gain the impression that it might seize them by force. Both exerted a major influence on Thatcher's own response to the crisis which, in turn, profoundly shaped her subsequent approach to British foreign policy. Accordingly, the debate about what was wrong with British policy towards the Falkland Islands is worth examining in detail, even though Thatcher was only indirectly involved with that policy before their loss. What is revealed is not who was to blame so much as the predicament in which satisfying an extensive and contradictory set of international responsibilities left Thatcher's government.

A POST-IMPERIAL ABERRATION?

According to multiple reports and interviews, the first two reactions of many people to news of the loss of the Falkland Islands was 'where are they?' and 'what is Britain still doing there?' Of course, a world in which military and political commitments were made only to places identifiable on the map by the general public would be a different world indeed. Why Britain was still trying to exercise its responsibilities to this and other far-flung residuals of empire is, nevertheless, a reasonable question to ask. With one exception, Hong Kong, these islands, peninsulas and territories had all out-lived their commercial or strategic usefulness and were not worth the effort it would take to defend them. Why not, then, let them go?

They were retained, according to one popular view, because the British political establishment, and the foreign policy elite in parti-cular, wanted to hang on to these symbols of former British power as long as possible, either out of habit or to remind themselves of better days. However, the claim is not persuasive because, rightly or wrongly, both the foreign policy professionals and their political masters shared the view that most of these commitments should be relinquished as quickly as was practically possible. The desire to retain what was left of the empire was to be found principally on the backbenches of Parliament, in some sections of the popular press, and in the colonies and possessions themselves. Rightly, however, the Foreign Office and successive British governments had determined that, should these commitments be relinquished, they would be so in a responsible manner. There would be no scuttles.

Avoiding the latter, however, presented a problem, for the hidden premise of those who advocated prompt exits was that they could be easily effected, and as the Foreign Office well knew, this was usually not the case. The people who wished one to stay often strongly identified with Britain and rejected its probable replace-ment: Gibraltarians, for example, disliked Spain, Belizeans feared

Guatemala, and the Hong Kong Chinese did not wish to be absorbed by the People's Republic. Further, even though Britain had successfully relinquished most of its vast empire in less than a quarter of a century, there was no clear pattern of evidence to suggest that the problems which they posed for British foreign policy would simply go away. In the three months between July and September of 1981, for example, Thatcher's government was faced by the rejection of its offer of compensation to islanders from Diego Garcia for their forced displacement to Mauritius, Barbuda's objections to being included in Antigua's independence, the British Virgin Islands' opposition to their new governor who had once worked for South Africa and, at home, criticism in Parliament of the use of public funds on infrastructure projects in the Turks and Caicos which served a new holiday resort but provided little benefit to the local population.[2]

To be sure, many of these problems could be easily dealt with and sometimes ignored because they were remote from the concerns of the public. Some, however, like those prompted by the publication of the new British Nationalities Bill in January 1981, could go to the heart of British politics. By this bill, the government sought to restrict the right of residence in Britain by developing several classes of citizenship, fulfilling Thatcher's promise to address the concern that Britain was being 'swamped by people of a different culture', to use her own notorious phrase.[3] And a few of the problems associated with colonial policy could become so intense as to raise the possibility of armed conflict and require the deployment of troops, warships and aircraft. The Falkland Islands were not alone in this regard. During its first three years in office and, indeed, beyond, Thatcher's government had to deal with two other potential armed conflicts which arose as it attempted to discharge the difficult responsibility of bringing former colonies to full independence.

The first of these concerned the Anglo-French condominium of the New Hebrides in the Pacific which was scheduled to become independent as the republic of Vanuatu in the summer of 1980.[4] A secessionist movement declared it would not recognize the new government, which promptly appealed to Britain and France for help. The problem was eventually solved, but not before both great powers had sent troops, fallen out with each other in such a way as to precipitate the threat of Australian intervention and had finally asked Papua New Guinea for military assistance. The episode shared all the elements of a Graham Greene novel: farce, tragedy and the exploitation of innocence for low motives of greed. The secessionists were reported to be cargo-cultists who had fallen under the influence of a shadowy organization known as the Phoenix Foundation which was committed to setting up its own political communities around the world. In all probability, they were motivated by local concerns and egged on by European, primarily French, residents who saw commercial advantage in secession. If ever the comic opera qualities ascribed incorrectly to the Falklands war applied anywhere, however, they did so here, as heavily-armed British and French assault troops prepared to act in uneasy concert against people armed primarily with bows and arrows. Even so, potentially dangerous issues were at stake involving the territorial integrity of a new, small state, plus the interests and sensibilities of two great powers, a regional one and a neighbouring state. Only when these were resolved, primarily by overriding the wishes of one set of local inhabitants, could Vanuatu proceed to full independence, its integrity intact.

Much more serious and intractable was the dispute over the future of the Central American self-governing colony of Belize, formerly British Honduras. Belize and its 150 000 people were threatened by a territorial claim from neighbouring Guatemala, and a British garrison had been stationed there since 1977 for the purpose of deterring this threat. The dispute was shaken out of a fairly dormant status by the UN General Assembly's decision in November 1980 to support the colony's request for full independence the following year.[5] Guatemala objected, and so negotiations were conducted in New York and London the following spring about the terms on which Belize would become independent before December and the end of the next session of the General Assembly. The talks went well, and an outline of a settlement, known as the Heads of Agreement, emerged. In return for economic assistance, certain rights along a road improving its access to the Caribbean and promises of a role in the exploitation of oil and gas deposits which might be found in the seabed off Belize, Guatemala would drop its claims. Both countries promised not to let their territories be used for subversion of the other, and the British said that, with the exception of training missions, they would no longer maintain a garrison in Belize. All that remained to be settled were the precise details of Guatemala's access to two Belizean Cays, the Ranguana and the Sapodilla.[6]

The British were pleased with the agreement, believing it to have reconciled Gautemala's commercial interests with Belize's concern for its security, but it was in trouble from the start. Honduras objected, its foreign minister, Señor Cesar Elvir Sierra, declaring that his country '...reserved its rights over the Sapodilla Cays.'[7] More importantly, Britain's sanguine view was shared by neither most Guatemalans nor most Belizeans. The former regarded Belize's concessions as insufficient and a military dimension to Guatemala's right of access to the Cays was sought.[8] Many Belizeans, on the other hand, believed that the agreement compromised both their sovereignty and their security, and in the last months before independence, a state of emergency was declared because of strikes and riots in protest against it. Following the pattern of the successful Lancaster House talks on Zimbabwe, however, the British decided to press ahead with the final round of constitutional talks in London. Neither Belize's prime minister nor its governor attended because of the troubles at home, and parallel talks with Guatemala at New York were broken off.

As the date for independence in September approached, Guatemala's position hardened. Diplomatic relations with Britain were severed during the summer. Guatemala's foreign minister declared there would be no occupation but, he added '...when the English leave Belize we will then be able to start the process of renegotiation.' Two weeks before independence, Guatemala made the final diplomatic break by severing consular relations, and called for the UN Security Council to discuss the situation. However, the Council endorsed Britain's timetable for independence, and against a tense backdrop of troop movements and Guatemalan complaints of violations of its airspace by the Royal Air Force, Belize became independent on schedule. Britain and six other Commonwealth countries pledged to consult with one another in the event of an externally organized or supported attack on the new country.[9] Isolated at the UN, and under considerable American pressure, Guatemala suspended its campaign against Belize until the following spring.

Then, however, with the crisis over the Falkland Islands building in 1982, the new government of General Rios Montt which had emerged in the course of a coup reasserted Guatemala's claim. As late as 1 April (on the eve of Argentina's attack), the British had declared their intention of withdrawing from Belize by the end of the year, but this position was reversed by the end of the month. As

Francis Pym, the foreign secretary, told Parliament, in framing its response to Argentina, the government had '...the situation in Central America very much in mind.' Indeed, as Guatemala called for talks to be reopened in early June and declared it no longer recognized either Belize or the Heads of Agreement, Britain reinforced its garrison and assigned a warship to the area. Fresh talks, the British representative at the first anniversary celebrations of the country's independence declared, might be welcome, and Britain would do what it could to help. Guatemala, however, must understand that Britain was no longer responsible for Belize's external affairs.[10] In the absence of an agreement, however, it would continue to exercise its responsibility for the security of the now-independent and sovereign state of Belize by retaining forces there.

THE PERMANENCE OF THE POST-IMPERIAL CONDITION

Far from being aberrations, therefore, colonial responsibilities were part of the routine of British foreign policy under Thatcher, presenting problems which were usually difficult and sometimes dangerous. As Sir Anthony Parsons has persuasively argued, it is perhaps better to think of post-imperialism as an enduring condition of the great and lesser powers which possessed overseas empires rather than as a passing phase from which they are in the process of emerging.[11] Former colonial powers are still expected to take some responsibility for the affairs of their former possessions, by the international community, by their own citizens and, not least, by the people who actually live in them. A few countries, Belgium and Portugal for example, have sought to make a complete break but, in practice, they find this difficult to achieve. Most, however, accept the claims against them with good grace, if not enthusiasm. They do so partly because they may hope to secure commercial or political advantages. More often than not, however, sentiment and the chance to show that their imperialism was not driven by entirely selfish motives explain their receptiveness to requests for help.

The practical problem for foreign policy, however, is that while these countries may be prepared to exercise their post-imperial responsibilities, the commitment which they bring to doing so is uniformly weak. The cases of Vanuatu, Belize and the Falkland

Islands all demonstrate that, while the problems they presented were of an enduring kind, then the operational expectation was that they were not. In each case, British policy was not driven by the desire to hold on at all costs, but by the need to reduce its commitment. Thus, if they became costly or controversial, the government's priority was to find reasonable alternatives to British rule as quickly as possible. If Papua New Guinea was willing to police Espirito Santo, then Britain and France were willing to let it do so. If Belize might be persuaded to accept an arrangement which, while hard to swallow, would secure its larger and unfriendly neighbour's recognition, then the British government was happy to make the attempt. If the Falkland Islanders could be convinced that a formula conceding sovereignty to Argentina offered the best chance of preserving their way of life, then Britain was prepared to transfer them to a country whose claim to the Islands was, to say the least, no stronger than its own.

The only major constraints upon British preferences in each case were the wishes of the majority of the local inhabitants. Any final arrangement had to be acceptable to them or all bets were off. The problem with this approach, however, was that it could create a situation in which the British promised one party that there would be no change in its condition without its consent, while they encouraged another to believe that such a change was possible. This is precisely what happened in the case of the Falkland Islands. Assurances were given to the Islanders and their supporters at home that so long as they wished to remain British they might do so, while, at the same time, the Argentinians were engaged in discussions which envisaged a radical change in the status of the Falkland Islands at some point in the future. It was this approach which provided the basis for the second school of criticism of British policy in the years preceding the Argentinian attack on the Islands. In a number of ways, it was claimed, from using only junior personnel in negotiations to being willing to discuss a future transfer of sovereignty, the British government conveyed the impression that the fate of the Islands was not very important to it and that, hence, it would not fight if they were invaded.[12] This, of course, was not the case and, therefore, it is claimed, the invasion took place because of an avoidable 'failure to deter' by the British government and, indeed, because some of its actions may even have been interpreted by the Argentinians as tacit encouragement of their ambitions.

THE FAILURE OF DETERRENCE ARGUMENT

In this view, the British government and the Foreign Office in particular, far from seeking to hang on to the Falkland Islands at all costs, were only too keen to get rid of them. This is not the case, but Carrington's subsequent account of his own approach to the problem illustrates all the difficulties of the weak hand with which the government was constrained and, indeed, had partly constrained itself to play. Claims like those of Argentina upon the Falkland Islands, he maintained, inconvenient or irrational as they may appear to others, are 'facts of politics' which have to be taken into account. This being so, Britain had three possible courses of action. It could have ignored Argentina's claims, stalled them by negotiating without concessions on sovereignty, or it could have tried to find, in Carrington's own words, 'a way forward'.[13] By this he meant exploring the compromise known as 'leaseback'. Britain would concede sovereignty over the Islands to Argentina which would, in turn, permit their continued administration by Britain and the local inhabitants.

Ignoring or stalling were both rejected by Carrington for they would result in either the loss of the Islands or a costly defence commitment. Leaseback, in contrast, offered the possibility of an acceptable *modus vivendi* for all concerned. Reasonable though it might seem to those who did not have to live with its consequences, however, the problem with leaseback was that virtually no one who mattered, least of all the Islanders and the Argentinians, wanted anything to do with it, for it satisfied neither the latter's sense of injustice and honour, nor the former's sense of security. The Islanders feared that once sovereignty was conceded, there was nothing to make Argentina live up to its obligations under the leaseback agreement and, certainly, nothing in the record of the military dictatorship in Buenos Aires suggested that self-restraint or promise-keeping were among its strong suits.[14] By default, therefore, British policy was left with pursuing option two, negotiations without concessions on sovereignty. These, Carrington conceded, were '... of a fairly meaningless kind,' but he hoped that they '... might buy time in which people could be educated about the realities of their situation. The case for leaseback, he believed, might then prove 'more persuasive'.[15]

The problem with his approach was that it still depended on the Argentinians being content to do nothing, while it allowed them to

charge that Britain was not negotiating in good faith and corrobor-
ated their assessment of Britain's weak commitment to the Islanders. If such indeed was the conclusion drawn by the Argentinians,
then the defence cuts announced in the summer of 1981 arguably
served only to confirm this impression. A principal target of these
cuts was the surface fleet of the Royal Navy, and among the ships
whose schedule for withdrawal was announced were the only two
amphibious assault ships in the fleet and a lightly-armed ice patrol
vessel which operated in the waters between the Falkland Islands
and the islands and territory of British Antarctica. Once these cuts
had been made, then the defence of the Falkland Islands would
depend completely upon a very small garrison of Royal Marines,
and their recapture, should they be taken, would be almost impossible.[16]

It can be plausibly argued, therefore, that by the spring of
1982, Britain had signalled that it lacked the will to defend the
Falkland Islands, and would soon deny itself the means if faced by a
modest yet determined threat. All the signs suggested that
Britain would do little to resist and, indeed, some of them suggested
that the government might welcome being gently nudged out of
this particular post-colonial predicament. Small wonder then, in
this view, that on the receipt of such signals, Argentina's desperate
and unscrupulous government succumbed to the temptation of
fulfilling a national aspiration by invading. For two principal reasons, however, the argument does not hold up. First, while the
British government had certainly indicated there might come a
time when it would relinquish control of the Islands, at no point
did it indicate that it was prepared to override the wishes of the
inhabitants to achieve this solution. And any evidence that some
members of the government, at least, were looking for a military *fait
accompli* on the part of the Argentinians to bring a merciful end to
the impasse remains highly ambiguous at best. Indeed, all the
postwar evidence suggests that Britain responded to anything
beyond the most minor demonstrations by non-combatants on
remote islands in British Antarctica with naval demonstrations of
its own.[17]

Secondly, there is little evidence to suggest that British actions
weighed heavily in Argentina's decision to invade, and some to
suggest they did not. If, for example, its government had been
paying attention to Britain's defence cuts, then why did it not wait
for their implementation before attacking? If one accepts the

notion of a tacit deal by which an Argentinian *fait accompli* allowed Britain to make an honourable but decisive exit, then perhaps the announcements, rather than actual cuts, could be regarded as signals that, tired of the Islanders' recalcitrance, the door was wide open. Again, however, the evidence does not support this view, for far from initiating a low-keyed affair between gentlemen, Argentina staged its invasion as a major Goa-style act of violent national self-assertion.[18] The British were not given the opportunity to bow to *force majeure*. Rather the message which Argentina sought to communicate to the rest of the world was that it had imposed its will upon Britain by driving its troops off the Islands. Lest anyone had doubts about this, photographs of the captured British garrison, spreadeagled and prostrated by victorious Argentinian troops, were circulated to the world press to confirm the point. It may be that the Argentinian strategy rested on the sentiment that Britain would bow to the inevitable, but if this is so, perhaps the best that can be said is that they gave little thought to how the British might be encouraged to share the sentiment.

In fact, the extent to which governments allow the decisions and announcements of their fellows to weigh in their own calculations is generally overestimated. Argentina's military plans for Las Malvinas were probably no more determined by Britain's proposed defence cuts than Britain's Falklands policy was shaped by Argentina's announcement of a 10 per cent reduction in defence spending made a month before the invasion.[19] Like most foreign policy, Argentina's decision to invade was driven by multiple concerns organized in terms of their domestic significance, of which its negotiations with Britain constituted only one, and not a prominent one at that. Political and economic difficulties at home combined with the country's new and flattering counter-insurgency partnership with the US to provide the government with the motive and the confidence, respectively, for acting as and when it did. It was for these reasons that Argentina behaved 'irrationally', ignoring or discounting the likelihood of a British response, and to the extent that it did, it must be concluded that there was little the government could have done, within the normal parameters of British foreign policy, to forestall the invasion. This is not to say that British conduct was beyond reproach, however, for, despite Argentina's culpability, the key to Britain's part in the whole affair is still to be found within these parameters.

THE PROBLEM OF CONSTRAINED DETERRENCE

In retrospect, it is clear that the possibility of leaseback should not have been raised once it was clear the Islanders were not interested in it. The only reason for doing so would have been to undermine their confidence in the British guarantee and make them more flexible, and it did not succeed in accomplishing this. It is not clear how the offer of the leaseback possibility affected Argentinian calculations, but one thing is certain. It made it harder for Britain to meet its responsibilities to the Falkland Islands, for the rejection of leaseback by the Islanders left Britain committed to the defence of a threatened territory which it had previously expressed a willingness to give up.[20] Having raised the possibility, only to see it rejected, however, Carrington and the Foreign Office should not have trusted to time to educate the Islanders to the realities of the their circumstances. Instead, they should have emphasized the real costs of exercising Britain's responsibilities to the Falkland Islands to the full.

Had they done so, they would have strengthened their own position by putting pressure on those in Britain who supported the Islanders' unwillingness to contemplate any change in their status. Once the costs of an adequate defence commitment and the dim prospects for any quick return on commercial investments were made clear, then the Islanders' supporters would have found themselves as politically exposed as those who sought to negotiate the Islands away. At minimum, the scope for making concessions to Argentina would have been broadened. This still might not have made a difference, but the diplomats could have been satisfied that they had discharged their duty and, in so doing, raised the costs of ignoring their advice. There was always the chance, also, that the government might have listened and decided to commit a modest force to the Falkland Islands, thereby strengthening Britain's political commitment to them while raising the costs of a successful invasion to Argentina.

In retrospect, this course of action appears so reasonable, and its consequences so attractive, that it may seem difficult to understand why it was not taken. With such a commitment, instead of talking of leaseback, Britain could have avoided not only the war, but also the far more extensive commitments to the Falkland Islands necessitated by its subsequent victory. Even if Carrington had advised his colleagues to make up their minds about Britain's going or staying and strengthening its commitment to the chosen course of action, however, it is unlikely that they would have listened. All of them, including Thatcher, were trapped by the assumptions about responsibility and influence which were still guiding British foreign policy.

Britain could not abandon the Falkland Islands; their intrinsic worth as British territory made them hard to vacate, even willingly. The inhabitants wanted Britain to stay. Most of the government probably did too, as did the general public once it learned of the Islanders' predicament, and before it was presented with the bill. A responsible great power like Britain did not walk out on its responsibilities, particularly if to do so would look like giving way to a third-rate power. Besides, this was one of the rare occasions where an international sentiment, support for national self-determination, worked in Britain's favour. So how best to stay? The answer to this question was shaped by two considerations. First, and most obviously, the Falkland Islands were far away and not worth much in instrumental terms. There were sheep, undeveloped fisheries, the possibility of offshore oil and gas deposits, and the Islands themselves occupied a strategic location. The colony, however, was in long-term decline. A major investment in its defence, therefore, would have seemed outlandish and an easy target for the political opposition to exploit.

The second consideration concerned Argentina's response to any attempt by Britain to strengthen its commitment to keeping the Falkland Islands. The great fear, of course, was that such steps would provoke Argentina to do things it otherwise would not have done. The low instrumental worth of the Islands compounded this problem. While governments may accept that extreme measures can be threatened to safeguard supreme values, with low instrumental values a strong posture is more likely to be regarded as evidence of bullying and disrespect than as an indicator of serious and legitimate commitment. Far from forcing the other government to reconsider whether what it wants is worth the new price, raising the stakes is likely to become a new, and possibly primary, source of conflict.

Thus, an assessment had to be made of just how important the Islands were to Argentinians. The latter's powerful rhetoric was one guide, but this had been constant over busy and quiet years alike in terms of substantive actions. The actions, themselves, were another guide. While not infrequent, they had tended largely to be demonstrative in character. The British also used their own sense of the

Islands' worth as a guide to the Argentinian position. This led them to hope that the Argentinians saw them in a similar light: of negligible instrumental value; a potential headache if Anglo-Argentinian differences were not handled carefully; and an issue over which neither side wished to be forced into action by the mistakes of the other. If the British were right, then the situation demanded that they kept a presence on the Islands which was just sufficient to prevent the Argentinians from simply 'walking in', for without it they might be compelled to do precisely that. This presence, however, had to be sufficiently invisible so as not to constitute any sort of provocation to which Argentina might regard itself as compelled to respond.[21]

What never seriously seems to have been asked, however, was how Argentina would have responded if it had regarded itself as provoked. The worst case was an invasion and, indeed, one subsequently materialized, but it did so only with the possibility of a virtually bloodless victory guaranteed. Had Britain staged its own *fait accompli*, however, placing a force of sufficient size to prevent this possibility, the Argentinian response to the 'provocation' might have taken a diplomatic rather than military form. Unfortunately, even this the British government was not prepared to countenance because it did not wish to be the target of Argentinian, South American and, indeed, hemispheric diplomatic pressure at the United Nations and in other international organizations.

Thus, the same self-image of a responsible great power which prevented Britain from leaving the Falkland Islands also inhibited the steps it needed to take to permit it to stay, for to be seen as a source of international problems would damage Britain's international reputation and its influence. Muffled by these concerns was any clear consideration of where British interests lay in the matter, until Argentina provided its own dramatic and unwelcome clarification by passing the point of no return. This it did, when it decided to support a party of scrap-dealers which had landed without a British permit on the island of South Georgia and had raised the Argentinian flag. Carrington was slow to recognize the seriousness of the situation initially, and did not let the pantomime on South Georgia disrupt his own diplomatic itinerary, a decision which he and Thatcher both subsequently regretted.[22] Returning from Brussels to make a statement on the crisis, he then left again to pursue his Middle East initiative, and was in Israel when the invasion took place.

Once it was clear that Argentina was going to invade, however, the British government made every credible diplomatic and military threat it could to prevent the attack. Nuclear-powered hunter-killer submarines were ordered to the South Atlantic with maximum publicity, and Reagan was asked to get the Argentinians to change their mind, but by then it was too late. Once they had decided to act, there simply was not enough time for Britain to respond effect- ively, and the Thatcher government had been prevented from acting effectively earlier by foreign policy preoccupations which long-predated its own existence. This, however, was cold comfort. The claim that an unwanted development was beyond the govern- ment's control can sometimes provide politicians with an effective alibi. A poor economic performance at home, for example, can be blamed upon a sluggish world economy or the misdeeds of one's predecessors. It rarely works, however, for something as specific and emotionally laden as a military defeat.

This defeat had happened on Thatcher's watch, and her govern- ment's defence policy could plausibly be regarded as a contributing factor. Worse, it was hard to counter the charge that the whole episode was symptomatic of precisely the sort of post-imperial fail- ure of nerve which Thatcher herself had so strongly criticized. Argentina's success mocked everything for which she stood and posed a deadly threat to everything she valued, not least her own political future.[23] In so doing, however, it also finally provided the British government with an unambiguous national interest to pur- sue. Perhaps Thatcher could not have prevented the loss of the Islands. The important question now, however, was what, if any- thing, could she do to get them back.

5 Recovering the Falklands: the Diplomacy of War

After its successful invasion, Argentina refused to withdraw from the Falkland Islands without a promise from Britain that negotiations between the two over their future would resume. Britain would have to agree in advance that these negotiations would last for a limited time only, after which it would relinquish its claim to sovereignty in favour of Argentina. This was unacceptable to Britain and, accordingly, within a day of the attack, Thatcher announced that a naval task force would be dispatched to the South Atlantic, declaring that the government's objective was '... to see the islands were freed from invasion and returned to British administration at the earliest possible moment.'[1] Meanwhile, Argentina declared them a province and began to strengthen its own garrison. In the course of these events, several attempts at mediation were made by third parties, the Peruvian president, Belaunde Terry, the UN Secretary General, Pérez de Cuéllar and the American Secretary of State, Al Haig, all without success. The British recaptured the Falkland Island dependency of South Georgia on 26 April and military operations to recover the main Islands began in earnest on 1 May after a last British peace proposal which amounted to an ultimatum had been rejected by Argentina. A landing was made on 21 May and on 14 June after a series of defeats the Argentinian garrison surrendered.

The war captured international headlines for the few months of its duration, but subsequent interpretations of the episode have stressed its significance in terms of domestic politics. Victory made Thatcher's political reputation and defeat destroyed the military junta in Argentina, paving the way for the re-establishment of democracy in that country. As an international event, however, the conflict has widely been regarded as an avoidable aberration, an inter-state war in an age of non-state and intra-state violence, waged over a territory whose symbolic value clearly outweighed its practical value. It was widely agreed, both in Britain and abroad, that, whatever the merits of Argentina's claim to the Islands, nothing justified the use of force to settle the dispute, but there also existed a widespread uneasiness about Britain's willingness to respond in kind. The Islands were not worth much, and the government had been more than half-willing to give them away before they were taken. Just before the invasion, David Watt judged the argument to be '...one of the most incongruous and unnecessary international disputes which has ever broken out between states' and, afterwards, even Thatcher maintained in her memoirs that '...the Falklands were always an improbable cause for a twentieth century war.'[2] Why, then, did the Islands have to be recovered, and how was the case for being ready to go to war to get them back to be made?

PRESERVING THE GOVERNMENT

The most pressing concern driving the government's policy to begin with was its own survival. The general public, the political opposition and even Thatcher's own Conservatives were appalled at what they understood to be the circumstances of the Islands' loss, and informed opinion was divided only over whether the government should resign immediately or only if it failed to recover them. As Enoch Powell told the House of Commons the day after the invasion, while Britain was duty-bound to bring its complaint against Argentina to the UN, the only appropriate response to '...-unprovoked aggression upon one's sovereign territory' was '...a willingness expressed by action to use force'. To this, he added his now-famous observation that while Thatcher enjoyed being known as the Iron Lady, she would learn in the next few weeks of what metal she was made. Thatcher acknowledged Powell's barely disguised challenge in the Commons and, by her own account, took it very much to heart, but a *Times* editorial on the same day captured the government's predicament more accurately. Failure to recover the Islands, it noted, would destroy the authority of the government, but one could not be optimistic about the prospects for success.[3]

The sources of this angry combination of pessimism and goading were ambiguous and complex. More than just the loss of the Islands, or even the national humiliation which it represented at a time of general failure, fuelled the attacks. Thatcher's personality had guaranteed her many enemies in her own party and had added venom to the political opposition's attacks on her domestic policies. The worst consequences of these, particularly in terms of unemployment, were still very much at the forefront of the political agenda. For a variety of motives, therefore, personal, political and patriotic, many people saw the loss of the Islands as an opportunity for getting rid of Thatcher, and she, being who she was, responded in kind to this threat to her political life. Thatcher would recover the Islands, even if it entailed being prepared to fight a war, 'The War of Thatcher's Face', as one critic called it in parody of an eighteenth-century conflict which Britain had fought with Spain, ostensibly over the severed ear of an English sea captain.

This characterization is plausible and satisfying, particularly if one does not like Thatcher or politicians in general. She was challenged, not just by Buenos Aires but in London too, and she responded in a way which confirmed her opponents' image of her, launching a war to secure her survival. However, Thatcher was driven to accepting a war policy by more than concern for her own political survival, just as those who dared her to fight or resign were driven by more than concern for their own prospects. The real crisis remained the international one, and in connection with this, it should be noted that Thatcher more than agreed with her opponents' demand that she either recovered the Islands or got out. If she failed, not only would she probably have to go, Thatcher thought, but she ought to. In her memoirs, she says she would have resigned if she had been pressed into a compromise which prevented Britain re-establishing the status quo *ante bellum* for such a 'conditional surrender' would have been 'completely unacceptable'.[4]

At several points before and during the fighting such compromises were put before the government, and several of Thatcher's senior colleagues were inclined to see them as offering a reasonable way out of a difficult situation. Had Thatcher been concerned with her personal political survival alone, she might have been tempted into agreeing with them on the calculation that Carrington's dismissal and the mere dispatch of the task force had satisfied the demand for action. However, she did not, for at best acceptance offered only her transformation into the greatly weakened prime minister of what would be, in all probability, a greatly weakened country.

PRESERVING THE COUNTRY

This was the second string to the government's argument for why the Islands had to be recovered. The whole country could not be held responsible for their loss. That failure belonged to the government alone, for which it might atone by recovering the Islands. If it failed in its attempt, however, or, worse, made no attempt at all, then this would reflect not just on the government, but on the whole country. It was Britain's competence, honour and reputation, Thatcher and her supporters argued, which were now at stake. This was a difficult argument to make for it involved the culpable claiming that the blameless had a responsibility to help them correct their mistakes. What the government did, therefore, was to attempt to lay the question of blame aside, while it made the case for why putting matters right served a vital national interest, and stressed its own absolute determination to do this if it enjoyed support. In effect, the government issued its own counter-challenge to its critics and the country at large.

Thatcher's emphasis was on a fundamental and emotional appeal. The British government, she said, had a responsibility to do '... everything we can' to uphold the Falkland Islanders' right to live as they wished, because their way of life was British, they were 'an island race' like 'the people of the United Kingdom' and their allegiance was to the Crown.[5] Confronting Argentina's aggression against such a people was a matter of Britain's honour as a nation, 'its self-confidence' and, hence, 'its standing in the world.'[6] A week after the task force had sailed, the scale of the military challenge started to become clear and the first doubts were expressed, even among those who had called for the dispatch of the fleet. Thatcher, however, was unmoved. The operation had to go ahead, she said, '... because the reputation of Britain is at stake' and, therefore, she added in most un-Thatcherite terms, '... we cannot look at it on the basis of precisely how much it will cost.'[7]

It was a powerful, if primitive and problematic, appeal. What kind of people would not allow their government to stand up for its own, and what would the rest of the world think of such a people? Previous Falklands policy, especially the government's attempt to deny residency rights in Britain to the Islanders, was an embarrassment, perhaps, but it was not effectively exploited by the opposition because it did not materially affect the substance of Thatcher's case. In so far as they were anything besides Falkland Islanders, the people whom she said Britain had a duty to save were demonstrably British and certainly not Argentinian. Nevertheless, other supporters of the government tended not to build upon kith-and-kin arguments, but rather situated them within a broader picture of

Britain and its international commitments. *The Times*, for example, extended its earlier argument about the government's authority being at stake to the country as a whole. The Islands had to be recovered, it claimed:

> ...to re-establish the evidence of British willpower, because the whole structure of this country's standing in the world, her credibility as an ally, as a guarantor of guarantees, as a protector of her citizens, depends on that willpower existing and being seen to exist.[8]

Status arguments of this kind appeared far more sophisticated than Thatcher's appeals to blood and soil. If Britain was still a great power, if it was to remain capable of independent action and merit consultation on important issues, then Argentina's transgression required an assertive response. However, such arguments also carried their own, arguably, even more primitive appeal, for the question 'Is Britain still a great power?' which the status argument raised, implied the corollary, 'or has it sunk so low that a country like Argentina can do this sort of thing without fear of retaliation?' On either level, however, Thatcher and her supporters hoped, the answer was clear. Britain had to recover the Islands, according to a petty officer in one of the warships, '...so that our children can walk about in the world with their heads held high.'[9] Without them, there could be no walking about the world for Britain would have ceased to be a great power. With them its reputation would not merely be recovered, but elevated. As Alan Clark, a Conservative member of Parliament, told a journalist towards the end of the war, the victory had:

> ...enormously increased our world standing. You asked about world opinion – I mean bugger world opinion – but our standing in the world has been totally altered by this. It has made every other member of NATO say 'My God, the British are tough.'[10]

In Clark's international political world where right without might rarely prospered, it was important to be regarded as strong and feared for the tenacity with which one pursued one's interests and defended one's principles. To judge by her subsequent foreign policy, Thatcher clearly agreed, particularly with Clark's distinction between world opinion and world standing. The peaceful resolution of all disputes involves somebody making concessions, and as the government well knew, relief that someone is prepared to make concessions to avoid war does not necessarily translate into respect for them. Had Britain agreed to a compromise by which it did not regain the Islands, neither its international position nor its remaining colonies would necessarily have been immediately threatened. Indeed, world opinion would have been so relieved that Britain had decided not to push the matter to a fight that the Thatcher government would have found itself the recipient of fulsome international praise for its courage and statesmanship. Even as 'world opinion' praised Britain, however, it would also be passing judgement on its new 'world standing' – here is a country which is no longer willing to fight for territory it claims as its own – and this would have undermined its standing as a great power.

Abroad, no one would be so rude as to challenge directly Britain's claim to a seat on the Security Council, for example, or its senior partner status in Nato, but such roles would become harder to perform all the same. At home, in contrast, no such restraint would prevail, and similar questions would have been asked more openly and aggressively about why the country retained extensive international commitments and powerful armed forces. Over 25 years of emphasizing the multilateral character of the way the latter now performed their primary mission did not change the fact that their mission remained the defence of British territory, even if this was located outside the primary area of operations. If British forces could not defend British territory from real attacks, then what was the point of having so many of them permanently preparing to deal with a hypothetical one? This would have been a reasonable, though not unanswerable, question, but fortunately the government did not have to deal with it. For the duration of the crisis, at least, it garnered sufficient public support for its claim that Argentina would have to be removed from the Falkland Islands, by force if necessary, if Britain's self-respect and international standing (however the public defined them) were to be preserved. And its eventual success in this regard provided a reason why it was good to be a great power which was difficult to counter.

Nevertheless, considerable opposition to the status argument for why Britain should act did exist. Honour, prestige and credibility, the vital elements of an international political reputation for those engaged in the business, have long been objects of deep suspicion among its observers, particularly when immaterial causes appear to entail all too material and damaging consequences like the extensive loss of life. At their worst, appeals to reputation can be entirely fraudulent, and at their best they may still be seen as providing dangerous infusions of emotion at the very moment when cool heads and sober reflection are required. Three days before Argentina's invasion of the Falkland Islands, for example, *The Times* had said that the Islanders had:

> ... to face the unpleasant fact that Britain is no longer a world power and that the rest of the world is unlikely to come to their rescue. If they are to stay where they are in the next century it can only be on the basis of an arrangement with their South American neighbours.[11]

Only a week later, however, the editorial quoted above about Britain's willpower, reputation and standing in the world depending on its retaking the Islands appeared in the same newspaper. It did so to the accompaniment of an extensive quotation from Donne and echoes of Thatcher's claims about the commitments of island races to one another, all under a heading which claimed improbably that 'We Are All Falklanders Now'.

What had changed beyond the Argentinians use of force to settle the argument? The sceptical response was nothing at all or, at least, nothing which necessitated the use of force to serve a vital national interest. Britain could discharge its responsibilities to the Islanders in other ways besides fighting to free them. Settling them on a Scottish island with a similar habitat was one suggestion, cheaper and preferable to a war which, won or lost, would probably destroy the very way of life it was ostensibly being fought to preserve. Better, surely, to work out some mutually face-saving compromise with Argentina for which the international community would think none the worse of Britain, than to precipitate a war which it could only regard with incredulity. After all, other countries had experienced the forcible seizure of their overseas territories and had not launched wars for their recovery. They had swallowed their pride, and despite the loss their national life in all its essentials had gone on much as before.

Beyond observing the dangers of allowing pride and anger to dictate one's actions, however, the opponents of the status argument divided into two clear types. There were those who regarded all the language of status and responsibility as mere cant designed to rationalize the fact that being a great power involved little more than cultivating the ability to use force and take life for selfish and oppressive purposes. Britain, because of its longer experience and greater wealth, merely happened to be still a larger and more successful bully than Argentina. Little can be said about this claim. It is based on an ordering of values to which most people subscribe in principle, but which is rarely validated by their sentiments or their actual practice. It also tends to assume that the impure motives, if such they are, of the most important protagonists provide the dramas in which they are involved with their primary or only moral significance. Suffice it to note, therefore, that objections to the government's status argument on the grounds that great powers are about violence and all wars are bad were marginal to the debate in Britain at the time, although arguments of general principle were deployed when found useful by those who were opposed to the war for other, more particular, reasons.

The second, more common source of opposition to the war was from those who did not reject the idea of being a great power in principle, or even the use of force to secure it. All other things, especially living standards, remaining equal, it may be better and more interesting to be a great power, or to live in one, than not, they conceded. The attempt to maintain such a standing should be relinquished, however, once its costs became exorbitant, and this was Britain's problem. The effort had become too much. If Britain's credentials as a great power had been in order, Argentina would have been unlikely to risk a war with it in the first place. A sober and unsentimental consideration of concrete indicators like trade patterns, military commitments and institutionalized political links strongly suggested that Britain was a regional power with few substantive interests elsewhere. This being so, then the very possibility of a war over a leftover like the Falkland Islands was just one more compelling reason why it ought to start acting like one.[12]

Nor was the government necessarily a prisoner of public opinion in this regard, for it was possible to argue that the latter was shifting to an even more modest conception of Britain's international role than that of a regional or middle power. A much-quoted Gallup poll suggested in 1985, for example, that only 26 per cent of those surveyed believed that Britain should 'try to be a leading power,' while 55 per cent said it should try to be '...more like Sweden/ Switzerland'.[13] Clearly, if these findings were anything to go by, the process of adjusting from a global to a regional self-image would be fraught with problems. The principled and limited (although not nearly so principled and limited as most of the respondents probably imagined) foreign policies of Sweden and Switzerland might sound more attractive to the dyspeptic ratepayer or unemployed worker alike when contrasted with the more extensive role which Britain was still attempting. In practice, however, this was a fragile sentiment and, at a visceral level, few people felt that Britain should respond to the invasion of the Falkland Islands in the same way that Portugal accepted the storming of Goa or the Netherlands acquiesced in the UN-sponsored transfer of West Irian to Indonesia. If it was in a position to do something about the affront, then the initial reaction was that Britain ought not to turn the other cheek.

Difficult though the task might be, however, the critics maintained that a responsible government would have worked hard to steer public opinion away from the oscillations between the great power of its increasingly second-hand memories and the Switzerland conjured up by its daily insecurities to focus on something sensibly regional in between. Then, neither government nor people could have been coerced by the sentiment to which *The Times* had given expression with its claim that Britain's ability to meet its commitments to allies in Europe or to protect its citizens at home depended on the assertion of its will over Argentina. Instead, the government could have concentrated on damping down the first emotional response to the attack. Visceral feelings, it should have argued, are a poor substitute for reason, and if the best reason Britain has for recapturing the Falkland Islands from Argentina was to save Belize from Guatemala, then Britain did not have a reason to go to war. The logic of colonial dominoes, even if substantially correct, should not matter to British foreign policy anymore. Indeed, if Thatcher really was the radical and classical liberal she claimed she was, then she should welcome the loss of the Falkland Islands as a glorious opportunity for the break with the past which she allegedly sought to make. The predicament in which the country now found itself, she could have argued, was a consequence of the preoccupations and the incompetence of Britain's landowning and military elites. Shorn of these, Britain could finally get on with the serious business of making money. Instead, she took the easy way out, going to war because the British people were not ready to make this reappraisal and certainly did not want it thrust upon them in this manner by Argentina.

That Thatcher and her supporters did not seize this allegedly radical moment should not be surprising. A government which was in the midst of an international political crisis was unlikely to precipitate a fundamental crisis of national identity to add to its burdens, even if it believed one to be in order. One crisis at a time, and this one could be best dealt with by presenting it as a test of old British strengths and virtues which Thatcher had always claimed still existed. More importantly, the claim that going to war amounted to taking the easy way out was not only intuitively implausible, it also revealed a major inconsistency in the pragmatic opposition to the status arguments for going to war. One could either oppose the defence of status on principle and then berate the bullying to which it easily lead, or one could oppose the defence of status on the pragmatic grounds that it had become too draining and point to the risks which it entailed. What one could not do was make the pragmatic argument and then accuse those who were prepared to accept the risk of taking the easy way out.

Of course, Argentina's invasion of the Falkland Islands did not present the British government with a choice between the easy and self-indulgent ways of business and bullying as usual in defence of its status, and the difficult, but upward, path of remaking itself as a regional, conscientious, social-democratic, or even bourgeois, state. In so far as they had ever really existed, gunboat operations providing easy victories and cheap popularity had vanished long before the First World War. Being prepared to go to war to maintain the country's standing as a great power required that the government and the country be willing to court real risks and costs up front. Embarking on change, in contrast, would have allowed both difficulties to be ducked. As the subsequent course of the fighting was to show, however, neither the risks nor the costs were as large as many had originally feared. The fate of the nation did not sail with the task force or, if it did, then it sailed in conditions of considerable security, for the military challenge proved to be well within Britain's reach.

However, it did so not merely because of the balance of power between Britain and Argentina, about which there existed so little confidence among the critics of British policy to begin with. That balance was revealed only as a consequence of choices made by Thatcher's government. For her, Britain's great power status was a critical element of the country's national identity, maintained not by the dead weight of history but, as it had been created in the past, by a combination of choices, courage and good fortune. In embracing the risks and costs of leading the country to war, therefore, she effectively confirmed her intention of maintaining this status and, to judge from the high level of support the war enjoyed, the majority of the public agreed with and expected her choice.

PRESERVING INTERNATIONAL LAW AND ORDER

To be a great power, however, involves accepting a measure of responsibility for the rules and institutions which maintain international order, and this responsibility provided the third and final set of arguments for why Britain should recover the Falkland Islands, by force if necessary. To do so would be to do no more than its duty, for Argentina's invasion had violated two important principles of international conduct. The first of these was the principle of self-determination. For most of the crisis, it was the British position that the Falkland Islanders had the right to live under political arrangements of their own choosing, and on several occasions Thatcher declared that their wishes must be the 'paramount' consideration in any final settlement.[14] Secondly, the government argued that armed aggression should not be rewarded and should not be allowed to change the status of a territory or its inhabitants. If Argentina was not forced off the Islands, then international law and the order which it helped to sustain would be weakened, aggressors encouraged and weaker parties to territorial disputes around the world put at risk.[15] She could not '. . . rule out the use of force', Thatcher told the House of Commons just before the recapture of South Georgia, because:

> You have to be prepared to defend the things in which you believe and be prepared to use force if that is the only way to secure the future of liberty and self-determination.[16]

Both claims posed problems. The self-determination argument rested on the hostility to Argentina and determination to remain British to which the Islanders' representatives gave expression whenever they were consulted on their future. Once again, however, the limited say which the Islanders enjoyed in their own affairs hurt the argument. The company which owned the sheep farms, its managers and the colonial administration appointed by London were more influential, and it has been argued that they were the most vocal supporters of the link with Britain. Indeed, there is evidence to suggest that a silent, indeed reticent, majority existed whose views about their future may have been more flexible, although this might be said of any body of public opinion.[17]

The second principle cited by Thatcher, that aggression should not be rewarded, was also vulnerable to the claim that it was undermined by Britain's own policy. There was, for example, a troubling similarity between the invasion of 1982 and the way in which the British had established their control of the Islands in 1833. Both had involved sending a large force to order a weaker one to depart, and the only major difference seemed to be that the Argentinians had gone quietly, bowing to *force majeure*, whereas the British had made a show of armed resistance. Worse, after they assumed control of the Islands, the British had removed the people they found there while the Argentinians announced their intention of letting them stay. However, there were also important differences. In the period between independence in 1810 and the British seizure in 1833, Buenos Aires had experienced great difficulty securing recognition of its authority both on the Islands themselves and abroad. The inhabitants had regarded themselves as subject to no one and, indeed, the British had exploited a period of anarchy following the murder of the Buenos Aires' governor to establish themselves.[18] In contrast, the 99 years of continuous British occupation were peaceful, broadly uncontested in material terms, and enjoyed the full support of the inhabitants.

There was another problem with the argument that aggression should not be allowed to pay. An international consensus quickly emerged that Argentina should not have invaded, but it rested on two different principles. The first was derived from the fact that history leaves few states, even the most democratic and pacific, unembarrassed about their origins in acts of violence. This being so, a broad agreement has emerged that the good to be achieved by calling into question every territorial settlement which someone regards as unjust would be outweighed by the threat to peace which trying to satisfy it would pose. The second principle was that states should not use force to settle their disputes. Taken together, they implied that while the consequences of past violence should be accepted, the present or future use of force should not and, thus, a country could not expect sanction for recovering by force what it had lost to force in the past.

Until Argentina seized the Falkland Islands, both principles favoured Britain, but once they were lost, the second, at least, worked the other way. If the international community could not consent to Argentina's benefitting from the use of force, then how could it support Britain's aspiration to do likewise? The British government's response, of course, was that Argentina's use of force had been to advance a national ambition and was, therefore, illegitimate, whereas Britain's use of force was in self-defence, to right a wrong and, in so doing, to uphold international law and order. The extent to which anybody accepted this claim is very hard to ascertain, but what the government discovered was that no governments abroad and very few people at home were prepared to oppose it substantially.

Such attacks as were made on the appeal to high principles were usually fuelled, once again, by dismay at the costs of violence and the suspicion that Thatcher and her supporters actually cared nothing for upholding international law or freeing oppressed peoples. An exception was the argument made by Anthony Barnett. He called into question the principle of self-determination by pointing out that it was neither a moral absolute nor automatic evidence of a strong stance against appeasing aggressors. The Sudeten Germans, for example, should have been denied the right of self-determination, he argued, for the price of granting it was the effective destruction of Czechoslovakia, the strengthening of Adolf Hitler's prestige and confidence and, hence, a greatly increased possibility of a general European war on terms advantageous to Nazi Germany.[19] Even so, such arguments were difficult for people on the left to make effectively, for they involved acknowledging that on occasions the requirements of peace, order and stability involved subordinating the aspirations of people to the interests and reasons of states. More importantly, in this particular case, opposition to Thatcher's appeals to principles was hamstrung by the fact that the Argentinian government was a military dictatorship with a miserable human rights record. To oppose her, as opposed to merely doubting her sincerity, was to imply that the Islanders should be left in the hands of a South American junta, either because it could be trusted, or because one simply no longer cared.

As a consequence, the most effective criticism of the government's appeal to international principles came from an entirely different source, Enoch Powell. Powell took the Hobbesian position that where there was no common power there could be no common morality by which to justify one's actions. In his view, the UN was a 'bogus democracy... devoid of democratic responsibility for the results of its deliberations', and the right of nations to act in self-defence did not depend upon its approval.[20] It followed that the government should not attempt to reconcile its policy with the combination of national interests which made up the UN's position. To do so would be to give way to humbug and might put the country's diplomatic position at risk. Powell was especially concerned that the right of self-defence, and not the principle of self-determination, should provide the basic justification for British policy. In mid-April, in a report on Haig's mediation efforts, Thatcher had assured the House of Commons once again of Britain's position that '... the wishes of the islanders should remain paramount.' This position attracted criticism in that it gave the Islanders an effective veto over any negotiations with Argentina and, since they wished to remain British, this would almost inevitably lead to war and prevent a future settlement. Powell's position, however, was that the Falkland Islands were British, whatever their inhabitants happened to think at any particular time. By suggesting that Britain's rule was conditional upon expressions of the local popular will, however, its claim to sovereignty over the Islands would be rendered more vulnerable to contestation as, of course, it had in Northern Ireland.[21]

Thatcher shared Powell's concern that bogus principles might obstruct the pursuit of genuine interests. Just over a month after he had made his point about self-determination and just before British forces landed on the main Islands, she again gave a summary of Britain's diplomatic position. Now, however, instead of paramountcy, she talked of a 'full account of the wishes' of the Islanders being taken in future negotiations with Argentina and on 28 May, with the ground war in progress and going well, she promised the House of Commons that once the war was over, the government would 'consult' with the Islanders on what they wanted.[22] It was thought at the time that this choice of words indicated a softening of Britain's position and a shift towards the idea that the Islanders' 'interests' rather than their 'wishes' should occupy the centrepiece of any final settlement with Argentina. Subsequent events, however, showed the reverse to be the case. As victory became more likely, the British position hardened, and Thatcher showed by the extensive resources she was prepared to commit to the Falkland Islands' future defence that she, like Powell, placed a high value on sovereign territory. It would be defended even though it possessed no great instrumental worth, and even if this involved some disruption of the Islanders' established way of life.

Sympathetic though she was to any deprecation humbug, however, Thatcher did not share Powell's view of international law and morality. She took the idea of international order from which these principles were derived far more seriously and approved of much in its postwar manifestation. She accepted the idea of great powers taking responsibility for order and the principles on which it is organized, whereas he asked for no greater virtue from nations than that, in the normal course of events, they should seek to mind their own business. She shared none of Powell's hostility to the US and did not see it as a rival which had nudged Britain off the world stage and was, even now, seeking to drive it from the Falkland Islands.[23] Rather, she identified the US as the primary upholder of an international order which was good, from which Britain benefited greatly and which, hence, it had an obligation to help maintain.

For Thatcher, therefore, to argue that in recovering the Falkland Islands, Britain was performing a service to the cause of international order was not humbug. It was a fortunate, but unsurprising, example of how British interests and the requirements of international order and morality coincided. Not only did Thatcher want to take international principles more seriously than Powell did, however, she had to as a political leader. Unlike him, she could not indulge the scepticism which they shared if she was to be successful, because success depended on maintaining a coalition of support both at home and abroad, and this involved a willingness to compromise. Thatcher was, for example, only too aware of the obstacles to British policy which might emerge in the UN. 'We knew', she says in her memoirs, '. . . that we had to try to keep our affairs out of the UN as much as possible.' The Cold War was still underway, and an 'anti-colonialist attitude' prevailed among many of its members.

Nevertheless, the first priority of British diplomacy had to be to obtain a Security Council resolution denouncing Argentina's aggression and demanding its withdrawal. Such a resolution would provide an international justification for what the government wanted to do should Argentina refuse, and make it easier for other governments to support Britain's policy. It would also help maintain support for the government's policy at home among, what Thatcher called, '. . . a coalition of opinion . . . composed of warriors, negotiators, and even virtual pacifists'.[24] Indeed, once it had been decided to use force to regain the Falkland Islands, and until the moment when the Argentinians submitted or were defeated, the principal challenge confronting the government was to preserve this coalition, abroad, at home and even within itself, while the armed forces went about their business.

PRESERVING THE COALITION ABROAD

Most governments adopted a position of neutrality on the substance of the dispute. They expected that Argentina would eventually gain the Islands, for this appeared to be the salient solution from a distance, but the most frequently expressed sentiment was that the two countries should settle their differences peacefully. Once it had invaded, therefore, Argentina enjoyed very little support for what it had done. Even the admiration which existed in the region for what was presented as an act of anti-colonial and national self-assertion was tempered by the precedent that success might set. Most of Argentina's neighbours, for example, were, or had been, the subjects of its other territorial claims. One of them, Chile, offered barely disguised support to Britain, and many island states in the Caribbean became concerned about their 'offshore' status in the eyes of others. Thus, substantive assistance to Argentina remained minimal while declaratory support gathered strength only as the course of the fighting made it easier to present the country as a victim, rather than a perpetrator, of violence.[25]

For the rest, neutrality on the point at issue between Britain and Argentina provided a poor guide to how they should behave in the crisis. Of course, the use of force as an instrument of policy, particularly as an instrument of someone else's policy, was unconscionable, but everyone was aware that a complete taboo would reward only those who were prepared to violate it. That is why the right to use force in self-defence and, less certainly, to punish violators of the taboo was widely recognized. What other governments had to ask themselves, therefore, was whether a British use of force would be justifiable in these terms. It was not an easy question to answer for it involved them in making another set of judgements, for example on the legitimacy of Britain's presence on the Islands in the first place, on whether it had exhausted all other means before resorting to force, and on whether the restoration of British rule was the necessary first step to finding a solution. Even if it was generally agreed that Argentina had committed a trespass against Britain, it was by no means clear to everybody that the war which Thatcher's government was prepared to fight was a reasonable and proportionate response to that trespass.

The answers governments gave to questions such as these were greatly influenced by both the interests they had in the dispute and the general state of their relations with either or both of the parties to it. Unsurprisingly, those who were least tolerant of the Thatcher government's willingness to use force were those who enjoyed a poor relationship with Britain or a good one with Argentina. Thus, for example, once the fighting began in earnest with an escalation by the British, the torpedoing and sinking of an Argentinan warship with heavy loss of life in uncertain circumstances, Italy and Ireland began to withdraw from the economic sanctions imposed by the EC on Argentina. The Italian government was not prepared to confront a large domestic constituency which, as a result of immigration, enjoyed personal ties with Argentina. The Irish government was sensitive to the charge that it had compromised the country's neutrality in the most embarrassing way possible by supporting a war to further the ambitions of British colonialism. At the time, Ireland's change of policy seemed to threaten dangerous consequences, for it involved calling for a meeting of the UN Security Council in circumstances which would have been disadvantageous to Britain. In retrospect, however, it is possible to conclude that both Italy's and Ireland's policy changes were calculated to have maximum domestic impact while doing little of substance to affect the final outcome of the conflict.[26]

More surprising to Thatcher's government were the responses of some of those it regarded as friends. Like Britain, France and the Netherlands possessed vulnerable overseas possessions and were understanding, but others found it hard to accept that Thatcher would risk the use of force for so little cause. Although Argentina was wrong to have invaded the Falkland Islands, the result, at least, could be seen to be in keeping with the post-colonial spirit of the times. By invading, Argentina had merely tried to hurry the flow of history, but by trying to recapture the Islands, in contrast, Britain would be attempting to swim against that tide at terrible risk to itself and others. Once its honour was satisfied by a military demonstration and some Argentinian concessions, therefore, many of its friends believed that Britain ought to accept a settlement by which its control of the Falkland Islands was reduced and Argentina's influence over them increased. Such a compromise would represent an honourable way-station on the road to a full transfer of sovereignty at some point in the future.

For much of the conflict, the clearest and most important exponent of this view was the US. At Britain's request, President Reagan had asked the Argentinians to suspend their attack before it went in, but to no avail. Then, to the dismay of the British, the Americans decided to attempt a mediation with the Secretary of State, Al Haig, shuttling between London and Buenos Aires in search of a compromise. The invasion presented the US with a difficult problem, a conflict between two allies, each demanding support, and its dilemma was complicated by the existence of tensions within the American government over the control of foreign policy. Fights over this had spilled over into fights about the content of policy. Haig advocated maintaining the European focus of US policy while others like Jeanne Kirkpatrick, the ambassador to the UN, believed that hemispheric relations with countries like Argentina should be built up. By the mediation, therefore, Haig hoped to appease the concerns of those like Kirkpatrick while establishing himself as the senior US diplomatist by resolving a difficult foreign policy problem.

In retrospect, the mediation was a mistake. Success in such efforts depends on whether the parties to the conflict are prepared to settle on any but their own terms, and, if they are not, then on the ability of the mediator to secure concessions through persuasion, the threat of punishment and the promise of rewards. Haig lacked all of these resources. Neither side was sufficiently moved by any threats he may have made, and no reward could compensate either government for the loss of the Islands. All Haig could do, therefore, was offer various formulae for establishing a temporary joint or neutral executive, and instead of using superpower leverage to broker a settlement, he found himself in the unflattering position for a US Secretary of State of duplicating similar efforts by the UN Secretary General and the leaders of several minor powers with about as much success.

Failure, however, is not the worst possible consequence of mediation efforts. If it were, they would always be worth undertaking, for no one, except perhaps the mediators, would be worse off than if the attempt had never been made. The danger lies in the possibility that a failed mediation makes the conflict which it seeks to avert more likely. This concern was raised by the British when they first heard of Haig's mission. Thatcher was told that the Americans had adopted a mediatory position to retain as much influence for as long as possible over Argentina's actions.[27] What, however, if such respectful treatment merely encouraged the Argentinians in the hubris resulting from their new security and counter-insurgency relationships with the US? Worse, what if the mediation effort reflected a lack of commitment to Britain on the part of the US and was designed to undermine Britain's determination to press ahead? Memories of the Suez crisis in 1956 and the US refusal to support Anglo-French efforts to repossess the Canal and topple Nasser were aroused.

Understandably, the British preference was for an immediate declaration of American support followed by substantial military assistance, including a commitment to the security of the Islands once they were repossessed. If Argentina was to be brought to its senses, it would be by the shock of having the real balance of power in the conflict made completely clear and not by diplomatic court-ship. This was not to be, however, and British diplomacy never completely overcame American reservations about the need to fight a war for the Islands. Haig's mediation effort failed at the end of April, and the US abandoned its position of neutrality because, as he put it, Argentina would not accept the American peace proposals.[28] However, this was not before Haig had attempted to restrict Britain's use of the US facilities on the British island possession of Ascension as a staging post for its forces while peace talks were going on and, for the same reason, considered giving the Argentinians notice of British operations against South Georgia.[29] Even after the US abandoned neutrality, on two occasions it asked Britain to compromise, once after British honour had been satisfied by a successful landing on the main Islands, and again as Port Stanley was about to fall to avoid completely humiliating the Argentinians.[30]

The British government's response to American attempts at even-handedness had to be carefully weighed. Any indignation which its members felt at being treated by the US, that most moralizing of nations, as the moral equivalent of Argentina was restrained and the mediation accepted. If the Americans believed that a mediation offered the best chance of influencing Argentina and securing US support for a tilt towards Britain in the event of failure, then Britain would participate in the exercise.[31] However, Thatcher made Brit-ish expectations very clear by stressing that Haig would be received in London not '...as a mediator but as a friend and ally', here to explore how the US might best support Britain's efforts to get Argentina to leave the Falkland Islands.[32] The US should not expect Britain to accept any settlement which ruled out its resump-tion of full control there. At the most, Britain would consider a temporary administration sponsored by the US with a minimal Argentinian involvement while the Islanders decided what they wanted.

The strategy was not without its risks. A willingness to accept mediation at all might be interpreted by others as evidence that Britain had been bluffing all along and was looking for a way out. The possibility also existed that Haig would produce a compromise which was acceptable to the Argentinians but which, while falling far short of what Britain wanted, might become very difficult to refuse. Could Thatcher refuse such a settlement if it enjoyed American support and the support of the international community in general? However, these risks were never very high. The government's resolve was not called into question by accepting the American effort because in the early stages, at least, Britain was not in a position to act. It was three weeks before the task force reached the Falkland Islands and when it did, its own precarious circumstances dictated that it would have to be used directly, if it were to be used at all. The British were also fortunate that the opening steps of their own preferred solution were rejected by Argentina but sounded reasonable to nearly everyone else. The Argentinians must leave the Islands before talks about their future resumed. These talks must not rule out any particular outcome in advance, but the Islanders' preferences would have to be a primary consideration. The Argentinians judged this to be a formula for restoring the status quo and insisted, therefore, on keeping some people on the Islands while talks were conducted. A time limit should be set, and the participants should agree in advance that at the end of the talks, sovereignty would be transferred to Argentina. As a result, they rejected several proposals which Thatcher would have found it equally difficult to accept or refuse.

Most importantly, however, the British established early on that neither the US nor anyone else would raise severe objections if, in the absence of a reasonable agreement, they decided to use force. Indeed, while disputes within the higher levels of US foreign policy-making were damaging the coherence of American diplomacy, those responsible for its defence policy were already responding to the requests of their British counterparts for equipment, supplies and intelligence which would help put the issue, when it came to a test of arms, beyond doubt. The real challenge to British policy, therefore, came not from abroad but from within. If Britain had an excellent chance of winning, as her military advisers said it did, and if the worst the diplomatic community was prepared to do involved withdrawing support for economic sanctions or forcing Britain to veto a ceasefire resolution at the Security Council, then Thatcher and her supporters were prepared to go to war. Others, however, including members of the government, were not so sure. After the first flush of anger, they began to share the concern of the international community that the course on which Thatcher had embarked, the complete restitution of British authority by force if necessary, was neither prudent nor necessarily right.

PRESERVING THE COALITION AT HOME

When Thatcher announced the dispatch of the task force in the House of Commons on 3 April, only a handful of members disagreed, and while the mood of the House of Commons may have been ahead of public opinion in its bellicosity, there was little to suggest subsequently that it was at odds with it. If sending a task force to the South Atlantic was something about which nearly everyone could agree, however, why it was being sent was another matter. Three views with different implications are identifiable. First, sending it would provide a catharsis for the emotional stress generated by the loss of the Islands, satisfying the need for what Michael Foot, the leader of the opposition Labour party, called 'deeds not words'.[33] On the long voyage south, cooler sentiments would prevail on both sides and a compromise would be worked out. Second was the view that the task force represented a bargaining signal, a demonstration to Argentina of how seriously Britain took the issue. Argentina had miscalculated, and perhaps British actions had contributed to error, but now negotiations could resume without any doubt about how matters really stood. Third, the force was seen as an instrument of a more direct British policy. Sending it might be emotionally satisfying at home and, with any luck, it would communicate British resolve. Its primary function, however, would be to provide the threat or use of force necessary to ensure that the Argentinians left the Islands.

The first two views were little more than hopes that the problem would somehow go away. The first was quickly exposed as such. Whatever cathartic release the task force may have provided on the day it sailed, the problem it was sent to solve remained while those associated with the military option loomed larger with each successive day. In contrast, the idea that the task force would concentrate the Argentinian mind on looking for a way out by signalling Britain's resolve was more resilient. As such, it reflected the tendency to hope for the best even as things are clearly getting worse. It also reflected, however, an ironically naive inference from the popular and cynical conviction that life, and political life especially, is all staged, namely that things will turn out alright. In this view both governments were engaging in a pantomime to satisfy themselves and their various constituencies. They were pretending to arm for war and, unless one or both parties were crazy, once their performances brought them to the brink of real consequences, they would back away. A case can be made for saying that even some members of the government were victims of this particular delusion, for the force initially assembled was completely inadequate if negotiations failed and it was ordered to storm the Islands. If this is so, however, then to judge by the steady and extensive flow of reinforcements which the task force began to receive, those charged with prosecuting the war soon disabused them of it.

The obvious question raised by viewing the crisis as political theatre was what should Britain do if Argentina refused to abandon the pantomime when it became dangerous. If it brought the task force home, Britain's solo return to reality would look like a capitulation in which its bluff had been called. As the prospect of war increased, however, those who called for further talks were increasingly made to look like the bluffers. Foot, for example, declared that force should be used as a last resort, only after every possibility of a peaceful settlement had been explored and exhausted. Speaking for the Labour party in the days between the recapture of South Georgia and the first raids on the main Islands, he called for the reconvening of the Security Council now that the US mediation had failed and, again, just before the landings towards the end of May, he asked Thatcher for a full debate in Parliament on the final British peace proposals.[34]

Thatcher refused because, she argued, it can never be demonstrated that the last prospect for a peaceful settlement has been exhausted, especially if one's principal objective has become to avoid fighting. Someone will always be willing to launch one more political initiative even if it is only, in the words of the Irish representative on the UN Security Council, to 'shout stop'.[35] The military option, in contrast, was all too exhaustible. If the task force remained at sea, thousands of miles from its nearest base, while every possible peace proposal was explored, then it would quickly become incapable of recapturing the Islands and the Argentinians would succeed by default.[36] There is nothing in Foot's record to suggest that he regarded the task force as a bluff, or that he was prepared to leave the Falkland Islands to their fate if the bluff was called. He may not have known how narrow was the window for action in the South Atlantic. If this is so, however, Foot must take some responsibility for his ignorance because he had excluded himself from the closest consultations between Thatcher and other party leaders, the better to fulfil his constitutional duty to oppose. And knowledgeable or not, the practical consequence of his calls for delay would have been the loss of the Islands.

Thatcher, of course, was committed to using the task force as an instrument for recovering the Islands and, as such, she had little patience with Foot's interventions. Any actions or words which might lead the Argentinians to believe that Britain was less than fully committed to its course of action were to be avoided at all costs, for in strengthening Argentina's own resolve, they would only strengthen opposition to Thatcher's policy in Britain, forcing her to abandon it and resign, or, if that did not happen, simply make a shooting war far more likely. Potentially damaging though she judged such requests to be, however, Thatcher was not seriously troubled by anything the opposition might do. She enjoyed an unassailable majority in Parliament and Foot was the ineffective leader of a weakened party which, in her judgement, had completely lost its grip on political and economic realities. Thatcher neither respected nor feared opposition from this source and Labour's subsequent defeat in the 1983 election confirmed her judgement in this regard.

What she did fear, however, was the emergence of similar arguments from within her own 'War Cabinet' and the Foreign Office. The problem, as Thatcher saw it, was Francis Pym, who had become foreign secretary upon Carrington's resignation. By her own account, their relationship was a difficult one, for his pragmatic qualities, while they made Pym a popular party choice, were ill-suited for handling this particular crisis.[37] Many of Thatcher's supporters saw him as embodying the defeatism which had prevailed in postwar Britain and working with his diplomats to summon up the old uncertainties which might snatch defeat from the jaws of victory. Whether out of personal ambition or personal conviction, in their view, Pym did everything he could to undermine Thatcher by suggesting she did not mean what she said or did not speak for Britain. The counterpoint, of course, was that Thatcher was a woman in need of rescue, chiefly from herself, and that Pym was the man to do it. In this view, Thatcher's personality and inexperience combined to make Britain's task more difficult than it needed to be. A willingness to negotiate a little more and preach a little less might not produce a settlement, but it would neutralize some opponents and put some of Britain's allies more at ease. And if it did produce a reasonable compromise, then so much the better. What the world needed to know, however, now more than ever, was that British diplomacy had not become a captive of conviction politics, but remained sensitive to the concerns of its friends and allies.

Both views are overdrawn. Pym was neither the cold-footed subversive of Thatcher's recollection, nor was he the zoo keeper of Healey's earlier imagery restraining a woman driven to desperate and bloody vengeance by a failure for which she was not prepared to take responsibility. However, the differences between them were real and did not result from some finely calibrated good cop/bad cop strategy of psychological warfare directed at the Argentinian government. The most obvious one concerned the place of force in British policy. Throughout the crisis, Thatcher was sceptical about the ability of either diplomatic or economic measures to solve the problem. After Carrington's resignation, for example, she claimed that no one could have been 'more active diplomatically' than Britain but '. . . it failed.' Britain would continue with this effort, she continued, but it was '. . . difficult to see how it could succeed now when it failed before.'[38] Two weeks later, just before South Georgia was recaptured, Thatcher told Parliament that she could not rule out the use of force, not least because the '. . . history of economic sanctions and their effectiveness has not been good.'[39] Once military operations were underway she was firmly opposed to reverting to diplomatic measures which might interfere with their momentum. There would be no pause, she said, after the capture of South Georgia to allow the Argentinians to reconsider their position now that Britain had demonstrated its willingness to use force. 'Negotiations', she told Parliament, '. . . are more likely to succeed if military pressure is kept up', and she reiterated this position once the fighting had started in earnest and resulted in considerable loss of life on both sides. Any ceasefire, she argued, would simply allow the Argentinians to consolidate their position on the Islands.[40]

Pym, in contrast, saw force as but one instrument of a broader diplomacy. Britain's policy, he told Parliament at the end of April, was one of diplomatic, economic and military pressure upon

Argentina, designed to achieve a peaceful settlement, although no one should doubt Britain's willingness to use force. He reiterated this in mid-May, following Argentina's rejection of the Peruvian peace initiative and Britain's subsequently positive response to it. Britain, he told the House of Commons, '...had a clear and decisive preference for a negotiated settlement.' Military pressure, however, was necessary to bring Argentina '...to negotiate seriously and to strengthen the British negotiating hand,' and there were '...encouraging signs that the message is beginning to get through.'[41] As a general description of British policy, there was little to which Thatcher could object in this except, perhaps, its optimism. The frequency with which Pym stressed Britain's preference for a negotiated settlement, however, and the circumstances in which he chose to do so were another matter. Between early April and late May, by which time British troops had re-established themselves firmly on the Islands, Pym expressed this preference in public on at least eight occasions.

Even this might not have been remarkable except for the timing of his pronouncements. Pym's intention seemed to be to balance, or even counter, Thatcher's attempts to make it clear that Britain was prepared to use force. For example, on 7 April with the task force two days out from Portsmouth and on the same day that Reagan announced Haig's mediation, Nott went before Parliament to inform the world of the first of a series of operational zones which the British were to declare around the Falkland Islands. The defence minister had not performed well in the 3 April debate and had offered his resignation. Initially, he had also been pessimistic about sending a task force to recapture the Islands. As the man with immediate political responsibility for the military operation, therefore, Nott had some lost ground to make up. Accordingly, he made what is known as a strong speech, embellished by Churchillian flourishes about not wanting to see bloodshed but refusing to acquiesce in unprovoked aggression. He concluded by declaring:

> We are in earnest and no one should doubt our resolve...We have made no estimate of cost. We are concerned with the success of the operation.

Pym, in contrast, while agreeing that dictators should not be appeased, made clear Britain's preference for a diplomatic solution and added that:

The naval task force on its way to the south Atlantic was a formidable demonstration of this country's strength and its strength of will.[42]

In other circumstances, the distinction between the language of resolve and that of demonstration might be judged to have been too nuanced to matter. In the midst of a crisis such as this, however, the latter could be regarded as words of reassurance, not just to people in Washington and New York who were hoping that Britain did not seriously mean to fight, but to those in London and Buenos Aires who hoped so too.

This pattern was repeated on several occasions. In the House of Commons debate over the final Haig proposals on 29 April, for example, Thatcher stressed their problems. They were, she said, complex, difficult and couched in the language of compromise. Britain's own efforts were critical to getting the Argentinians even to look at Haig's proposals, and she challenged anyone to suggest that the government's willingness to use the task force in '... self-defence for the recapture of British territory' was not a 'proper use of force'. Pym, in contrast, while agreeing that Britain was prepared to use force, reiterated his strategy of pressure in three dimensions, diplomatic, economic and military, designed to get Argentina to accept a peaceful settlement.[43]

He may have seen himself as balancing the impressions given by his more bellicose colleagues, the better to retain international support, or he may simply have thought that they were forgetting other options in their preoccupation with the task force. Research suggests that the pressure of crisis on a government greatly strengthens the phenomenon of 'group think', the tendency of people to build a shared view of their problem which discounts contradictory evidence and alternative perspectives. Some have even suggested that a deliberately contrary participant, a devil's advocate who resists the consensus, is a good idea.[44] If this is how Pym saw his role, however, then he gave a poor performance. Managing the impressions a government conveys abroad requires coordination if it is to accomplish more than conveying the existence of disagreement at the centre, and devil's advocates belong within the policy process, not in Parliament or at press conferences where their interventions can interfere with or under-mine policy at the operational level. On 21 April, for example, just before he made his first visit to the US with a British response to

Haig's proposals, Pym was asked in Parliament if Britain was on the point of using force. He replied 'I will exclude it so long as negotiations are in play.' Military operations already set in train against South Georgia would have quickly made a liar of him and his country, so he returned to the House of Commons to correct any wrong impression he may have given by saying that '...the use of force cannot be ruled out.'[45] At the least, this suggested that Pym was not privy to the military side of British policy, but his detractors took it as evidence of his doubts about Thatcher's policy.

Mistakes do happen, and it is reasonable to suppose that with his Washington trip looming, the diplomatic context of British policy was foremost in Pym's mind. However, this charitable view could be maintained only if his unhelpful interventions had been restricted to this one notorious episode, and they were not. Less than two weeks later, and just after the cruiser *Belgrano* was sunk and Britain was attempting to increase the military pressure on Argentina by naval and aerial bombardments, Pym was in the US on his second visit, 'as an ally', as he expressed it, now that the Americans had abandoned their mediation and thrown their support behind Britain. There, and having told the Falkland Islanders over the BBC World Service that war was 'quite probable' a few days earlier, he declared that:

> No other military action is envisaged at the moment other than making the total exclusion zone secure.

On his return home, he maintained this position. Britain did not seek to humiliate Argentina, he said, and a diplomatic solution was still being sought, which was why the government had made a constructive response to the Haig proposals.[46] His position was not altered by the sinking of the destroyer *Sheffield* on the same day nor even, indeed, after worse setbacks at the end of the month when two warships supporting the main landings were sunk within three days. Negotiations, Pym maintained, remained an objective of British policy.[47]

For Thatcher, Pym's willingness to reiterate Britain's commitment to negotiations in the midst of difficulties rather than to have it dragged out of him on the appropriate occasions as it had to be from her, signalled his lack of resolve. What confirmed it, however, was his willingness to think out loud about the possible outcome of any negotiations which might finally take place. In a television interview in April, for example, he affirmed that the Islanders' wishes must be 'the dominant factor' in any final settlement. 'After all,' he continued, '. . . they are the people who live there and what they feel like after this awful experience who can tell?' He thought they would be 'very much more pro-British' and doubted whether the lease-back proposals would be of interest to them any longer.[48] Again, there was nothing substantially wrong with this, but Pym's speculative approach to what the Islanders might want and his willingness to voice an alternative institutional relationship in public, if only to cast measured doubt upon it, were not in keeping with the image of resolve and certainty of purpose which Thatcher was seeking to project. The same was true of his Commons performance a week later in which Pym had to correct himself about the use of force while negotiations were still in progress. The 'critical points', in Washington, he said, would be:

> . . . the arrangement for an Argentine withdrawal; the nature of any interim administration for the Islands; and the framework for negotiations on the long-term solution to the dispute for which the United Nations resolution called.[49]

As *The Times* commented, these words had '. . . the ring of Foreign Office draftsmen'. Nothing in them precluded the restoration of the status quo *ante bellum*, but uttered by Pym rather than Thatcher, they conveyed that something other than the status quo was a possibility. This was borne out a few days later when fighting had broken out in earnest and both sides had begun to suffer losses. On his return from Washington, according to Thatcher, it was Pym who had pushed for acceptance of the final Haig plan, and he succeeded in persuading the Cabinet into making a warm response to its Peruvian successor, much to Thatcher's discomfort. Doing so, according to Pym, demonstrated 'flexibility' on Britain's part and, he might have added, at little cost because the non-prejudicial nature of the proposed negotiations remained a sticking point with the Argentinians. They did not want the British to stall as they had done so in the past. On replying to an opposition question about the interim arrangements, however, Pym said that the government had not '. . . ruled out any particular option', although he imagined that one which gave '. . . the Argentines a predominant position would be unacceptable.' The Islands were 'British sovereign territory', he continued, but then he added:

We acknowledge the Argentinians feel they have a claim to it. We
believe that claim is invalid, but we acknowledge that they have
that claim and let that be negotiated about in a peaceful way.
That is the crunch point.[50]

It was, indeed, the crunch point. Beyond it, Thatcher and Pym
went their separate ways. As the fighting intensified, Thatcher
successfully argued for a hardening of the British position. By her
own account, the final British proposal before the landings was
made secure in the knowledge that Argentina would reject it. Britain had to appear reasonable, she recalled, and maintained that she
regarded an interim administration set up to return the Islands to
Britain as 'reasonable'.[51] As the fortunes of war tilted decisively in
Britain's favour, however, even this device was abandoned. On 28
May, with British forces firmly established and advancing, Thatcher
said her objectives were to repossess the Islands, restore British
administration, reconstruct the Islanders' way of life and 'consult'
them on what they wanted. A few days later, she asserted that
Argentina could have no sovereignty role on the Islands and
talked about their economic development, increasing the population, and seeking multilateral military guarantees for them after the
war.[52] As Whitelaw, the home secretary, made clear a week later,
Britain had been willing to negotiate so long as the outcome was not
prejudged, but now it was '... unthinkable to negotiate about the
future of the Falkland Islands as if everything was as it had been
before.'[53]

Pym, in contrast, continued to stress his preference for negotiation. As late as 18 May, and as Thatcher was declaring that
nothing short of an Argentinian withdrawal would delay military
operations, he told Conservative backbenchers that there was still a
slight chance of peace. On the same day that Thatcher declared
that British policy was directed at repossessing and reconstructing
the Islands, he gave an interview in which he talked about the
Islanders' need to live in peace with the Argentinians after the war
was over. And on 9 June, even as he explained the reasons for
Britain vetoing a UN Security Council call for a ceasefire, he
reiterated this point. 'It remains true ... ,' he said:

> ... that at the end of the day there has to be a settlement what-
> ever form it may take, if there is to be prosperity in that region
> and for the islanders.[54]

The differences between Pym and Thatcher on Falklands policy were not contrived for diplomatic effect. Their subsequent mutual antipathy is testimony to that. Nor, however, did it result from political rivalry in a simple sense. Pym might have been asked to replace Thatcher if her policy had resulted in a military defeat or stalemate, but he adhered to his line, even as its popularity declined in inverse proportion to the prospects for a British military victory. He did so primarily because he believed he was right. Pym believed it was his duty to speak to all the awkward facts of the problem presented by the Falkland Islands, as he and the Foreign Office saw them, especially at the moment of victory with its danger of hubris. He was also a good diplomatist, in that he believed that Britain's commitment to a negotiated settlement entailed more than simply hoping that all one's demands could be satisfied without going to war. Britain ought to make real concessions if these could avoid a war *and* allow the Falkland Islanders to retain their way of life. Just after the *Belgrano* and the *Sheffield* had been sunk, his thinking on this was revealed in Parliament. The government, Pym maintained:

> ... has an open mind about what might be the ultimate solution. Most certainly, the United Nations trusteeship concept is one of these possibilities. It might in the end prove to be highly suitable.[55]

In looking for a settlement along these lines, Pym was not alone. Had Argentina been more conciliatory, many of his colleagues might have happily accepted a trusteeship solution rather than fight a war, and Thatcher, less happily certainly, might then have been forced to do likewise. Pym differed from other supporters of compromise, however, in that he was not just looking for a way to avoid fighting. A trusteeship appeared to him as a fair settlement and, therefore, if the Argentinians rejected it, one for which it was proper to fight. Nearly every statement in which he expressed Britain's preference for a negotiated settlement included a declaration that Britain was prepared to fight if Argentina was not prepared to be reasonable. The obvious weakness of this position was exposed by the course of events. 'In the end', to use his own term, a compromise of the sort Pym wanted appeared, if not the least 'suitable' solution, then the least likely one. The Argentinians were never interested in such a compromise and, after fighting, neither were the British. The day after the surrender, Thatcher made this clear in Parliament responding to a question about the future from Michael Foot. She could not agree with him that '... these men risked their lives in any way to have a United Nations trusteeship.'[56] As one soldier was reputed to have remarked at the time, if the Islands were worth fighting for, then they were worth keeping.

This was a sentiment which the government was happy to foster because it put responsibility for everything on the shoulders of the Argentinians. They had forced a fight and, in so doing, had forced the change in Britain's Falkland Islands policy. This is not strictly true for Britain's response in both regards was the product of British choices. Despite the costs, the government could have chosen not to fight or, having fought and won, sought to resume the search for a long-term compromise, albeit at great cost to itself. What is true, however, is that the case for a compromise was completely undermined by Argentina's refusal to recognize the route to a settlement which Pym was trying to signal. The rejection of compromise is not grounds for condemning those who advocate it, but there was a second and less obvious weakness in Pym's position. The soldier's argument applied just as much before the fighting as after it. Thatcher might not have been able to say until late in the day that British policy was directed solely at restoring the status quo *ante bellum*. In effect, however, it could have be directed at little else, and certainly not at recovering British territory simply to put it under the immediate supervision of a third party because no one would have been willing to fight for that.

In effect, therefore, the course which Pym advocated would have amounted to a capitulation. This is not what he wanted, but whether he realized it or not, his own reasonableness in seeking compromise avoided the taint of capitulation because Thatcher, and not he, was prime minister, and because she argued for a stronger line. In her place, he could have hardly argued for less and expected to survive. What he advocated instead was not so much a policy as a sentiment, the need for a negotiated settlement, accompanied by observations about the consequences of failing to achieve one. Accordingly, Pym does not entirely evade the charge of political opportunism, for while he may not have aspired to replace her, his role in the crisis was made possible at Thatcher's expense, and the manner in which he gave expression to his views made the government's task more difficult.

'GREAT BRITAIN IS GREAT AGAIN'[57]

However, political opportunism, if such it was, was by no means a monopoly of Francis Pym's. Even before the war was over, Thatcher and her supporters used what they called the 'Falklands Factor' to good effect in local elections at the beginning of May, and a Conservative candidate in a parliamentary by-election likened the leader of a rail union threatening strike action to the Argentinian leader, General Galtieri.[58] Thatcher tried to use success in the war and the popularity it had engendered for the government to mobilize broader support for her programme of domestic transformation. Britain, she claimed in a speech at Cheltenham, '...had ceased to be a nation in retreat.' Its people had proved they could still excel, but the challenge before them was to apply the discipline and productivity they had demonstrated during the war to peacetime conditions. The virtues which had made victory possible in the South Atlantic would provide sound money at home, she claimed, and a start would be made if railway trade union members ignored the calls of their leaders for strike action and showed up for work.[59]

Others, however, disputed the idea of the war as a turning point in British history. E.P. Thompson, for example, maintained that the British

> ... would pay for it for a long time, in rapes and muggings in our cities, in international ill-will, and in the stirring up of ugly nationalist sentiment which will cloud our political and cultural life.[60]

The concern of many foreign policy experts was that the war had been a highly risky distraction from the real business of the nation. Worse, they feared, it had provided a powerful boost to all the attitudes and prejudices which lay in the way of Britain becoming a competitive, and hence prosperous, regional power. Proof that Britain remained capable of exercising its old skills might be used to draw the erroneous inference that it did not need to develop new ones. To judge by the way that she juxtaposed her own claims about how the whole country had been transformed with a concern over particular pay disputes in the public sector, Thatcher herself shared some of these concerns. She was the first to acknowledge, even in her most triumphal moments, that the ability to perform effectively in wartime did not automatically translate into a similar effectiveness in times of peace. Indeed, in her own understanding of

British history, the problems which now beset the country had their origins in the circumstances of the victory of 1945. Then, exhaustion had combined with the complacency of success to persuade the electorate into voting for the party which promised to take care of them. What, then, was the significance of the victory in 1982?

Argentina's invasion of the Falkland Islands created a moment of considerable danger for the country. Had the government decided not to fight, or in fighting had been defeated, the government would have fallen and a deeper crisis calling into question more fundamental institutions, practices and self-images might have occurred. There were a few on the left who imagined that such a set-back was precisely what Britain needed, in much the same way that Imperial Russia had needed to be defeated by Japan in 1905 to set in train the events which would lead to fundamental change. Only the most optimistic 'revolutionary defeatist', however, could have imagined that the Britain which emerged from such a crisis would be a freer and more prosperous place to live than it had been before. Nothing that happened in the Falkland Islands could materially effect the distribution of power and wealth on which the existing social order in Britain was built, and so it is likely that it would have survived the crisis and emerged in a more authoritarian form to remedy the 'weaknesses' which failure in the Falklands had exposed.

Fortunately, however, there was never really much chance of the crisis developing in this direction. Given its structure, it is remarkable in hindsight how seriously the possibility of the two countries not fighting was taken at the time. Their positions were mutually exclusive and both governments had pinned national prestige and their own survival on not backing down. Only a coup from the streets or within the cabinet could have changed either country's policies and in Argentina, no one was prepared to lead one in the name of retreat, while in Britain no one would lead one on behalf of turning the other cheek and leaving the Falkland Islanders to their fate. Compromise was advice which could be whispered from the wings or shouted from the audience of the political opposition, but it was impossible for the prime minister, as the leading character, to espouse it. Her own political survival was at stake, but so too was the country's international standing, and both depended on recovering the Falkland Islands. Thatcher, being who she was, responded effectively, and sometimes with relish, to this combination of pressures to act, but there were few who, in her place, would have been able to resist them successfully, except by resigning.

There was little chance that Britain would not go to war, there-fore, but could it win? In retrospect, it is hard to avoid the conclu-sion that both Thatcher and her advisors were not entirely sure of what they were getting into. The initial task force was too small to recapture the Islands, but whether the military planners were still thinking in terms of a demonstration force or were merely seeking a commitment on which they could subsequently build remains unclear. Thatcher herself, however, was surprised at the continuous requests for reinforcements which were made during the war and, to judge by the references to them in her memoirs, she continues to be so.[61] Indeed, from her passing observation on her husband's fascination with 'matters military' to her concern over the *Belgrano's* '6 guns with a range of 13 miles' rather than 'six inch guns' and her harsh words on the loss of the *Sheffield* resulting from 'mishaps and mistakes', there is evidence to suggest that the business of war was, and remains, uncomfortable and uncertain territory for Thatcher.[62]

Accordingly, she had to take her commanders on trust, but she was well disposed to do so and, on the whole, they gave her sound advice.[63] The war was winnable, they said, if they were provided with the necessary resources and political support and if the gov-ernment was prepared to accept losses. The operation was not without risk. If one of the two aircraft carriers were sunk or put out of action then the whole operation would have been crippled, but that is the problem with going to war, and in their judgement the risk was a reasonable one. With the benefit of hindsight, it is possible to conclude that this advice was sound. If anything, the vulnerability of the warships protecting the landings from Argenti-na's air force was underestimated. However, the two carriers were never hit, the loss of four warships and two support ships never put the operation seriously at risk, and the war was won at a cost of 255 killed and 777 wounded on the British side, including only three Islanders. It was, by any standards, a small war, but it was a real one.[64]

Britain was not transformed by the victory. Its most obvious consequence came in the form of political rewards for those who had taken the risk and were successful – Thatcher and the Con-servative party. The slow recovery which they were beginning to make in the opinion polls before the war became a surge of support which contributed to Thatcher's victory at the polls the following year. Less obviously, however, the episode provided Thatcher with two lessons which were of critical importance to her subsequent and enhanced international role. The first was that even (or especially) in a world increasingly dominated by the rhetoric of multilateralism and collaboration, how utterly alone a government or a country could be when something goes wrong. The whole world, friends and enemies alike, was watching to see what Thatcher and, hence, Britain would do. No one would solve Britain's problem for her. All they could offer were suggestions like the calls for a ceasefire which would make their own world more secure.

The greatest surprise for Thatcher in this regard came from the US. Haig's mediation was a source of insecurity, but even the extensive semi-covert military assistance from one defence establishment to the other had unpleasant resonances of other more serious occasions when the US had been prepared to provide the treasure if Britain supplied the blood. Throughout the crisis, Thatcher never came to appreciate the extent to which American interests were defined by considerations other than supporting Britain through thick and thin. Only this explains the repeated, and completely unrealistic, requests she made for American diplomatic commitments and troops '... to guarantee the islands against renewed invasion'. Even after Britain had recaptured the Islands, Thatcher returned to this theme when she told the House of Commons that she did not '... exclude the possibility of associating other countries with their security.' The Americans were not forthcoming and it is this, perhaps, which accounts for the frankness with which she describes the various errors of US policy during the war and Reagan's ignorance of his own country's position in her memoirs.[65]

At the moment of crisis, just when one needed it most, the international community was capable of evaporating into a self-help system where even one's best friends might let one down.[66] If this were so, however, then the second lesson which Thatcher learned was that this was not entirely a bad thing if one happened to be the leader of a wealthy and powerful country of 56 million people, and were possessed of the nerve to act. For such countries and larger, the international system was becoming a more permissive system than common wisdom had believed it to be since 1945. If most members of the international community were not prepared to give much help to one of their number in difficulties, then neither were they prepared to get in its way if it decided to help itself. Better, they were prepared to acquiesce in its definition of what it was attempting so long as this required nothing substantive of them up front, and best of all, they were prepared to reward success with support.

This, in effect, was what Thatcher discovered during the war for the Falkland Islands. Britain had a good case to put before the international community. It also had the means with which to recover the Islands by itself. However, neither of these alone was enough, and political leadership with the nerve do something which it judged to be right was necessary to bring them together. A less courageous and, indeed, less ruthless prime minister than Thatcher might have secured more international sympathy for Britain as victim of both Argentine aggression and the harsh way of the world with fading powers, before being thrown out of office for failing to recover the Islands. A less certain and, indeed, less self-righteous prime minister might have presided over their recapture before an uncomprehending world and a grim but guilt-ridden and uneasy British public. A less ambitious and, indeed, less egotistical prime minister, having won them back, might have reflected on her good fortune and decided that two months of war had provided enough excitement for a lifetime and left her nothing to prove.

Thatcher, of course, did none of these things. Not once, for example, after the first week of the crisis, did she allow Britain to be presented as a victim in need of help. Rather, it was the moral agent and leader of the righteous calling others to follow. So successful was she in this regard that by the end of the campaign, domestic opposition to her had been marginalized, compromised or co-opted into supporting her, while abroad she had made her country the recipient of accolades from all sorts of unlikely sources of admiration for Thatcher's Britain. As the Secretary General of the Commonwealth, Shridath Ramphal, was moved to say the day after the ceasefire:

> All the more has Britain's response in this instance been a service to the world community, which condemns the invader, but lacks the means to deny him the fruits of aggression.[67]

Nor, as far as Thatcher was concerned, was the Falklands War an anomaly or, as she put it in her Cheltenham speech, '...some last flickering of a flame which must soon be dead.' Rather, it was a platform from which to embark on greater projects. By her own account, just after the recapture of South Georgia, she had told a television audience what she was doing:

I'm standing up for the right of self-determination. I'm standing up for our territory. I'm standing up for our people. I'm standing up for international law. I'm standing up for all those territories – those small territories and peoples the world over – who, if someone doesn't stand up and say to an invader 'enough, stop'...would be at risk.[68]

At that point, the final outcome was still uncertain and this, perhaps, accounts for her over-use of the first person and a certain shrillness which pervades the passage even now. However, its significance lies not in the principles she iterates, which are unremarkable, but in the ego it reveals. Until now, that ego had been content to confine its operations to the domestic stage. Thatcher had accepted the prevailing consensus about Britain's international decline or, at least, that there was nothing much to be done about it until she had put domestic affairs in order. What the war for the Falkland Islands revealed, however, was that in the right hands, hers, the British state remained a powerful instrument. Britain could act independently and even use force without the skies falling either at home or abroad. Thatcher had always suspected as much and, indeed, in a small way, had acted on her hunch, notably on the question of Britain's contribution to the budget of the EC. Now, however, she had the confidence, as well as the inclination, to put her principles and prejudices about British foreign policy to a much more extensive test.

6 Thatcher's US Policy I: The Diplomacy of Support

Britain's success in the Falklands War thrust foreign policy upon Thatcher and launched her international career, but neither would have been possible without US support. Haig's mediation may have troubled the British, but the *matériel* assistance and intelligence information provided by the Pentagon and other US agencies greatly reduced the severity of the military challenge which confronted the British. Without it, their task would have been much harder and more costly. More importantly, had the Americans decided to oppose Britain's recovery of the Islands, then the war would have been impossible and Thatcher's political demise all but assured. That American support was eventually forthcoming is attributable to the Special Relationship which exists between the two countries. Britain and the US are allies, but the term suggests they are more than that. Precisely what, however, is a matter of some controversy.

Thatcher's view of the British side of the relationship was that 'We are close to the United States. We are by history, this government, this people, very pro-American.'[1] Enthusiasts maintain that this closeness on both sides has enabled the two countries to achieve a level of cooperation which is unusually high by the standards of international politics. Britain and the US, it is claimed, are even capable of deferring to each other's concerns in what can only be described as a spirit of altruism or self-abnegation.[2] However, the history of diplomatic relations between the two suggests that claims of altruism should be treated with scepticism. At times, Britain and the US have engaged in close cooperation on a wide range of issues. However, they have also fought two wars, engaged in intense commercial conflict and, arguably, tried to subvert each other's political integrity, Britain by encouraging the Confederacy, the US by encouraging independence movements within the empire. They have cooperated, therefore, only when a consideration of their respective national interests suggested that they should.

This is not to say that the idea of the Special Relationship is devoid of content, only that cultural closeness does not make Anglo-American relations qualitatively different from other bilateral relationships between states. What it does do is lead the governments of both countries to define certain international problems, their interest in them and their response to them in similar and compatible ways. Closeness also serves as a powerful mobilizer of support for cooperation between the two once this has been decided upon for other reasons. However, the question to be answered by any survey of Anglo-American relations is not whether ideals or self-interest drive their respective contributions, but how the interests of both countries come to be defined in terms of helping each other out.

Since the end of the Second World War, the answer on the British side has been shaped by the facts of America's ascendancy and Britain's relative, but precipitous, decline. Accordingly, British diplomacy has worked to keep the US engaged in maintaining the international order upon which Britain continues to depend. It has sought to maximize its own influence over the way the US exercises its leadership and, finally, it has tried to exploit American military and diplomatic resources to maintain Britain's standing as a great power. The principal strategy for achieving these objectives has involved asserting and demonstrating Britain's usefulness to the US as a uniquely valuable source of political and practical support. In return for such help, it has been hoped that the US will listen to Britain's advice on policy and be sympathetic to its attempts to pursue its own distinctive course as a great power.

As such, the strategy of making itself useful has produced another argument about the Special Relationship, this time over whether it worked in its own terms and at what cost to Britain's other interests, notably in Europe. By the late 1970s, many academic experts were arguing that international security issues had become dominated by superpower bilateralism, while economic problems were increasingly addressed by multilateral negotiations among rich countries and between them and the poor. Meanwhile others, principally on the left, claimed that the US could no longer lead because of its defeat in Vietnam, the Watergate scandal and other traumas. The assumptions about US strength on which these two views rested were mutually exclusive – one took American power as a given, the other saw it disappearing. However, both views fed the expectation that the Special Relationship, with its emphasis on close ties between intelligence, military and, to a lesser extent, diplomatic elites, could only decline. Even the cultural closeness which facilitated the relationship would become less significant in the emerging global popular culture based on American, not Anglo-American, referents.

Events were to prove the first view correct, at least for the whole of the Thatcher period. In retrospect, it is even possible to see that the key decisions which maintained the American link with Europe, increases in defence spending and nuclear force modernization, had been made before the full revival of East–West tensions and the emergence of the Reagan–Thatcher partnership.[3] Nevertheless, popular images of American weakness, uncertainty and, indeed, incompetence provided the opportunity for those like Carrington who sought to build a European diplomatic identity, not to replace a fading hegemon, but to provide a vehicle by which other views on Western interests might find more effective expression. Thatcher did nothing to obstruct Carrington's effort in this regard, but even before she began to take an interest in foreign policy, she had no sympathy for any of the views of American power on which it could be based. American decline she barely countenanced. As she was to say in an interview there in 1984, the US was'. . . the most powerful country in the world as you know'. It was going to remain 'the most powerful free country', Thatcher continued '. . . and we are very fortunate in that.'[4] Even more so than Britain's, its current problems resulted from mistaken policies of the past and the consequent loss of national confidence. Nothing was amiss, she maintained, which could not be corrected by pursuing the right policies.

SUPPORTING AMERICAN LEADERSHIP

If she rejected the notion of US decline, however, Thatcher did not believe that American leadership could be taken for granted. In particular, she believed, it was wrong to build up a European centre of influence which continued to depend on American wealth and power, but which justified itself by pointing to the alleged failings and weaknesses of the US. Thatcher expressed her own version of Britain's support for American leadership on her first visit to the US as prime minister in December 1979. The visit coincided with the British diplomatic triumph over the Zimbabwe-Rhodesia settlement, while her hosts, in contrast, were mired in the crisis which had been precipitated by the storming of the American embassy in Teheran and the taking of its staff as hostages the previous month.

There was, said Thatcher, 'enormous respect' in Britain for the 'statesmanship, calmness and courage' with which President Carter had faced this 'agonizing problem'. The Americans had asked their allies to back a request for economic sanctions to be imposed on Iran by the UN, and Thatcher provided strong support for this move. 'We do support you,' she said, '...we shall support you and let there be no mistake about it.'[5]

On this, as on other occasions, her strong statement of support for the US was to lead to considerable trouble. Four months after her visit, Britain, along with the rest of the EC, agreed in Naples to a package of economic sanctions against Iran developed principally by Carrington. These were not strong enough according to the Carter administration. As noted above, however, its disapproval turned to anger when Thatcher was forced by a backbench revolt to break with the Naples consensus that the measures should be retroactive to November of the previous year. Coupled with Thatcher's failure to insist that British athletes join the American-led boycott of the Moscow Olympics in protest against the USSR's intervention in Afghanistan, the sanctions episode provided an uneasy beginning to Thatcher's own special relationship with the US, which, the State Department let it be known, was 'extremely disappointed' with British policy.[6]

From the start, therefore, Thatcher accepted that British and American interests and opinions could diverge. She believed, for example, that while the government could encourage athletes not to attend the Olympics, it had no business curtailing individual liberties by insisting that they not attend. She could also be persuaded on occasions, as over the Iranian sanctions, that narrow British interests would sometimes take precedence over American conceptions of where the general interest of the Western Alliance lay. Nevertheless, such defections were never easily made by her and she was never attracted by the idea that differences with the Americans could provide a source of domestic or European political capital. Nor did her discovery of the possibility of such differences lead to any muting of the full declaratory support she was inclined to give to the Americans on public occasions. Indeed, with the election of Ronald Reagan, a politician with whom she knew she had already much in common, her expressions of support became even stronger.

As she said in her address to the annual 'Pilgrim's Dinner' shortly after Reagan took the oath of office: '...We need to say more clearly "we are with you" to the US.' The Americans needed to be told that '...Setbacks for them are setbacks for us' and '...greater recognition of the extent of the American effort which guarantees our freedom...' needed to be offered. At the Group of Seven (G7) meeting held in Ottawa that summer she declared that '...as for the leadership of the western world, ultimately the United States is the guarantor of the freedom of Europe and we should make it clear that we understand that and that we are grateful for it.' 'It is not for us...,' she told a Parliamentary debate on disarmament in the autumn of 1982, with the Falklands victory behind her, '...to tell the United States what to do about their strategic nuclear force. It is for us to recognize that their strategic nuclear force is the final guarantor of Europe's liberty.'[7]

No one had expressed the central objective of Britain's American policy so strongly or unequivocally since Churchill's attempt to secure the support of the US and its entry into the Second World War. And in public, at least, he had presented the relationship he sought as a partnership, not as an opportunity for the US to lead with Britain and others grateful to follow. Thatcher's willingness to do precisely this reflected political realities which had become impossible to ignore or obscure, but it was not without its costs. On those occasions where she had to defect from the American conception of the common good, for example, the Americans could be more upset than when they judged the French or Germans had let them down. And when she stuck by an unpopular American position, she always laid her government open to the charge that it was '...dancing to Washington's tune' and herself to the accusation that she was 'Reagan's poodle'.[8]

The benefits of being an enthusiastic follower and supporter of American leadership are harder to assess. Certainly, Thatcher did not keep the US engaged in world affairs. This objective was beyond her means, as it had always been beyond the means of British policy, but fortunately it was also an objective which she did not have to secure so long as US administrations could convince their people of a Soviet threat to American interests which had to be countered. Where she did succeed was in providing the corroborative evidence and sentiment which made it easier for the Reagan administration to secure Congressional and popular assent to what it wanted to do abroad. The emotive component of this support was more important than its rational or material aspects. Americans are no more likely than anyone else to do what foreigners tell them, but they do seem more concerned than most that they obtain 'positive feedback' and confirmation that their own good is, in fact, the general good. As a consequence, and whether it was her principal objective or not, Thatcher's personal political stock, and Britain's along with it, rose in the US and as they did, the reputations of both rose in the world at large also. However, the critical question was, as it had always been, whether Britain's capacity to influence American foreign policy increased correspondingly.

INFLUENCING AMERICAN LEADERSHIP

If one does not have power oneself, then the next best thing is having powerful friends over whom one enjoys a measure of influence. Cultivating such influence had been the second objective of Britain's American policy since 1945, for the British retained strong preferences about how the international order was to be maintained and strong doubts about how the Americans would go about it. In addition to agreeing with the US and providing it with support and encouragement whenever possible, therefore, the policy of making Britain useful also involved the cultivation of close personal relationships between presidents and prime ministers. The wartime partnership of Churchill and Roosevelt was the ideal, but no postwar British prime minister (including Churchill) enjoyed even the waning strength of wartime Britain. Accordingly, the best practical postwar alternative was held to be a relationship of the sort which existed between John F. Kennedy and Harold Macmillan. They liked each other and, by all accounts, the former was prepared to accept the seniority of the latter in their personal relationship up to a point.

Macmillan claimed that British historical experience and diplomatic expertise could help guide American foreign policy, as the Greeks had enriched the Roman Empire by which they had been superseded and absorbed. While the details of what this actually meant were rarely spelt out, they were plain to anybody with the sensibilities and prejudices of an Englishman. British experience would be deployed to modify the moral extremism and youthful *naïveté* which, it was believed, led the US to oscillate between trying to isolate itself from the wicked world and seeking to remake it in its own image. In retrospect, this depiction of the relationship itself appears naïve and arrogant. It was most plausible when the prime minister and president were close, as were Macmillan and Kennedy. Even then, however, it worked more to secure for British interests special consideration in the American scheme of things rather than to alter that scheme as a whole. In so far as British preferences had a role in shaping the latter, it would be as ammunition used by one group or another in the bureaucratic politics of US foreign policy-making. When relations between leaders were not close, however, British influence at the highest level had to be exercised from outside the American policy process. Then, as when Harold Wilson tried to modify Lyndon Johnson's conduct of the Vietnam war, success was not forthcoming and the attempt was not welcomed.

Thatcher succeeded in establishing a close personal relationship with Reagan after he was elected in 1980.[9] There was a strong element of calculation in this for, with the exception of his willingness stubbornly to defend what he thought was right at the declaratory level at least, Reagan was not the sort of man to whom Thatcher was usually attracted. He, in contrast appears to have conceded a measure of moral and personal authority to Thatcher, so much so that his own senior advisors saw her input as being potentially decisive when the president had not made up his mind, and sought to exclude it if it did not accord with their own preferences. However, the big difference between Thatcher and other postwar British prime ministers was that she did not establish her relationship with the Reagan in order to moderate or restrain American foreign policy. Her influence derived from the fact that she usually encouraged the Reagan administration to do what it wanted while others, especially other foreigners, were urging more restraint.

ENCOURAGING THE AMERICANS: MISSILES AND BOMBINGS

The most obvious expression of this was Thatcher's support for the expansion and modernization of those American armaments which she believed would deter the USSR from exploiting opportunities to expand its influence and power. In a series of decisions from 1976 onwards, Nato had committed itself to both modernizing its 'theatre nuclear forces' in western Europe, while simultaneously seeking arms negotiations with the Warsaw Pact. The Thatcher government confirmed this decision in December 1979 when, along with its allies, it announced that new American missiles would be deployed in Britain, West Germany, Italy, Belgium and the Netherlands.[10] The British had originally agreed to accept 124 Cruise missiles but, in contrast to Belgium and the Netherlands which were already hesitating, Thatcher agreed to accept an extra 36 which had originally been destined for the Federal Republic.

The purpose of these missiles was a matter of intense controversy at the time and has remained so. They and their Soviet counterparts had far longer ranges than the tactical missiles, bombs and shells whose use would be confined to the immediate battlefield, but they were also seen as something less than the strategic weapons with which the superpowers could attack each other's territory. The USSR's missiles, principally the SS 20, were intended either to provide decisive firepower for a surprise attack or to deter Nato from initiating nuclear exchanges in a conventional war which it was losing. Whatever their intended use, however, their existence posed a threat to European cities as well as Nato's means of controlling and supplying its forces. The public justification for the new Nato missiles was that they were to counter the SS 20s which had been, and were still being, deployed in far more plentiful amounts. As Thatcher expressed it in an interview given to *Time* in 1981:

> So long as those fantastic SS 20's in the Soviet Union are targeted on Europeans so long must I have a deterrent to those. We are very fortunate to have someone else's weapons stationed on our soil to fight those targeted on us.[11]

There were problems with presenting the new Nato missiles as merely balancing Soviet ones. All of them had the potential for striking targets deep within eastern Europe and possibly the USSR. The Pershing II, in particular, was regarded as a major threat to Soviet command and control centres because of its speed and accuracy. As a consequence, the USSR maintained that they were part of an American attempt to make Soviet territory vulnerable to nuclear forces launched from neither US territory nor US submarines, a non-strategic weapon with strategic effects. It also claimed that the short flight time of the Pershings would force it to adopt a policy of 'launch-on-warning' rather than waiting to confirm a nuclear attack, and that this would greatly increase the chances of accidental nuclear war. These concerns were shared by the Peace Movement and by some European military and strategic experts who also doubted that the credibility of the US nuclear guarantee to its Nato allies would be enhanced by attempting to decouple the US from the consequences of a nuclear exchange in Europe.

These fears were exacerbated by Reagan's claim in 1981 that he could '...see where you could have the exchange of tactical weapons against troops in the field without it bringing either one of the major powers to pushing the button.' Two weeks later, Haig spoke of '...contingency plans in Nato doctrine to fire nuclear weapons for demonstrative purposes' when the 'other side' were '...exceeding the limits of toleration in a conventional attack.'[12] The Haig statement was later disavowed by the Pentagon, and neither really signalled any departure from Nato's strategy of flexible response as it had been developed. The willingness to speak so openly about such disturbing matters, however, reflected an attempt by some members of the Reagan administration to look for ways of using nuclear weapons other than in support of a policy of deterrence by magnitude or threatening catastrophe. The best form of deterrence according to these circles was to create a situation in which an act of aggression would not risk bringing down annihilation on both aggressor and victim alike, but entail the virtual certainty of defeat for the aggressor, hence the attempt to develop doctrines of limited and controlled nuclear war-fighting which would result in victory as the best way of deterring the USSR. For the advocates of these, Cruise and Pershing missiles did not represent bargaining chips to be surrendered in return for similar concessions by the USSR. They, and other even more exotic weapons, were to be the instruments of the new strategy.

However, the new strategy had major implications both for arms control and the long term political relationship between the super-powers about which there was little agreement in the Reagan administration. On the one hand, there were those who believed, like Thatcher, that the arms build-up was directed at creating a position of strength from which the US could safely negotiate with the USSR about a broad range of issues including arms control. On the other were those who argued that strength was an end in itself because there was little prospect of successful negotiations over anything important with the 'evil empire'. This difference was resolved by the time the new missiles arrived in the autumn of 1983. Reagan had offered his 'zero option' of no deployment if the USSR destroyed its own systems two years earlier and Strategic Arms Reduction Talks (START) a year later. The radical significance of both proposals had been minimized, however, by the widespread belief that the USSR would find them unacceptable and that, therefore, the US had not been altogether serious when it made them.

Events were to show, to the surprise of Margaret Thatcher and many of his senior advisors, that Reagan was as serious about reducing the numbers of nuclear weapons in the world to zero if possible as he apparently was about scaring the USSR with them if nothing else would work. In 1983, however, this was not apparent, and the military reasons for deploying new American missiles in Europe had become much less important than the need to deploy them as a demonstration of Nato's collective political will. It was in these terms that Thatcher primarily saw the issue, and even when she argued against the withdrawal of the missiles five years later, there is little to suggest that she did so on strategic grounds of any sophistication. For her, nuclear weapons remained blunt instruments of last resort. Their acquisition and retention, however, provided both a test of political will and an opportunity to demonstrate resolve and, as such, Thatcher gave her full support to the deployment of the new systems by Nato.

Tests of political will were Thatcher's forte, of course, and the influence she enjoyed over US policy was never stronger than when she was encouraging the Reagan administration to meet its own tests with resolution and firmness. This applied on a broad range of issues: East–West relations, arms control, reducing obstacles to free trade and combating terrorism; and it was enhanced when the opportunity existed for providing material assistance in support of American policy. The most spectacular demonstration of this occurred in 1986 when, after a series of confrontations between the US and Libya in the Mediterranean, the Americans launched an air raid on Tripoli using both carrier-borne aircraft and planes based in Britain. Land-based aircraft were needed because only their ordnance possessed the accuracy required by certain aspects of the mission, namely killing Gaddafi and others close to him.

Other allies closer to Libya would not offer their bases, and the French reportedly even denied the use of their airspace. They disapproved of the mission and feared retaliation by terrorists. Britain's cooperation, however, was not accompanied by Thatcher urging the Americans to be firm for, in fact, the decision to permit the use of British bases was not easily arrived at. Britain's response to a confrontation between Libyan and American aircraft several years before had been distinctly cool, and the government shared its allies' concerns about the purpose of the mission. Indeed, Thatcher had seemed to rule out such an operation from British territory a few days before the attack by suggesting that it could not be reconciled with international law. Under American pressure to assist anyway, she obtained legal opinion about the terms on which the operation could go ahead and communicated these to the Americans before agreeing to help.

The raid was only partially successful. It frightened Gaddafi, but killed only a very young member of his family and several civilians. The domestic costs to Thatcher were considerable. Britain, it was claimed, was far more vulnerable than the US to Libyan revenge attacks and, indeed, three British hostages were found murdered in the Lebanon a few days later. As a consequence, Thatcher made it very clear that she did not wish to be put in a similar position again by the US. After the destruction of an airliner over Scotland at the end of 1988, for example, she stressed catching the perpetrators above revenge. Revenge she said, was '... never a good word to use because it can affect innocent people.' This position was reiterated a few days later, when the Americans shot down two Libyan aircraft in another confrontation over the Mediterranean. The British government accepted the American claim that this was done in self-defence but, in the words of William Waldegrave, one of the ministers of state at the Foreign Office, Britain had made it clear that it could not '... condone an action which did not have an appropriate basis in international law.' 'Great countries', he continued, '... like the United States and Britain must not be involved in any illegal activity.'[13] In the US, however, it was the original support, not the eventual equivocation, which was remembered. The domestic costs to Thatcher were seen as reasons for more gratitude which found its expression three months later in the Senate's approval of an extradition treaty making it harder for IRA terrorists to find sanctuary in the US.

RESTRAINING THE AMERICANS: PIPELINES AND INVASIONS

However, encouraging the Americans in their desire to be more assertive was one thing. In the more traditional role for a British prime minister of seeking to be a force for restraint on American assertiveness, Thatcher was far less successful. Such situations were aberrations from the main pattern of Anglo-American relations under Thatcher and Reagan, but they were always a source of discomfort and embarrassment to her for they exposed the limits of Thatcher's influence in the US. The most important argument between the two on East–West relations was conducted over the sanctions which the US imposed on the USSR at the end of 1981 as a consequence of the latter's Polish policy. These measures included a ban on the transfer of pipelaying equipment and technologies involved in pumping natural gas. The purpose was to block an agreement concluded the previous month by which the USSR would supply the Federal Republic with natural gas through pipelines yet to be built. Once again, Thatcher was quick to approve the US initiative. 'Ronald Reagan', she said '...has given an excellent lead and we must follow.' However, she qualified this by adding that the response of Britain and Europe '...would be slightly different', because of '...different treaties, with different conditions attached to the United States and Europe.' Even so, Thatcher told her audience, she was sure '...we can take some of the initiatives he has taken.'

In fact, the EC, although it accepted that the USSR was behind the repression in Poland, was reluctant to act. Before it did so, Carrington said, it would have to consider very carefully whether a policy of sanctions against the USSR would have any useful effect.[14] It would have economic costs and the West Germans, in particular, were worried at the possible political costs of raising the level of international tension. The US was unimpressed by this reticence, but maintained its own stand while the Europeans considered other approaches to the problem. Then, shortly after they had secured declaratory support for reducing commercial contacts with the USSR from the G7 summit in Versailles the following June, the Americans confirmed that the restrictions they had placed on their own companies' dealings with the USSR would be extended to their foreign subsidiaries.

The Reagan administration had been hostile to the pipeline from the start, believing that it would create a dangerous European energy dependency which the USSR would be able to exploit in times of tension. Even if they did not, Weinberger told the British press, the US did not believe that '...anybody's interest is served by giving them eight to ten billion dollars a year in new hard currency.'[15] Why the American position became so firm at this time is not particularly clear. There is speculation that American vagueness at Versailles and a subsequent Nato summit created a misunderstanding between the US and its European allies. Certainly, the arguments over foreign policy which had been distracting the Reagan administration came to a head during the crisis with Haig's resignation in June 1982. It may simply be, however, that the Americans regarded both the issue and the timing as right for an act of assertion within Nato. Perhaps they believed that they could count on British acquiescence to divide the Europeans in gratitude for the support they had given Britain in the Falklands War which had ended three days before, and because the British were still angry at the rest of the EC for agreeing to new farm prices over their own strenuous opposition.

If so, it was a miscalculation, for the British objected strenuously to the American move. Thatcher herself had warned Haig of her opposition to imposing such restrictions at the start of the year, and four days after the announcement she repeated her concerns forcefully in Washington to the president and Donald Regan, the Secretary of the Treasury.[16] This was followed by a request from the government under the 1980 Protection of Trading Interests Act for companies to submit evidence of how US export control regulations were damaging British commercial interests. It was easy to be angry at America's apparent high-handedness over the pipeline, and many British people, inside and outside the government, were. It was not clear why the Europeans should be penalized when the US continued to sell grain to the USSR although, as Francis Pym was constrained to point out, selling grain did not provide hard currency, quite the reverse.[17]

The sources of Thatcher's opposition were more complex, however, given that she lacked the anti-American instincts which easily fuelled the anger of some of her colleagues. To begin with, there was the financial loss to British companies that would result from the American ban. John Brown Engineering, a Scottish firm, had an order for turbines worth £104 million which was threatened, and when the government ordered four firms to ignore the American ban and honour their contracts in August, it claimed that they were worth a total of £220 million.[18] In all probability, Thatcher's own emerging scepticism about economic sanctions which had vague and unspecified consequences for the target at some point in the future, yet clear and present costs for oneself, helped strengthen her opposition. The case she chose to make, however, emphasized the fact that the US was asking, or attempting to force, its allies to break promises which they and their companies had made. This, she told the House of Commons, was wrong, and she said why on a visit to Japan the following September. If the US had been clear from the start that it would stop pipeline contracts, then she did not think that '. . . any of us would have attempted to make arrangements with the Soviet Union.' However, she added, it was '. . . not reasonable to suddenly stop a commercial contract when it has been honourably and freely made and entered into.'[19]

The dispute continued through the autumn, at one point becoming bound up with another disagreement over the question of whether European steel exports to the US were subsidized. Two weeks before Thatcher's comments in Japan, the US Department of Commerce placed a temporary denial order on exports to the four companies ordered by Britain to honour their contracts, and just over a month later US customs authorities in New York seized pipeline parts made by the General Electric Company under licence from an Italian firm. By November, Nicholas Ashford was claiming that Britain and America had taken 'the special out of the relationship' because of the pipeline dispute, and because the US had supported a UN General Assembly call for Argentina and Britain to begin negotiations over their differences.[20] Even as he did so, however, the Reagan administration was declaring the dispute nearly over. A steel agreement had been reached the previous month, and now an agreement was in prospect by which the Europeans promised to make their credit and technology transfer rules more strict and to reduce their dependency on raw materials and energy from the Warsaw Pact countries. In return, the Americans would drop their objections to the pipeline contracts. A few days later, Lech Walesa was released by the Polish authorities and the US set out the terms on which it would end the sanctions which it alone had imposed.

'The Great Pipeline Cave-In', as William Safire called it in *The New York Times*, was heralded in Britain as a success for European solidarity in general and Thatcher's diplomacy in particular. Much was made of the performances she had given in Washington shortly after the policy was announced, by which, it was claimed, she had established her European credentials and her independence from the Americans. It was, however, an untidy affair all round. The Reagan administration, or part of it at any rate, had attempted to assert itself by establishing stricter codes of conduct for both the

USSR in eastern Europe and Nato's relations with the USSR, but had ended up isolating itself. The European allies had not accepted the new approach. Instead, they had focused on not making matters worse, and had treated the USSR's reluctance to intervene in Poland in 1981, like its reluctance to use force in Czechoslovakia in 1968, as evidence of the further evolution of Soviet international norms, at least as far as Europe was concerned, away from those which had permitted the bloody reassertion of control over Hungary in 1956.

The episode was untidiest of all, however, for Thatcher. Her argument about the sanctity of contracts was certainly a respectable one and consistent with her liberal convictions. Her willingness to defend the contracts of British companies accorded with her nationalist instincts, her domestic political interests and her scepticism about the utility of sanctions as an instrument of foreign policy. However, none of this could be reconciled with either her preferences about how the US should conduct itself in the world or her policy of enhancing British interests by encouraging the Americans to act assertively in East–West relations. Her statement in Japan admitted as much. Had the Americans been clearer, Thatcher implied, investor caution would have prevented the moral dilemma over contracts and allowed the objectives of her American policy to override her doubts about sanctions or her desire to help British companies win export orders.

Even the extent of the tactical success of Thatcher's opposition to the pipeline ban is not clear. If her strong performance convinced the Americans that they could not overcome European opposition, it did not stop them trying. The dispute lasted for another five months, and even after it was settled in November, the USSR refused to purchase any pipeline equipment until the following August, when the Americans finally lifted their ban on the involvement of US-based companies in the project and the export of US-made equipment for it.[21] In fact, the greatest success of Thatcher's diplomacy was in obscuring the extent of the predicament in which the whole episode had placed her. Her stand against the Americans prevented her political opponents from exploiting her claim that the sources of the dispute ultimately lay in poor transatlantic communications, while that claim reassured the Reagan administration that there was no great difference on East–West policy between the US and its British ally. As a consequence, neither Thatcher's close relationship with the Reagan administration nor the claim that she exerted considerable influence over US foreign policy were significantly damaged by an attempt to restrain American policy which enjoyed only modest success at best.

The same cannot be said of the British government's appeal to the US to refrain from invading the Caribbean island of Grenada in October 1983 and Thatcher's subsequent reaction to the rejection of that appeal. Under the leadership of Eric Gairy, Grenada had obtained independence from Britain in 1974 as a member of the Commonwealth. Gairy's regime became unpopular, oppressive and increasingly eccentric, and in 1979 it was overthrown by a coup which brought Maurice Bishop, the leader of the New Jewel Movement, to power. Bishop and his supporters were Marxists. They believed that Grenada's poverty was a result of British and, latterly, American imperialism, and saw themselves, along with the Cuban and Nicaraguan governments, as part of a hemispheric popular movement seeking to break, or at least redefine, the old patterns of exploitation. Therein lay an argument, for Bishop increasingly sought accommodation with the outside world, encouraging, for example, a tourist industry and preserving Grenada's own private sector, while his rivals feared that this would eventually destroy the revolution and their own political influence along with it. As a result, they launched their own coup in 1983, in the course of which Bishop and many of his supporters were killed.

The British government did not approve of Bishop, but neither did they regard him as much of a threat to anyone other than himself and his own unfortunate people. British companies were involved in constructing the new airport which was to become so controversial, and trade with the island continued to be of some significance. Bilateral assistance, however, had declined from £303 000 in 1979–80 to £57 000 three years later. It was maintained that Grenada was a relatively prosperous place by the standards of the Caribbean, although the course it was pursuing cannot have helped it make its case for assistance in London.[22] Opinion among the centre and left of the attentive public in Britain was far more favourably disposed towards Grenada, based as it was on a generous assessment of Bishop as a courageous idealist pursuing a viable and humane road to socialism along with Castro and the Sandinistas which other poor countries might seek to emulate. Most people in Britain, however, had paid little attention to Grenada under revolutionary rule or before. It was a place from which occasional reports came of mysterious shootings, press restrictions and, what was called in a feature article in 1982, the medical school of last resort. Events in Central America, especially Belize, attracted more attention.[23]

This began to change in 1981 after Reagan's election. The new administration shared its British counterpart's distaste for the domestic policies of the Grenadian government, but also regarded its expanded relations with Cuba and the USSR as a threat to the stability of the region. Cubans, Libyans, Syrians and Algerians, a veritable checklist of *personae non gratae* in an American sphere of influence, were reported to be involved in the construction of the airport and in the summer of 1982, the USSR announced that it was making a line of credit worth £800 000 available to Grenada.[24] The latter was a piece of opportunism made possible by the campaign of diplomatic and economic pressure with which the Americans were trying to get Grenada to change course or collapse from within. In 1981, they had asked the EC not to assist in the construction of the airport. Later, they had excluded Grenada from the programme of economic and technical assistance to the region known as the Caribbean Basin Initiative and had asked the IMF and European banks not to provide it with credit. By the spring of 1983, US forces were practising amphibious landings, and Washington had precipitated a diplomatic crisis by refusing to accept the credentials of the new Grenadian ambassador while asking their own man in Saint George's not to present his.[25] Grenada, the Americans maintained, was being developed into a centre of Soviet subversion and a base from which interdiction operations could be conducted against shipping in wartime, about which something had to be done.

The coup provided the opportunity for an invasion, while the medical students, in the role of potential hostages of the new regime, provided the pretext. Just over a week later, therefore, American forces invaded on 25 October. Following a few days of fighting, the island was secured, several hundred Cubans were captured, the new leadership arrested and the American students brought home. In Washington, the operation was declared a success which would let the US put the humiliations of Vietnam and the Iranian hostage crisis behind it. It also served as a distraction from the collapse of American policy in the Lebanon, where over two hundred US marines had been killed by a suicide bomber the day before the invasion.

In Britain, however, the invasion precipitated a political crisis for Thatcher's American policy. It did so for several reasons. The attack was widely regarded as an example of American high-handedness and hypocrisy by the centre and as evidence of its imperialistic and counter-revolutionary ambitions by the left in British politics. Opposition along these lines would no doubt have been much more vocal had Bishop still been in power, but it was muted by the obviously odious character of his murderers. There was also opposition voiced by Conservatives who regarded it as a matter of regret that someone else should be in a position to use force in a British sphere of influence when Britain was not. Surprisingly, however, it emerged that the strongest opposition to the invasion of Grenada had come from the British government and Thatcher herself. For a few days, the foreign secretary, Sir Geoffrey Howe, sought to maintain a balanced position. He acknowledged the differences which existed between London and Washington over the matter and expressed his regret '... that consultations had been less than the Government would have wished.' However, he also stressed that Britain shared the American and Caribbean objective of restoring democracy, and that the government would not put pressure on the US while it was still engaged in fighting.

Then followed Thatcher's attack, expressed not for a primarily domestic audience angry with the US, but on the World Service of the BBC. She doubted the Americans' claim that they were responding to a call for help from Grenada, because there had been no such call to the British government. She also called into question the precedent which the action implied by saying that if the US was now going to intervene '... wherever Communism reigns..., even though it's happened internally... then we are going to have really terrible wars in the world.'[26] A number of factors contributed to the strength of Thatcher's reaction to what was, after all, a minor, if doubtful, affair. No doubt she meant what she said about the precedent set by the attack for every potential aggressor, and there were, indeed, embarrassing echoes of past Soviet interventions in the way the US ensured that it was invited in by someone, the Governor-General Sir Paul Scoon. However, this concern did not prevent Thatcher from making sure that the first message of support for President Bush came from Britain when the US invaded Panama to remove General Noriega six years later on. It is also probable that she possessed proprietorial instincts activated by the invasion of a member of the Commonwealth, even though, as she told Parliament towards the end of the fighting, 'The UK Government has no residual responsibility to the independent sovereign state of Grenada.'[27]

Thatcher also shared Howe's frustration at the way Anglo-American exchanges over the problem had resulted in maximizing the British government's embarrassment. The Reagan administration had consulted with allies before the attack. Indeed, it managed to secure a request for action from the Organization of Eastern Caribbean States and the promise of a few soldiers to help garrison the island once it had been captured. A similar request for British participation, however, had met with a refusal and strong advice not to go ahead. Evidently, the government, or some members of it, thought that this advice had been heeded, at least to the extent that some delay had been obtained. The day before the invasion, Howe had told the House of Commons that the US presence off the island '...in no way foreshadowed possible intervention by the United States in the island's affairs.' Like the solitary British warship on station, he continued, '...they were simply ready to evacuate their own citizens...should the situation deteriorate'.[28] A few hours later, however, when Thatcher called Reagan to press her 'considerable doubts' about the invasion, she learned that the Americans were already going ahead. This, she knew, would make the foreign secretary, and hence her government, look foolish. Worse, it would do so at a very sensitive moment, only a few weeks before the arrival of the first Cruise missiles in Britain and in the midst of a debate about who had final authority over their deployment and use, Britain, the US or both.[29]

Thatcher may also have been less than impressed by the performance of her own diplomats in the affair. Howe, naturally, blamed the Americans for failing to signal clearly the extent of their commitment to an invasion. Perhaps so, but his assumption that an American amphibious task force and a single British warship were both instruments of the same minimalist policy of waiting out events is difficult to defend, particularly when, as Howe must have known, the Americans were requesting British participation in a military operation. As Julian Amery argued, Britain should either have come out openly and strongly against the operation, which would have had the virtue of courage if little else, or it should have wholeheartedly supported the Americans and, indeed, taken a leading role. Instead, it had done neither, with the result that unnecessary damage had been done to Anglo-American relations by an issue on which there was '... only a marginal difference of view between them'.[30] Had American intentions been clearer, of course, then Amery's course of action might have suggested itself far more strongly to Thatcher. Those intentions were not clear, however, and not merely because the Foreign Office was slow to discern them, but also because the Americans may have chosen not to be clear. Far from being insensitive to British concerns and behaving, in the words of one member of Parliament, 'cavalierly, arrogantly and contemptuously' over Grenada, the Reagan administration, once it had learned of Britain's opposition, probably sought to ease its own problems and spare its ally by executing a *fait accompli*.[31]

However, had she realized this – and she did not – it would have been cold comfort to Thatcher. Less than a month before, she had been fêted in the US. She had talked with Reagan for two and a half hours and been presented with an award by the Churchill Foundation at a dinner in the British embassy. In a speech afterwards she had discussed the Special Relationship, maintaining that the differences between the US and Britain were '... nothing compared to the things we share'. After making her usual remarks about their shared resolve and confidence in the eventual 'triumph of freedom', however, Thatcher had gone on to launch a very forceful attack on the USSR. The Soviet leaders, she had maintained, did not share 'our morality', and the West had to avoid falling into the trap of thinking that they did. As David Watt noted, these were the sorts of things Americans might say about the USSR, but they sounded shrill and frightening in Britain and did not serve British interests.[32] Taking the two themes together, however, it may be seen that Thatcher was adopting an American rhetoric which extended the coincidence of Anglo-American interests to a coincidence of overall outlook and approach. This was the speech of someone who believed herself to be very close to the Americans and, since Thatcher showed little intention of automatically subordinating British policy to American preferences, it was also the speech of someone who believed she exerted a great deal of influence over US policy.

It is in this context that Thatcher's reaction to the invasion of Grenada can best be understood. Once Reagan knew of her government's objections, the British had been kept 'out of the loop' for as long as possible regarding his determination to see the attack through. By the time Thatcher knew for sure what Reagan was up to and called him in an attempt to halt the operation, she had no

influence over American policy whatsoever. She was left to endure
the gibes of Denis Healey about the '... cult of her special relationship with the American president', and Enoch Powell recalling
George Washington's advice '... that a nation indulging towards
another in habitual hatred or habitual fondness was in some degree
a slave.'[33]

Encouraging the US to assert itself in world affairs and do what it
wanted to do was easy. The Americans were receptive to and
grateful for such encouragement. Restraining them, however, was
much more difficult, for once committed to a course of action, the
US was unlikely even to consult with sceptics, let alone be persuaded by what they had to say. This, in itself, was not a major
problem for Thatcher's policy. She usually agreed with what Reagan was trying to do, and where she had her doubts, on Central
America for example, it was easy to keep quiet. There were others
in Britain willing to point out the faults and weaknesses of American
policy. The real problems arose, as in the case of Grenada, when
substantive British interests, even if relatively minor ones, were at
stake, because then the limits of the American partnership to which
Thatcher laid claim were exposed. Partnership was revealed as
followership, and followership was revealed to have its own costs
to set against the benefits to be obtained from a policy of strong
support for the US.

7 Thatcher's US Policy II: The Diplomacy of Interests

The costs of Britain's American policy were clear, sometimes painfully so, under Thatcher, while the benefits of its first two objectives, at least, were hard to demonstrate. It was beyond the power of British diplomacy to exercise decisive influence over the level of US engagement in the world. That depended primarily on the existence of external threats to American interests and secondarily on the ability of US administrations to convince their electorates of the reality of these threats. Influencing US foreign policy offered more scope, especially if the prime minister and president of the day liked each other enough to engage in close consultations. Thatcher enjoyed considerable success in this regard but even so, it is still hard to determine how much influence she actually exercised. Was she, for example, an independent source of opinion listened to by senior figures in the Reagan administration, or merely the instrument of one faction against another in the bureaucratic politics which characterizes much of the American policy process? Even the strong testimony of American officials, as opposed to their British counterparts, about the extent of Thatcher's influence in Washington provides no easy answer to that question.

However, the benefits from the third objective of Britain's American policy – exploiting American resources to maintain the country's standing as a great power – were both clear and considerable. The key success in this regard involved securing what will eventually be at least a half-century of US support for Britain's nuclear weapons programme. This has enabled the British to maintain, at a sustainable cost to themselves, a modern nuclear force capable of attacking multiple targets thousands of miles away. It is this force which keeps Britain in the front rank of military powers, at once capable of destroying the international order and responsible for its maintenance. In diplomatic terms, however, it was the exclusive character of this cooperation which was of importance. The US shared with Britain, to an extent which it did with no one else, some of the weapons and secrets which provided the foundation of its own power and position in the world. To begin with, this willingness had derived from other dimensions of the Special Relationship but by the time Thatcher became prime minister, Anglo-American nuclear collaboration had itself come to constitute its core. Without it, the other dimensions – the habits of consultation and the pooling of intelligence – would have been insufficient to mark the relationship out as special.

Extensive though Anglo-American nuclear collaboration came to be, however, it was often a source of considerable tension, both between the two countries and within each of them. Assisting Britain in this way usually suited the alliance-oriented priorities of American diplomacy, but it was not always consistent with the more monopolistically inclined objectives of the Pentagon or the agenda of the State Department's own Arms Control and Disarmament Agency. Britain's defence establishment, in contrast, was relieved to have its access to the latest developments in nuclear weapons and their delivery systems preserved, while its diplomats and politicians worried about how technical dependence on the US would affect Britain's claim to nuclear independence. These tensions were at their greatest in two circumstances: when the British required new systems to maintain the effectiveness of their deterrent; and when the Americans judged that developments in their strategic environment necessitated changes in their nuclear policy. Then, the controversies associated with the relationship would be aired on both sides of the Atlantic in debates which were made more intense by the contribution of those who believed that neither country should have anything to do with nuclear weapons at all.

THE NUCLEAR PARTNERSHIP

Anglo-American collaboration, of course, had been responsible for creating the first atomic bombs during the Second World War. As the research teams had come closer to their goal, however, British participants had been progressively excluded from work designed to solve the practical problem of how actually to build a bomb. As a consequence, the British decided to proceed with their own nuclear programme, detonating their first atomic, or fission, device in 1952. By the end of the decade, Britain possessed its own fleet of jet bombers equipped with more destructive thermonuclear, or fusion, weapons and was working on a ballistic missile, Blue Streak, which could also deliver them to targets in the USSR. By the end of the decade, however, it was also clear that Britain could no longer afford to stay in the nuclear arms race. Its bombers became operational just as improvements in Soviet anti-aircraft defences cast doubt over their effectiveness, and the missile it had struggled to produce was of an obsolete, liquid fuelled and, hence, vulnerable type.[1] Fortunately for Britain, however, the US had decided to relax its rules on nuclear collaboration, partly because of Britain's own efforts to develop a nuclear programme and partly because it had been cooperative in allowing American air and missile bases on British territory. One of the first fruits of this cooperation was an American offer of 100 Skybolt missiles, a standoff bomb which could be launched some distance from the target by aircraft. In lieu of the cancelled Blue Streak missile, bombers equipped with Skybolt were to be Britain's main nuclear strike force and, thus, it was an embarrassment and potential disaster for the British government when, with no consultation, the US cancelled the missile in 1962. A meeting was hurriedly set up between Macmillan and Kennedy in the Bahamas, as a result of which the US agreed to provide Britain with Polaris missiles and technical assistance to build the nuclear submarines from which they were launched. The Nassau agreement, as it was known, was a triumph for, instead of being an ignored dependent, Britain was now to be privy to some of America's most closely guarded nuclear secrets and a partner in operating its latest weaponry.

It was also a fortunate arrangement in strategic and economic terms, for by it and at modest cost Britain was provided with the sort of secure nuclear force which would have been beyond its economic, scientific and technical resources acting alone. By the late 1960s, therefore, the Royal Navy had acquired four British-built, nuclear-powered submarines. On each boat were sixteen American-made and maintained missiles, each with three 40 kiloton British-built warheads assigned to Soviet targets in a Nato plan, but at the disposal of the British government in the event of a dire threat to national security. Even the best weapons systems wear out or become obsolescent, however, and because of the time it takes to develop new ones, decisions about their replacement have to be made between 10 and 15 years in advance. The Polaris boats were due for replacement at some time in the first half of the 1990s and, thus, the decision about what, if anything, would replace them, had to be made by the Thatcher government soon after it was elected.

Predicting what one's security requirements might be 15 years in the future is difficult enough, but the choice facing Thatcher was complicated by other constraints. First, even if it was intended only to maintain the capability provided by Polaris, making the replacements which could do this remained beyond the country's economic and technological resources. Therefore, Britain remained dependent on the US, for no one else was willing or able to provide that capability in the necessary time at an acceptable cost. However, the US no longer manufactured, and no longer wished to service, Polaris missiles. It was already in the process of seeking a replacement for Polaris's successor, Poseidon, but there was uncertainty both about what it would be and its suitability for British purposes. Secondly, the nuclear experts were no longer sure that the damage which Polaris, or its equivalent if attainable, could inflict on the USSR was sufficient or certain enough to deter the Soviet leadership if it was contemplating attacks on Britain or western Europe. Indeed, under previous governments, a nominally secret programme known as Chevaline had been implemented to improve Britain's Polaris so that as many warheads as possible might pass through Soviet anti-ballistic missile defences to strike home. The programme had been plagued by technical difficulties, however, and its costs, in John Nott's picturesque phrase, had '. . . gone bananas.'[2]

The final constraints upon the government were the economic and political conditions in which this already difficult decision had to be made. Britain's economic difficulties and the public spending cuts with which the Thatcher government sought to alleviate them directed the defence establishment's attention to the costs of maintaining nuclear weapons. Some argued that deterrence could be achieved by alternative less expensive methods – patching up the Polaris system, for example, or buying cheaper Cruise missiles. Others claimed that within projected defence spending, the deterrent could not be maintained without weakening one of the other primary missions of the armed forces.[3] Public attention, in contrast, was drawn by the government's opponents to the worsening international context in which Britain's decision to acquire nuclear weapons was being taken. Was it right, they asked, that Britain should be acquiring new nuclear weapons just when a newly belligerent US appeared set on confronting an equally stubborn USSR? As a consequence, by 1981, the problem of replacing Polaris had exploded into an argument between the government and its opponents over whether Britain should have nuclear weapons and whether the US should be allowed to retain its nuclear bases or any military bases on British territory.

Francis Pym, then defence minister, announced the decision to acquire Trident I missiles from the US in July 1980. He justified the decision in the same way previous governments had explained Polaris. Trident would be '... an essential affirmation of our commitment to security and to cooperation with our allies'. Like Polaris, it would be assigned to Nato, and only in '... the extraordinary circumstances of some situation in which our national security is threatened' would Britain's '... ownership and sole operation come into play.' In response to a jibe from the Labour spokesman on defence that acquiring Trident amounted to a '... pathetic effort to pretend we are still a superpower', Pym added that there was '... no question of prestige and status'. Only cold analysis of the facts of the situation had informed the government's decision.[4] The following year, Nott clarified this analysis. Britain had a responsibility to make a nuclear contribution to Nato, he argued, because the alliance could not be defended without nuclear weapons. This being so, for Britain '... to wash its hands of nuclear matters' while enjoying the protection of the alliance would be '... a dangerous and dishonest pretence'. He added that Britain's deterrent should also be regarded as an '... insurance premium against any Soviet supposition' that the US might '... seek to insulate itself from nuclear consequences while abandoning Europe.' Britain's nuclear capability would force an aggressor '... to face two gambles instead of one'.[5]

Opposition to Trident was intense. The Campaign for Nuclear Disarmament, which had been established in the 1950s, revived as a mass movement. It organized demonstrations attended by tens of thousands of people, and the Labour party adopted its policies advocating British unilateral nuclear disarmament and the closure of American bases in Britain. The protestors claimed a large reservoir of popular support. In 1983, for example, the year that Cruise and Pershing missiles were to arrive in Europe, polls suggested that some 60 per cent of the population did not want them, and that 55 per cent were opposed to Trident. In 1985, a month before the superpowers resumed summit diplomacy with the meeting between Gorbachev and Reagan in Geneva, opposition to Trident had risen to 60 per cent of those polled, and only 40 per cent agreed with a defence policy involving any sort of nuclear weapons.[6] In retrospect, however, it is hard to ascertain what these figures revealed beyond the fact that most people regarded nuclear war as a bad thing of which they were scared and the possession of nuclear weapons as a matter for regret. As Thatcher's election victories in 1983 and 1987 over a Labour party committed to unilateral nuclear disarmament seemed to confirm, no one, or almost no one, liked nuclear weapons, but most believed that Britain should not give them up while other countries retained them. This being so, and mass demonstrations notwithstanding, the biggest obstacles to Thatcher's nuclear policy were not posed by her domestic opposition, but by the policies of Britain's great nuclear benefactor, the US.

REAGAN'S POLICY: USING OR LOSING NUCLEAR WEAPONS?

The first of these had been hinted at from the very start of the Trident programme. The Americans were not sure whether they were going to proceed with the C4 missile or switch to a more sophisticated Mark II version called the D5. This could travel 6000 miles, compared to 4000 for the C4 and 2800 for Polaris, it could carry up to 14 warheads, compared to eight on the C4 and three on Polaris, and it needed a larger submarine to carry it.[7] The proposed acquisition of such a weapon would fuel the arguments of those opposed to the C4. It would be more expensive. Early Ministry of Defence estimates suggested that the total cost would be between £7.5 and £10.5 billion as opposed to £4.5 to £5 billion for the original replacement.[8] It would also be potentially more destructive because of the greater number of D5 warheads and their greater accuracy. This, the system's critics argued, posed an unjustifiably greater threat to the USSR, particularly if, as they claimed, D5's primary purpose was to contribute to the American nuclear warfighting doctrine of attacking missile silos and command centres. Finally, it would be less independent, since the D5's full potential could only be realized when it was deployed in conjunction with American space-based navigation and guidance systems.

In March 1982, the government announced that it was, indeed, the Trident II system with D5 missiles which would eventually replace Polaris. Another Skybolt crisis had been avoided by the early signalling of this possibility, but the other problems remained to be addressed. With regard to the project's costs, the government maintained that the new arrangement was, in John Nott's words, 'a bargain,' when compared to financing continued American production of C4 or sustaining an independent British effort, although he had earlier suggested that it would be beyond the capacity of a Nobel prize winner in mathematics to arrive at a precise figure. For Trident, however, Britain would spend some 3 per cent of its defence budget, which contrasted favourably with the 20 per cent he claimed France was spending on its own nuclear weapons, and it would not be dependent on the US for '...communications, targeting or...day-to-day operation of the force'. As to the potentially offensive character of the weapons, Nott assured the House of Commons that no more warheads would be placed upon the D5 than had been planned for C4, and pointed out that this represented no more than 3 to 4 per cent of the total Soviet inventory. He also spoke of the 'essential lunacy' of the superpower nuclear build-up, but beyond this, all he could do was reiterate his earlier views on the matter. 'A localized tactical nuclear war', he had stated the previous spring was '...an absurdity'. Any kind of nuclear exchange '...would be crazy and madness...' for the purpose of deterrence was '...not to fight a war with nuclear weapons, but prevent one.'[9]

Assuming Britain required the destructive capacity delivered by the D5 missile, the arguments about alternatives and price were strong ones. What the government found hard to address, however, was whether Britain needed that much destructive power given the hostile reaction which this might produce in the USSR. Understandably, Moscow was no more impressed by Nott's assurance that Britain would only place 128 warheads on each boat, as opposed to their full capacity of 224, than London was by Soviet assurances that a nuclear-free Britain would never be the target of Soviet nuclear weapons.[10] Thatcher herself, however, was not troubled by such concerns for she operated on a simpler and more effective calculus concerning nuclear weapons and their uses, which practically discounted hostile diplomatic reactions to deployments. The government's position, as summarized in a Defence Council Memorandum published in 1980, was that deterrence would not be achieved by a capability which '...offered only a low likelihood of striking home to key targets', or which the '...Soviet leaders could expect to ward off successfully from large areas of key importance to them.' As far as Thatcher was concerned, if this were so, then obviously Britain needed Trident because it was '...a much more powerful weapon', and, addressing the diplomatic dimension, she added later that if relations with the USSR did improve, '...it would be better to negotiate disarmament from a position of strength.' Strength, in terms of the certainty of doing damage, offered more security and better prospects for real progress on arms control.

Nor was she bashful about the other reasons why Britain needed Trident. Contradicting Pym's earlier claim that concerns about prestige had played no part in the decision, she told the Conservative party conference in 1980 that '...it was important for Britain's reputation abroad that we should keep our independent nuclear deterrent', and on the sensitive issue of why independent control of the weapons was so vital, Thatcher was even more forthright. This was usually dealt with by emphasizing, as had Pym, the 'extraordinary' and 'horrendous' circumstances in which the force would revert from Nato to the sole control of the British government. Thatcher herself in her 1980 letter to Reagan requesting Trident had stressed their Nato assignment except in '...supreme national interest cases', and Nott had made the case for independence in terms of making it impossible for the USSR to believe it could escape nuclear retaliation on the miscalculation that the US guarantee to Europe was no longer operative. What was being edged around, of course, was the question of the reliability of that guarantee. Would the US expose itself to nuclear strikes to save Europe? To judge by the case she made for retaining an independent deterrent the day the Falkland Islands were lost, Thatcher had her doubts. 'We have been alone before,' she declared, and '...I trust we will never be alone again.' However, it was '...reasonable and prudent to make proper provision for the defence of this country if we were.'[11] Thatcher's Churchillian vein drew as much on June 1940 as it did on June or December 1941 and what followed.

Thatcher's parsimonious nuclear doctrine allowed her to ignore the problems posed by the lavish character of the assistance the Americans were prepared to provide. Packing a punch one was certain of delivering remained the key to effective deterrence, and the war-fighting doctrines into which the new weapons were supposedly to fit were far too exotic to be taken seriously. However, subsequent developments in US nuclear strategy were not so easily ignored for they exposed a weakness in Thatcher's nuclear hand and forced her to reveal an aspect of it which had formerly not been clear at all. In March 1983, Reagan announced his Strategic

Defense Initiative (SDI), known to critics and sceptics alike as 'Star Wars'. The initial purpose of SDI was to support research into the feasibility of developing weapons capable of destroying missiles before they reached their targets. Reagan spoke of '...countering the awesome Soviet threat with measures that are defensive', but the 'ultimate goal' involved '...eliminating the threat posed by nuclear missiles'.[12]

This announcement precipitated a debate within the US, within the Nato alliance, and between them both and the USSR. Most of the polemic addressed two basic questions. Could such a system be developed; and what would be the consequences of doing, or even trying to do, so? On the question of technical feasibility, the British shared the scepticism which had been orthodoxy since the 1973 anti-ballistic missile (ABM) treaty. The high performance standards which any such system must meet, particularly if it were to satisfy Reagan's goal of providing a shield against all missiles, entailed that the programme was, in Howe's words, '...geared to a concept which might prove elusive'. Only a few warheads penetrating the defences would spell disaster. Thus, anyone who claimed that an alternative to nuclear deterrence as the basis of security was realizable in the near future was engaging in what Thatcher herself called a 'perilous pretence'. Nevertheless, the government's position was that research on the project should go ahead, for it was prudent to suppose that the USSR was conducting research of a similar nature. The US should '...seek to match the present stage in Soviet programmes.'[13] In addition, there emerged a financial incentive for supporting SDI research. In 1985, the US government invited bids by other countries for SDI work. By participating, Michael Heseltine, the defence minister, argued, British universities, research institutes and companies would gain access to high technology which could be obtained no other way and which would go to others if Britain held back. He spoke of attracting contracts worth £1.1 billion pounds, but only a fraction of this amount materialized eventually.[14]

British support for SDI, however, applied to the research phase of the project only. This was because concerns existed within the government about the possible political, diplomatic and strategic consequences of trying to develop ballistic missile defences. Least important of these was the one which had most exercised the public imagination, namely that SDI was part of a comprehensive and insane US attempt to achieve a strategic superiority which would allow it to win nuclear wars. Evidence existed which supported this view. The Reagan administration spoke of gaining a military advantage with SDI as well as imposing strains on the USSR's technical and economic resources, and an advantage can be used not only to deter, but also to intimidate and fight. Further, after the original announcement, most of the Reagan administration, although not the president himself, began advocating a scaled-down version of the project capable of protecting vital targets rather than the whole country. This, arguably, was more consistent with preparing to fight nuclear wars than with making them impossible and obsolete.

The British government, however, did not take these claims seriously, except as domestic political embarrassments which had to be explained away from time to time. They, and Thatcher in particular, seem to have accepted that the purpose of SDI was to enhance deterrence by creating a position of strength, although there is a suggestion that when they learned from the Soviet defector, Gordievsky, how scared SDI had made the Soviet leaders, the offensive aspects of the project became a source of concern. What bothered the British far more than the US rationales for SDI were the real political and military consequences of the way it was acquiring it. The ABM treaty had placed restrictions upon the systems which the two superpowers could deploy and, while it permitted some research and testing of systems incorporating new technologies, it made the deployment of anything else a matter for further negotiation. As SDI became a possibility, however, some members of the Reagan administration argued that work on it should not be constrained by what they began to call a narrow interpretation of the ABM treaty. The treaty permitted testing, and testing, they claimed, involved deployment. Thus, the treaty permitted some deployment. If it did not, then the US should follow the USSR's example and act as if it did anyway.

Whatever the legal ground on which this case was built, it certainly violated the spirit of the ABM treaty as far as the USSR and America's Nato allies were concerned. For the US to break out of the treaty's restrictions in this way, they argued, could only increase East–West tension, whether or not the Americans were actively seeking superiority. More importantly, as the British and French quickly realized, the first practical consequence of an American rush to develop limited ballistic missile defences would be an intensification of the USSR's attempts to do likewise. This might not be overly bothersome to the US with its several thousands of warheads, but it would greatly reduce the effectiveness of their own smaller and, hence, more vulnerable nuclear forces. Accordingly, Thatcher's own response to SDI was to obtain Reagan's assurances at Camp David in December 1984 that US strategic and arms control policies were still guided by four principles on which both countries agreed. These, in summary, were that the US, like its allies, did not seek superiority over the USSR, would negotiate any SDI deployment as obligated by existing treaty commitments, would do nothing to undermine deterrence, and would engage in arms control talks to reduce existing levels of offensive systems.

This episode has become part of the Thatcher legend as the first occasion on which, as British sources like to see it, an uncertain President Reagan was steered by her firm and guiding hand. Certainly, the manner in which the four points were negotiated – the British presenting a piece of paper to which the Americans assented – provides a glimpse of Thatcher's own high standing with the Reagan administration at the time.[15] However, the substance of the agreement and the fundamental character of the principles which the British needed reaffirming underline the unease with which even Thatcher viewed the priorities which were appearing to guide the policy of her closest ally. The possibility that even modest improvements in ballistic missile defence could reduce and perhaps nullify the effectiveness of a system on which Britain was committed to spend some £10 billion over 15 years was a source of concern. Scarcely better would be to have its effectiveness maintained by the USSR's willingness to refrain from deploying the systems which could nullify it. The extent of Britain's strategic dependence on the US could be embarrassing enough at times, but to be also dependent on Soviet restraint as part of a superpower agreement, while conceivable, would have been politically embarrassing.

On their own, however, even these possibilities were not much to lose sleep over. The SDI programme became mired in technical and funding problems, and even the 'modest' improvements associated with a partial deployment were not easily achieved. Nor was it clear that, in Soviet hands, they would be able to protect the sort of targets – large cities – which *in extremis* the British might be expected to go after. Ballistic missile defences might be something to worry about in the future, but it is likely that the British government believed that cheaper countermeasures, such as launching more missiles at different speeds on different trajectories, would always be a disincentive to deploying such defences. More troubling to the British government were the competing and contradictory imperatives driving American grand strategy during the Reagan era, of which SDI and its several rationalizations were but symptoms. War-fighting or, more properly, deterring the enemy by convincing him he would lose a war was the newest of these imperatives, but its advocates competed with those who shared the more established concern with preserving stability by collaborating with the 'enemy' to make victory impossible for either side. It was this latter view, preventing nuclear war by making the costs of it catastrophic, which the British defended when they spoke of enhancing deterrence and doing nothing to undermine it.

There was, however, a third possible approach to nuclear security which involved getting rid of the weapons entirely. This approach, long-advocated by the Peace Movement, had been revived in American foreign policy by Reagan's original SDI address in 1983 and echoed by Gorbachev on Soviet television and by the Delhi Declaration in 1986.[16] As a declaratory preface to policy, or as an aspiration for the future, the British government took no great exception to the idea of a nuclear weapons-free world. It provided little constraint on practical policy. Arms control measures designed to achieve stability at lower levels could be easily reconciled with it. Reagan's 'zero option', for example, announced in November 1981, by which Nato would refrain from deploying new missiles in Europe in return for the USSR destroying its own theatre nuclear forces, was presented both as a stabilization measure and as a first step down the road to nuclear disarmament. More remarkably, even SDI could be presented as stability-enhancing, as the key to nuclear superiority or as the quickest way to get rid of nuclear weapons. The trick, of course, was to know which imperative was actually guiding US policy and, as arms control negotiations between the superpowers gathered pace following the Geneva summit in November 1985, of this the British became increasingly unsure.

The big surprise, in these terms, came in October 1986 when the British learned that, at their summit in Reykjavik, Reagan had nearly accepted Gorbachev's proposal to eliminate nuclear weapons completely over two five-year periods. Only Gorbachev's insistence that SDI must also be abandoned had prevented Reagan's agreement. Initially, the view that only Reagan's stubbornness had prevented a major and desirable breakthrough dominated even conservative opinion in Britain. *The Times* speculated that Thatcher would delay a visit to the US so as not to be seen to be adding to the pressure on the president to give up SDI. Within days, however, the implications of the agreement for European security were being given fuller consideration. Thatcher and President Mitterrand of France jointly declared in London that nuclear deterrence continued to provide the basis for the West's defence. When Thatcher travelled to Washington the following month, to confirm Nato's support for the weapons reductions envisaged in the first five-year phase, it was to smother the second phase in which the remainder were to be destroyed. At Camp David, Thatcher and Reagan went off in a golf cart without their aides and, according to Thatcher legend, she lectured Reagan on the fundamental principles of nuclear deterrence and its place in Nato strategy. On returning, Thatcher produced a piece of paper from her handbag on which, she said, was written their agreement. Once again, Thatcher's influence over Reagan had been confirmed, but once again, it had so in potentially difficult circumstances from the British point of view.[17]

Whether Reykjavik was a near miss brought about by a momentary lapse or the sort of deal which would have died a natural death for lack of support within the foreign and defence bureaucracies of the superpowers is hard to say. So too is the extent to which Thatcher was the instrument, rather than the architect of damage control, used by the Americans because of her personal influence over Reagan on unpleasant matters. Either way, however, she was effective in preserving British and Nato security interests from this particular threat. Much harder to deal with was the long-term trend in Soviet-American arms control agreements increasingly dominated by the rhetoric of reducing weapons levels to zero. This development posed two sorts of challenges. It undermined the axiom that so long as the Warsaw Pact retained an advantage in conventional weapons, then no matter what the USSR's nuclear policy was, Nato required at least some nuclear weapons to deter or defeat an attack. Further, zero rhetoric, with its assumption that all nuclear weapons were eventually to go, led easily to the expectation that cuts could be made across the board. Such an approach would result in Britain and France making disproportionate sacrifices in that all their nuclear weapons would be gone before the arsenals of the superpowers had been reduced by barely 3 per cent.

Long before, Reykjavik, Reagan's zero option, while politically successful, had been a source of British concern on both counts. So long as the USSR rejected it, as was expected, then it was an acceptable gesture. To the surprise of its authors, however, Gorbachev eventually accepted the zero option unconditionally and the Intermediate Nuclear Forces (INF) Treaty was signed in 1987.[18] From that point, British policy worked, ultimately unsuccessfully, to prevent the extension of the zero principle to other systems on which it maintained European security continued to depend. One of those threatened was Britain's own force, for the USSR had responded to the zero offer by requesting that both it and the French *force de frappe* be included in any calculation of the European balance. The British and French both responded that their nuclear weapons were instruments of national, strategic policy rather than alliance, theatre forces. However, they also claimed that they could not be included in the Strategic Arms Reduction Talks (START) for they were already at, in Thatcher's words, an 'irreducible minimum' from which cuts could not be made without destroying their effectiveness completely. Only if both the superpowers agreed to 'substantial reductions in nuclear weapons' and there was no increase in their defensive capabilities would Britain reconsider its position.[19]

The problem which accepting the rhetoric of zero did not answer was what would the British to do if deep cuts in the nuclear arsenals of the superpowers started to be realized. Only once did a British minister seem to acknowledge the consequences of acceptance. Shortly after Reykjavik, and still perhaps sensitive to optimism generated by Gorbachev's initiative, George Younger, the defence minster, told the House of Commons that:

> ... if, in due course, taking into account all factors, including conventional and chemical weapons, we can approach a period of deep reductions, or even zero, of course we would be able to have a part in that process, but not only taking one part of it on its own.[20]

Even this cagey acknowledgement of the possibility of British involvement in reductions to zero, leaving open as it did the possibility of conducting a glacial retreat over the years, did not reflect Thatcher's views, however. Her initial response to Gorbachev's and Reagan's calls for a nuclear-free world was that she could not see it coming about. The knowledge of how to make the weapons existed and, thus, governments should not work too hard for that 'pie in the sky'.[21]

However, as the process of cutting gathered momentum after the INF treaty, Thatcher was forced to give a more explicit defence of her position and the assumptions on which it was based. On her visit to Moscow in the spring before the INF treaty in 1986, she had told Gorbachev that the West '... was not prepared to accept the denuclearization of Europe.' At the time, she made the arguments about the conventional and nuclear imbalances which existed between Nato and the Warsaw Pact. In an interview a month later, however, she provided a very different rationale for the retention of nuclear weapons. We know, she said, that conventional weapons do not deter wars. Therefore, in a world which people supposed was free of nuclear weapons, wars would break out. When one did, then just as in the Second World War, the race would be on to develop nuclear weapons, the knowledge of which still existed. Victory, she concluded, would go to whoever succeeded in developing them first and, in all probability, that would be the country which had '... stowed a few away, just in case' in the first place.[22]

The possibility that an aggressor might possess nuclear weapons dictated that Nato should always retain some. Therefore, only days after the INF treaty was signed, Thatcher declared that '... we must keep a few American atomic weapons in Europe,' and pledged '... I will never give up' Britain's '... independent nuclear deterrent and neither will France.' The alliance aspect of her nuclear policy was less successful than the national one. By 1989, although she had offered to accept more nuclear-armed American F111 aircraft in Britain to help compensate for the withdrawn missiles, she had failed to hold her allies (and George Bush, the new American president, in particular) to Nato's commitment to modernizing its short-range missiles. And when she spoke of the denuclearization of Europe, it was no longer to tell Gorbachev that this was Nato's policy, but to tell her allies that this was something which '... We must at all costs avoid.'[23] Trident, however, was successfully kept out of both the new arms control agreements between the US and the USSR and the Senate's plans for cutting the defence budget. Gorbachev accepted that the Trident programme was unaffected by the START talks but, he argued in June 1990, subsequent transfers would have to cease to deny the US a channel for improving its forces outside the framework of arms control agreements between the superpowers. James Baker told the British that this was the major obstacle to a further agreement. However, this was not to be Thatcher's problem but her successor's, and the difficulties it posed for replacing Trident as Britain's independent deterrent would not arise for another quarter of a century.[24]

THE LIMITS TO THE SPECIAL RELATIONSHIP

Britain's acquisition of Trident and the subsequent struggle to pre-serve its effectiveness epitomizes the story of Anglo-American rela-tions since 1940. After much skilful diplomacy abroad and politicking at home, complete success on the specific objectives of policy was achieved and disaster averted. Even complete success, however, could not dispel unease about the circumstances which forced Britain to seek American help and the dependability of that source of help in the future. As long as Britain seeks to advance its interests by maintaining a close partnership with a country which, no matter how friendly and sympathetic, has over four times as many people and an economy which is up to eight times larger, the insecurities which these discrepancies engender will be a cost of that policy. It has been the judgement of successive British governments, however, that the benefits, particularly in terms of security, far outweigh the costs of working to maintain the Special Relationship. It is hard to disagree with this judgement, and it must be concluded that by the standards of postwar British diplomacy, Thatcher's American policy enjoyed a success of Macmillanesque proportions. Indeed, in terms of the boost to her own international standing, as opposed to the country's, which she obtained from her policy, her success bordered at times on the Churchillian.

Her Washington insider role was far more effective than Mac-millan's performance as a detached, elder statesman in providing the position of personal influence with other states which they both pursued. Macmillan premised his statesmanship on the fact that, in a world dominated by the outlook of the superpowers, he took an older British or European approach to them which had much to offer if anyone would listen. In contrast, Thatcher's influence over the Americans was not based on a claim to shared fundamental values bolstered by a superior 'British' understanding of the world. Rather, it was derived from the fact that she saw the world much as they did. Indeed, to judge by the stories of her stiffening the resolve of George Bush to respond forcefully to Iraq's invasion of Kuwait,

Thatcher had, on occasions, more 'American' instincts than some of the Americans themselves. She encouraged the Reagan administration in its efforts to overcome Carter's 'malaise' and reassert US leadership of the liberal capitalist democracies. She attempted, with some success, to influence the way in which the US exercised its leadership around the world, and did so with far more in mind than simply moderating American gaucherie to mollify the feelings of its allegedly horrified allies.

However, Thatcher's closeness with the Americans was accomplished without becoming 'Reagan's poodle' or subordinating British foreign policy interests to US preferences. As the pipeline episode demonstrated, Thatcher was capable of disagreeing with even high political acts of American self-assertion when she thought they were wrong. Indeed, she was nearly always reluctant to accept the American use of sanctions, be they economic, sporting or just plain bloody-minded like the denial of airport facilities to diplomats visiting the UN. Nor did she exhibit much tolerance for US actions which expressly ignored British sensibilities or opposition. Over Grenada, for example, rather than allowing the requirements of operational secrecy to provide an excuse for the breakdown in communications with the US and Howe's subsequent embarrassment Parliament, she relaunched the controversy after it had begun to subside.

Neither did the closeness of her relationship with Reagan prevent British foreign policy running to its own rhythms in other parts of the world, even where there was a strong American presence. In the Middle East, for example, British participation in various American military projects from the Rapid Reaction Force to peacekeeping operations in the Sinai and Beirut was restricted by concerns for the predicament of the Palestinians which the Americans did not yet share. Britain's own initiatives in the area were calibrated to fit with the EC's attempts to create a Middle East policy, involved a willingness to work discreetly with the PLO and, less discreetly, to engage in criticism of the Israelis, sometimes undertaken by ministers as they visited camps within the Israel-occupied territories.[25] Even in the Gulf, except after Iraq invaded Kuwait, British policy did not automatically coincide with American requirements. Britain sold landing ships to Iran, delayed the deployment of minehunters in 1984 and 1987, and prevented its own 'presence' in there, the Armilla patrol of two or three warships, from following the aggressive posture adopted by the Americans after Iranian attacks on shipping intensified in 1987. The prospect of arms sales, both legal and illegal as it transpires, the need to coordinate Britain's actions with the EC, a long-running, on-again-off-again attempt to re-establish full diplomatic relations with Iran, plus the government's belief that Britain could still make its own distinctive contribution to the Middle East peace process, all ensured differences with the Americans.

The combination of Thatcher's obvious closeness to Reagan with the fact that she and Britain retained a capacity for independent action secured her an entrée with one international figure in parti-cular, Gorbachev, and enabled her to become an international figure herself. Successful though she was in this regard, however, the fact remains that most of Thatcher's influence over the Amer-icans was expended on protecting British interests from oscillations in US policy. As Reagan said, the offer of Trident was a demon-stration of '. . . the great importance' which the US attached '. . . to the maintenance by the United Kingdom of an independent nuclear deterrent capability. . .'[26] and throughout the period, the Americans protected it from inclusion by the USSR in arms control negotiations. Having, in their own minds, given the British the bomb, however, the Americans were understandably ill-disposed towards having the broad brush strokes of their grand strategy spoiled by Britain's reminders of what it took to keep Nato's and its own minimum deterrent threat credible.

Just like her predecessors, this is precisely what Thatcher found herself doing. It was rendered tolerable by her closeness to Reagan and her admiration for the US in general, but towards the end of Thatcher's time in office, the tensions between the nationalism and atlanticism in her statecraft began to show. She opposed the Amer-ican response to the collapse of the Cold War order in Europe, for example, because she believed it was taking place on terms which threatened British interests. She opposed the superpowers' declared objective of negotiating away all nuclear weapons as 'pie-in-the-sky' and, in so doing, revealed the most innovative and lasting legacy of her American policy. Britain's possession of an independent nuclear deterrent might be justified as a responsible contribution to Nato, but, for Thatcher, its primary purpose was to serve as life insurance, and prestigious life insurance at that. In declaring her commitment to keep nuclear weapons, therefore, Thatcher was yearning neither for the days of former British greatness nor even the certainties of the Cold War. She was merely prefiguring the logic which would drive the security policies of those with means in a world no longer dominated by the superpowers.

This tension between the nationalism and atlanticism in Thatcher's statecraft was always overshadowed by its other controversial aspects and, indeed, European and domestic politics conspired to remove her from office long before it could become fully exposed. Had events been otherwise, however, it is clear that Thatcher would have resolved the tension in favour of her nationalist imperatives. She would have done so because, in retrospect, it is possible to see that she would have had very little other choice. Her American policy, successful though it undoubtedly was in making the best of and, indeed, exploiting Britain's Special, but hugely asymmetrical, Relationship with the US, was dependent on contingencies over which Britain exercised no control. Thatcher was able to exploit the climate of emergency which the US confronted and contributed to in the early 1980s, and the relationship she established with Reagan. However, she could neither create a climate of emergency if the US refused to recognize it as such, nor ensure the election of a president with whom she got on. As a consequence, though the relationship with Reagan's America was an opportunity to be exploited and enjoyed, both of which Thatcher did very well, the legacy of her American policy to her successors would be virtually empty. Relations with Europe, in contrast, were of the order of a necessity, for there, as Thatcher consistently maintained, was where Britain's future lay. It was also where Thatcher's statecraft could have a lasting impact both on British foreign policy and on the way the European great powers conducted their relations with one another.

8 Thatcher's European Policy I: The *Demandeur*

Europe was, indeed, the realm of necessity for British foreign policy. As Thatcher herself made clear in her famous address to the College of Europe at Bruges in 1988, Britain's ties with Europe were '...the dominant factor in our history', and Britain's destiny lay '...in Europe as a part of the Community'. Returning again to the theme of 'Britain's destiny' during a speech she made in Aspen, Colorado three months before her resignation in 1990, she declared that it lay '...in Europe as a full member of the Community'. Britain would not be 'standing on the sidelines or...watching from the bleachers.'[1] There is no doubt she meant what she said on both occasions, but what still remains very much in doubt is what she, or anyone else for that matter, meant by 'Europe' and the European Community.

'Europe' or, more properly, European unity was not a new idea when the present enterprise was begun by the parties to the Rome Treaties signed in 1957. The French under Napoleon and the Germans under Hitler had both created European orders of a sort by conquest. Further back, the Romans had succeeded in creating a far more resilient European community, although still by imposing their own way upon others, and a sense of European identity had emerged, based upon intellectual and religious traditions held in common, as individual European powers made contact with, and subsequently assumed control over, much of the rest of the world. What was new about the European Economic Community (EEC) and its counterparts in Coal and Steel and Atomic Energy, however, was the extent to which they resulted from collaboration rather than imposition. This impulse was driven by fear among the original six members, Belgium, France, Italy, Luxembourg the Netherlands and West Germany, that divisions among them would lead, as they had in the past, to war. It was also encouraged, however, by the prospect of economic recovery and, eventually, the prosperity which the combination of their efforts might deliver.

Consequently, the organization which emerged was a strange and ambiguous composite. Economically, it combined elements of a free trade area and customs union between economies which remained national in character with the sectoral integration and common policies of an attempt to create a new and larger economic entity. Politically, the nascent bureaucracy, executive, legislature and judiciary of a continental authority, the Commission, Parliament and Court of Justice, existed alongside an instrument of intergovernmental collaboration – the Council of Ministers. And all the institutions and practices of the Communities were permeated by an ideology, or sense, of forward and upward movement towards a contested destination, now quicker now slower but always such that the Communities could be said to be engaged in a permanent process of becoming. What this all meant, experts and academics had a terrible time defining. Was the European Community (EC), as the merged executives of its former components became in 1967, an instrument of its members' foreign policies, a modifier of their behaviour, or an actor in its own right?[2] And where was it all going? Would it eventually become a new state – a United States of Europe? Was it developing into a looser association more like the UN or was it, developing or no, *sui generis* and not much like anything else at all?[3]

Successive British governments had not attempted to answer such difficult questions, for the issue with which the EC had presented them was that of membership. Would Britain's national interests and its capacity to advance them be enhanced by joining the Community? The initial answer, once British diplomacy had failed to prevent the customs union aspect of the project back in 1957, was no. Self-confidence or hubris suggested that the trade-off between prosperity and independence was not nearly so attractive to Britain as it was to those who had undergone the catastrophe of defeat during the war, and accepting the common tariff would have resulted in a serious disruption of Britain's commercial ties with the rest of the world, principally the Commonwealth. Neither the self-confidence nor the trade patterns lasted very long, however.[4] Within three years, the Macmillan government and, subsequently, its Labour successors, all applied for British membership of the EC. They were unsuccessful because De Gaulle believed that Britain did not accept the principles on which the EC was organized and would subvert them from within. Only after he died was the Heath government to negotiate successfully the terms of Britain's entry in 1973, and membership was confirmed by a national referendum two years later.

One result of this delay was that the British debate about membership was greatly prolonged. The arguments, however, remained remarkably constant. The economic case for membership was straightforward. By joining, Britain would eventually enjoy unrestricted access to the European markets where an increasing percentage of its exports were already being directed. If it did not join, these exports would be penalized by the common tariff. Britain would also have to open its markets to the Europeans but this, it was claimed, would bring the stimulus of competition to British industry. However, the political case was much less clear. To begin with, it was claimed that Europe would somehow restore the power base from which Britain's international influence could continue to be exercised. Indeed, it was asserted by some, George Brown for example, that its diplomatic experience and connections would result in Britain establishing itself as the leader of the Community.[5]

However, as Britain's weakening performance, relative to the members of the Community especially, made this claim implausible, the emphasis in the political case shifted. Instead of providing the opportunity to lead Europe, membership would, as the Heath government argued, allow Britain to participate in the decision-making of an entity which was already, by some indicators, bigger than either of the superpowers. As a third force or as a second pillar of western security, the EC offered the necessary scale to be an effective participant in world affairs which, by themselves, Britain and the other European great powers no longer enjoyed. Inside the Community, Britain could help to build 'Europe' and the sort of Europe it wanted. Outside, it would be condemned to irrelevance, and yet increasing dependence on the decisions of a Community over which it had little influence.

The case for membership was, ultimately, an instrumental one. British power and British prosperity would be enhanced by joining the others. The United Kingdom had been created to solve the problems of the English, Welsh, Scots and Irish, and now a bigger Community existed which could solve them more effectively. The problem with this was the price which would have to be paid in terms of the country's sovereignty and formal right to determine its own affairs. Even in instrumental terms, the case for why an advanced country of 56 million people should no longer be regarded as viable in some sense was never really made clear. More importantly, however, the instrumental argument for membership tended to ignore the fact that most people do not identify with the communities of which they are members for primarily instrumental reasons; they do so because they feel and believe themselves to belong.

The opponents of membership never effectively exploited this weakness. Usually, they focused on the transitional costs of membership – for example, more expensive food and lost jobs in uncompetitive sectors of the economy – and, in so far as they defended British sovereignty, they did so for reasons which were just as instrumental as those being advocated for membership. The trade unions and much of the Labour party, for example, regarded the Community as a place in which a regionally unified capital would find it much easier to triumph over a nationally fragmented workforce. If the welfare state was to be preserved and genuinely socialist policies put into place in Britain, therefore, British sovereignty had to be preserved. While they effectively pointed out the costs of membership, however, its opponents were never able to make a convincing case, in instrumental terms, that the costs of not joining would be less.

The task of those who regarded British sovereignty as an issue in itself was even harder, however, for it was easily lampooned by talk of pints and pounds or discredited by accusations of xenophobia and racism. Further, and paradoxically, the stark simplicity of the case – either we are sovereign or we are not – seemed to repel rather than attract support, and those who made it, notably Enoch Powell, found themselves marginalized by their own efforts. More importantly, however, the defence of sovereignty was outflanked by claims that Britain's membership of the Community would enable it to counter the very threats about which those who conducted the defence were concerned. It would enhance, if not the country's formal independence, then what supporters of membership liked to refer to as its real capacity to control its own destiny in the face of challenges from the superpowers.

In this, they were greatly aided by the condition of the Community in the first few years of British membership. Thanks largely to de Gaulle, who had opposed the supranational elements of a way of financing the Community's policies to which the others had agreed by instructing his government to stay away from meetings of the Council of Ministers, the precedent for an effective national veto known as the Luxembourg Compromise had been established.[6] As a consequence of this and other factors, the momentum which had characterized the early years of the Community had been dissipated. Certainly, proposals for further institutional development continued to emanate from Presidents of the Commission and their allies among the smaller states, but by the late 1970s, it could be quite reasonably claimed that the EC had stabilized as an exercise in intergovernmental collaboration centred upon the Council of Ministers. To be sure, there were common policies left over from the first phase of development which troubled Britain and would have offended the sensibilities of any honest economist. However, there was also a precedent for taking care of some of Britain's specific concerns at the way these policies operated, and in compensation, there was also the growing area of European Political Cooperation (EPC), by which the Community, or the enthusiasts like Britain, sought to create a common diplomatic identity for the EC on the world stage. In short, and in contrast to what was to follow, the EC of 1979 appeared to confirm everything which pragmatic supporters of British membership, at least, had been saying about it all along.

ARGUING OVER MONEY

This is not to say, however, that the Community of the 1970s presented no problems for British policy. It did, the most important being the way in which Community finances were levied and the uses to which they were put. The EC needed money to cover its operating costs, to pay for its common policies, and to provide assistance to regions and people either because they were disproportionately hurt by the operations of common policies or in line with the principle that living standards throughout the Community should be helped to converge. In a broader sense, the Community also needed its own resources, and more of them, if it were to become a strong political and economic actor in its own right. However, the money for all this was collected by the member governments from three sources: the common tariff on industrial goods from outside the EC; the levy under the Common Agricultural Policy (CAP) on foodstuffs from outside the EC; and a small percentage of the Value Added Tax (VAT) on domestic commercial transactions. Britain had never liked the formulae by which transfers to the EC were assessed or the uses to which these funds were mainly put, a system of price supports to encourage agricultural production. The net effect was to transfer money from countries with large industrial sectors and a history of importing food to those with large agricultural sectors and a preference for self-sufficiency in food production. Upon joining the EC in 1973, Britain had been given a 10-year transitional period before it fully participated in the Community's system of financing, at the end of which it was hoped that benefits from other regional and social policies would help offset its burden on the CAP. Only two years later, however, a 'Budget Correction Mechanism' had been established to ease Britain's burden. By this, it was determined that should the amount of money which a member paid into the Community exceed the amount it received from it by a specified amount, and if its GNP per capita and growth rate fell below the Community average, again by a specified amount, then it would be entitled to a rebate of a proportion of the money it had paid in.

Even with this mechanism in place, however, Britain's situation had not improved. By 1979, Britain contributed about 20 per cent of the Community's budget, second only to the Federal Republic with nearly 30 per cent, and ahead of France with 19 per cent, and it was doing so on the basis of an economy which accounted for 15 per cent of the Community's total GNP. A year later, the government maintained that Britain was contributing 20 per cent of the Community budget but only getting 5 per cent of it back. In 1975, its contribution had amounted to £150 million but now it was estimated at £1124 million. Although after adjustments its net contribution would be in the order of £370 to £450 million, this compared unfavourably, in the British view, with the net receipts which everyone else except the Federal Republic obtained from the system and, as British officials pointed out, 70 per cent of the Community's budget continued to be expended on its farm policies.[7]

As is so often the case with figures, particularly when they represent money, several interpretations of their significance could be and were made. Brian Lenihan, the Irish Minister for Agriculture, pointed out in 1980, that members' contributions to the EC budget amounted to, on average, 0.9 per cent of their GNPs.[8] In other words, their expenditure on the Community was of the order of their foreign aid budgets rather than their expenditures on defence or social welfare. The British government, for example, would be shortly contemplating spending something like twice this amount a year for 15 years on the Trident programme, one element of its defence policy. To people like Lenihan, therefore, whose country was one of the primary beneficiaries of the CAP and other common policies, this seemed like a small price to pay for a great deal. Farm price stability, secure and plentiful food supplies, the family farm at the heart of French and south German life, the narrowing of incomes between rich and poor, one of the few Community success stories and, hence, a foundation on which the European idea might eventually be realized, all these at various times were presented as the fruits of these small transfers. To meet Britain's demands by reducing the CAP would be to put all these worthy consequences at risk. The only alternative would be to shift the financial burden elsewhere, to the Germans who were already paying more than the British, or to those who, in their own view, were supposed to be the financial beneficiaries of an effective CAP.

Not surprisingly, British governments did not appreciate a situation in which they continued to be one of the principal providers of a series of vaguely defined, imperfect European public goods. The Conservatives had campaigned in 1979 on the promise of a better relationship with the rest of Europe. Thatcher herself had spoken of Britain's 'total commitment' to the EC, but she had also stressed that Britain would be no 'soft touch' when it came to the Community's demands upon it.[9] She appears to have assigned herself the primary responsibility for securing British satisfaction on its contribution to the budget. Indeed, this was the first substantive foreign policy issue which Thatcher addressed in any sustained manner. She raised it at her first European Council meeting in Luxembourg, and was reported as jubilant over the reactions of her fellow leaders to her concerns. 'We have achieved', she had claimed upon returning to Britain in June 1979, '... everything we came here to achieve.' This amounted to little more than an agreement to undertake a study of the budget, and even this had probably been made possible by the British agreeing to an increase in farm prices.[10] Study or not, however, Britain was still being presented with bills and, accordingly, Thatcher's position very quickly began to harden.

The general objectives of Britain's policy were laid out by Sir Geoffrey Howe, the new Chancellor of the Exchequer, in November just before the next summit in Dublin. Britain would not seek to become a net beneficiary of Community financing, even though this would be reasonable. However, it could not accept year-to-year fixes justified by either the promise of a long-term solution or the claim that the problem would eventually be self-correcting. What Britain wanted was a settlement which acted on the problem of its high contributions and low receipts from 1980 onwards until the

CAP was reformed. It also wanted about £1 billion back from the approximately £1.2 billion it paid in, some 80 per cent of its contributions, while the Community was prepared to offer £0.3 to £0.4 billion, around 30 per cent at best.[11] While Howe provided the objectives, Thatcher embraced the issue and led the attack. Just before Dublin, she pledged, 'I will go on until I get a solution.' Britain could not '... go on any longer being Europe's most bountiful benefactor.' At the Council, she told her colleagues that she did not want a crisis, but she did want a billion pounds back. When the meetings ended in failure with only £350 million being offered, Thatcher came home declaring that she was now '... ready to precipitate a crisis'. Britain would not leave the Community, she said, '... We are in the EEC and we will stay in and no one has the right to throw us out...', but we want what she called 'our money'.[12]

'RIDICULOUS, PAROCHIAL, THIRD RATE MATTERS'[13]

How was this sudden escalation from an argument over money to a general crisis over the operations of the Community and the terms of Britain's membership to be explained? Several factors contributed to the explosion. To begin with, the domestic agenda upon which Thatcher's attention remained predominantly focused involved an extensive effort to make deep and painful cuts in public expenditure. Politically, therefore, it would have been very hard to reconcile parsimony at home with even the appearance of profligacy abroad. Secondly, and appearances aside, there was a real problem with the fact that Britain, 'the seventh poorest out of nine' as Thatcher was willing to call it on occasions such as this, should, in effect, be subsidizing and encouraging unwanted agricultural production in countries like France and Italy.[14] It has also been suggested that Thatcher's insecurity as a woman and new prime minister, her contempt for foreigners, and her ignorance of the appropriate ways for handling diplomatic disputes all contributed to her taking, in this view, an inappropriately combative approach.

In fact, however, neither ignorance nor insecurity were the driving forces behind her effort to secure a greater rebate for Britain. As Thatcher had said on returning from Dublin, other nations in the past had 'pointed the way' to achieving satisfaction on issues such as this. She was obviously thinking of de Gaulle's refusal to participate in EC deliberations in the 1960s when the other members had agreed to what were in his view excessively supranational ways of making decisions on the budget and farm policy. Thatcher said she would take the £350 million on offer, calling it '... not bad as a start' and demand further substantial progress on the issue by the next Council. Otherwise, Britain would be forced to consider preventing further progress on other decisions the Community wished to make on matters requiring unanimity or withholding all or a portion of its contributions to the Community budget. Both measures could quickly result in bankruptcy or the imposition of emergency supplementary levies on the other members. As Thatcher told Parliament, she did not think '... boycotting and leaving an empty chair was an effective way of going about things' because decisions could still go through, and she added that the government had not '... so far seriously considered...' withholding. She hoped that Britain would '... get a great deal further before applying either of these.'[15]

Thatcher's qualifications about the efficacy of such threats and her expression of the hope that they need not be carried out were of far less significance than the fact that she had actually uttered them in a public setting. By doing so, she served notice to her Community partners and sought to commit the British government to acting if its demands were not met. As a consequence, there followed four years of rancorous deadlock on the finance question. Britain sought, in Thatcher's words, a 'broad budgetary balance' with a '... modest contribution on top of that'[16], and to this end it began blocking farm price increases in the spring of 1980. The block was immediately lifted on the condition of a budget agreement and at the end of May, a deal offering £371 million back to Britain in 1980 followed by £445 million the following year was accepted by Carrington. A number of difficulties emerged to threaten this agreement during the summer, among them the need for New Zealand to reduce its lamb exports to the Community, and so by September, it was clear that there were going to be further problems with Britain's claimed reimbursement for the following year.

Not all the arguments which resulted were between Britain and the rest, however. France had responded to Britain's first obstruction by raising its own farm prices unilaterally, much to the anger of its fellows, and during 1981 there were at least two other distinct arguments being conducted. One was between the Council of Ministers, less Britain, Ireland and Italy, on the one hand, and the Commission and European Parliament on the other, over the legality of supplementary budgets to cover shortfalls caused by the British demand. The other, later in the year, ranged Italy, Ireland and Britain against the Federal Republic and France over whether spending on agriculture or the regional and social funds should be cut. It was, however, Britain's willingness to block the farm package in March which gathered the most attention and left Carrington with a very difficult task in conducting Britain's presidency during the second half of 1981. At the beginning of his term, Chancellor Schmidt had made some encouraging remarks endorsing the principle that the rich rather than just the West Germans and the British should be net contributors, but by the London summit in December, Britain was isolated and its presidency praised only for its successes in strengthening the staff supporting the President of the Council and coordinating the EC's positions at the UN.

At the start of 1982, a foreign ministers meeting on the budget collapsed with Carrington complaining that he could get no 'rational reply' to his call for long - term reform from his colleagues. They agreed with the logic but not the justice of the position, and even Carrington began to talk openly of blocking the Community's business; he could '. . . not see anything can be done until we have a solution.'[17] In March, Britain was offered an arrangement by which an agreed lump sum would be paid for three years followed by two years of negotiated sums, but while Carrington welcomed the attempt to move away from yearly wrangles and *ad hoc* solutions, he said the sums on offer were insufficient and so Britain resumed its tactic of blocking farm price increases. However, what was by now becoming the usual pattern of disruption was itself disrupted by Argentina's invasion of the Falkland Islands at the beginning of April. The EC condemned the attack and all its members initially agreed to Britain's package of economic sanctions against Argentina. Timely and impressive though the EC's diplomatic solidarity initially was for once, it is clear that some sort of *quid pro quo* from Britain on farm prices was expected.

When the sanctions were due for renewal in mid-May, however, Britain's minister for agriculture, Peter Walker, made it clear that his government was not prepared to 'buy' them with a concession on farm prices. Neither was Britain prepared to accept a joint proposal by Gaston Thorn and Leo Tindemans, the Presidents of the Commission and the Council respectively, to accept a one-year offer to return half the £900 million Britain had contributed if it accepted an agreement on farm prices. The government wanted £600 million. Accordingly, the other members of the EC threatened to ignore the British veto and raise farm prices themselves and, in spite of Walker's warnings of the 'terrifying consequences' of such a course of action, this they did in the second half of May with Britain, Greece and Denmark abstaining.[18]

This action, it might be thought, would have brought matters to a head for it was in Thatcher's view 'without precedent' and seemed to pose a challenge not just to Britain's basic strategy but also to the Community's way of doing business. It did not, however, for the episode coincided with one of the most difficult and costly phases of the Falklands War for Britain, and the government accepted a £500 million rebate. The Community, in the words of Douglas Hurd, then a minister of state at the Foreign Office, had been 'plain wrong' to ignore Britain's invocation of the Luxembourg compromise, and the Community seemed to agree in so far as its foreign ministers reaffirmed a month later that the compromise still existed.[19] Nevertheless, by the end of the year, the budget process was once again in chaos. Britain's rebate together with one which the Federal Republic was due to receive were frozen by the European Parliament until it received assurances that these would be the last *ad hoc* transfers. Howe threatened retaliation, saying that this time Britain was considering withholding payments. Withholding had barely been mentioned since Thatcher had first considered it, and then only by press sources which considered it less disruptive than blocking decisions and, hence, preferable to it. However, the EC's *finesse* of the government's blocking strategy had forced it to consider what was in its own view an escalatory alternative.[20]

Even so, an escalation did not follow. At the end of January 1983, Britain accepted the European Parliament's conditions placed on its rebate while still contriving to maintain that a further transitional arrangement might prove necessary. In March, Thatcher, with strong support from Helmut Kohl, the new Federal Chancellor and President of the European Council, sought a 'firm commitment' from the other heads of government to have settled the rebate issue by the end of the German presidency. She arrived at Stuttgart in June, fresh from her electoral landslide victory at home, seeking £650 million (two-thirds of the total Britain had contributed) and demanding that the others keep their promise of the previous spring. She obtained only £450 million. The French said they

would block this in the absence of an overarching budget agreement, and threatened to leave the summit if there was no agreement to make an explicit link between the size of the Community's
'own resources' and the Council's conclusions on how the EC and
its policies were to be financed in the future.[21]

Nevertheless, the British government regarded the Stuttgart summit as important. This was not, extraordinarily enough in retrospect, because of 'the Solemn Declaration on European Union'
which emerged from it, but because of another set of principles to
which the members had also agreed. According to the 'Stuttgart
principles', as Howe called them, everyone now agreed that: a
lasting solution was necessary rather than yearly haggling; that any
deal for limiting burdens on a member should reflect its ability to
pay, using GNP per capita as probably the best measure; that a
solution should be on the revenue side of the budget, with over-
payments discounted from next year's assessment instead of rebates;
and that the new system should work for 1984 and subsequent
years.[22] Before progress was made along these lines, however, one
more catastrophe had to be endured under the Greek presidency
during the second half of 1983, and the first three months of the
succeeding French presidency.

For a small state, assuming the European presidency represented
a major organizational and diplomatic challenge at the best of times
and Greece, unlike some of the other small states, did not enjoy a
reputation for handling its Community affairs well. It was a double
misfortune, therefore, that it took the chair in July 1983 just as the
consequences of the failure to achieve a lasting budget settlement
were beginning to mature. The Community budget was now
unable to meet its existing commitments, and it was widely accepted
that the CAP would be bankrupted by Christmas if European
farmers enjoyed good harvests. Existing commitments, however,
were not all the Community had to worry about. Spain and Portugal were about to join, and as relatively poor countries with strong
agricultural sectors they would make additional demands on the
EC's money for which they would compete with Greece. Further,
Britain's resistance had clearly affected the mood in which negotiations were being conducted so that, for example, even so *communautaire* a member as Ireland had exercised the veto to prevent an
attempt by its colleagues to reduce milk production through the
imposition of a super-levy. Finally, in November, Greek diplomacy
was distracted by the need to orchestrate a response to the declara-

tion of an independent republic in northern Cyprus by the Turkish minority with the support of the government in Turkey.

By the end of the Athens summit in December, therefore, none of these major questions had been settled. The French had retreated to looking for an *ad hoc* arrangement for the coming year. The European Parliament was blocking Britain's rebate, and Thatcher spoke of withholding once again if the freeze on its rebate did not collapse as it had done the previous year. It was rumoured that the legislation to permit withholding had already been prepared the previous October.[23] Thus, the new year under the French presidency began with threats and counter-threats. The Commission claimed £450 million from Britain (a sum very close to the rebate which Britain was due) for violations of Community regulations on UHT milk, and suggested that Britain might face over £2 billion in penalties for subsidy violations by the English and Welsh milk marketing boards. The Community was now looking for an increase from 1 per cent to 1.4 and eventually 1.6 per cent in its share of VAT revenues. However, Britain's position, in Thatcher's words, remained that there could be no increases in the EC's 'own resources' without '... a fair and responsible system of financing. You can't have one without the other.' Accordingly, a summit in March broke up without agreement. Thatcher rejected a deal sponsored by Kohl because it lacked a permanent mechanism, although it offered £600 million a year for five years. Mitterrand called for a complete relaunch of the Community with or without Britain, and Thatcher returned to Britain declaring she did not think '... one could go on as if nothing had happened.'[24]

THE SETTLEMENT

Nevertheless, within a week two developments which would make a settlement possible occurred. The first was that it became clear that Thatcher's government were reluctant to withhold monies from the EC in retaliation for the delayed payment of its rebate. The Cabinet Committee responsible for European Affairs which had examined the practical steps to be taken to prevent payments from the Treasury's relevant EC account had concerns about the legality of the move. According to Howe, who was now foreign secretary, Britain was refusing to make an early payment requested by the Commission to cover the cost of paying rebates because these were still blocked. However, the decision not to withhold scheduled payments was confirmed by Thatcher two months later when she told Parliament that although the rest of the EC had gone back on its word that the budget would be settled by the end of March, they were '... technically ... not in default, but ...' she added, '... if we were to keep back our contributions, we should be acting contrary to international law.' She confirmed this point again when the European Parliament appeared to be threatening the settlement which was eventually reached by the Council of Ministers. 'I have not withheld ...', she said, '... because I don't believe we should default on our undertakings, even if others default on theirs,' at least, she added, '... until the end of the year.'[25]

The second development was a concession made by Britain either at the Brussels summit or at the conference of foreign ministers which followed it. According to Ian Murray, Thatcher accepted that some duties and levies collected by Britain belonged directly to the EC and were not, in any sense, British money transferred to the Community. The advantage of this was that Britain's claims would, in future, be based only on its VAT payments to the part of the EC budget financed by VAT, a lower figure which produced a smaller gap between what it paid in and what it received.[26] In return, the rest of the Community reconfirmed the Stuttgart agreement that a permanent mechanism was required, and Kohl's proposal had reportedly brought the two sides to within £150 million of each other, although it had not been a permanent offer.

As a consequence, in late June, just before the final summit of the French presidency at Fontainebleau, the outlines of the final settlement were worked out. Britain, the French proposed, should receive a fixed rebate from the Community every year topped up by a fixed percentage of the difference between what it had paid in and what it was to receive. This amount, however, could never exceed two-thirds of its contribution. In return, Britain would agree to increasing the EC's share of VAT to 1.4 per cent. The British accepted this proposal, as did the rest of the Council of Ministers. There were further scares, particularly from the European Parliament, and it soon became clear that the Fontainebleau agreement had done little to address the fundamental problems of the Community's budget and farm spending. It did, however, defuse the direct conflict between the British government and its partners on

the European Council and in the Council of Ministers. By the
following October, Nigel Lawson, the Chancellor of the Exchequer,
was not only praising new Community spending rules as '...a
considerable triumph for the United Kingdom', he was also offering
an extra £120 million to the Community to help cover its shortfall
for the following year, provided that the European Parliament
followed the advice of its own financial committee to release Britain's rebate.[27]

WHO WON?

This is a very difficult question to answer. As a result of the Fontainebleau agreement, Britain was to receive its 1983 rebate of £457
million, plus £600 million for 1984 and 66 per cent of its contribution in subsequent years. According to *The Times*, this meant that
Britain had retreated from initially demanding over 75 per cent of
its money back, through 70 per cent down to 66 per cent. However,
this compared favourably to the £300 to £400 million originally
on offer back in 1979, and very favourably to the £1.2 billion
bill which, Thatcher maintained, Britain would have been
presented with in the absence of a deal which improved upon the
formula negotiated by the previous Labour government.[28] This
point was reinforced, but expressed more accurately, by Malcolm
Rifkind, minister of state at the Foreign Office, when he told Parliament that without an agreement even the existing rebate would
have been put at risk. What he stressed was that the cash offer was
both better and placed on a permanent basis, and he tried to
minimize the consequences of agreeing to a VAT-only-based formula. This, he claimed, resulted only in a small loss, although the
French, for their part, maintained that the new formula cost the
British an extra £115 million a year and that the whole arrangement would last only for some four years.[29]

   If the financial gains were substantial, there were grave doubts,
both inside and outside the British government, about the price
which had been paid to secure them. Those expressed in *The Times*
about Thatcher's introverted 'Little England' sentiments have
already been noted. Carrington, unlike Thatcher, sought to minimize the significance of the dispute, calling it a 'family squabble'
which, he insisted, had no impact on European Political Cooperation.[30] Indeed, in an interview he gave to David Spanier when

Britain assumed the European presidency in the summer of 1981, he failed to mention nearly all the internal reform priorities which were absorbing everyone else. The most important task of any presidency, he said, was to promote the interests of the whole Community by '...the efficient conduct of business and the constructive use of its international influence'. It would be wrong, therefore, to see it as an opportunity to advance '...any narrow national interest'. The presidency was a '...chance to reaffirm to our partners our commitment to the Community'.[31]

One of the fault lines within the government on this aspect of its European policy lay between the Carrington's Foreign Office and Howe's Treasury. A glimpse of this divide was provided in the summer of 1981 after Howe, still Chancellor of the Exchequer at that time, had made a speech in The Hague on the reform of the Community's finances. He was reported as saying that Britain did not see why it should be a net contributor to the budget but, at a subsequent Treasury briefing on the speech, an official was quoted as saying '...at least the Treasury does not.' The Foreign Office subsequently denied any rift between it and the Treasury, confirming that it regarded Howe's speech as '...a full statement of the Government's approach'. To give the affair a final twist, however, *The Times* had noted the previous day that, while Howe had called for budget principles which provided for the transfer of money from rich to poor countries in The Hague, the Treasury's position before the House of Lords' Committee on European Affairs was that Britain would be satisfied with a transfer mechanism which limited the costs to the whole Community, '...rather than ensuring benefits for low income countries such as Britain.'[32] As his memoirs were subsequently to confirm, even Howe, among the driest in Thatcher's cabinet on money matters at that time, was concerned about the manner in which Britain pursued its objectives on the budget and the amount of upheaval it was prepared to create in order to gain its way.

The source of the unease, of course, as far as men like Carrington and Howe were concerned, was Thatcher herself. The great fear was that she did not understand the costs of speaking to people like Giscard d'Estaing and Helmut Schmidt as though they were, in James Callaghan's phrase, 'mentally deficient'. It was not good to have President Mitterrand of France calling, as he did on at least two occasions preceding Fontainebleau, for a relaunch of the Community with or without Britain. Nor was it good to provoke the

President of the Commission into declaring, as did Gaston Thorn after the Athens summit in 1983, that Britain seemed set on destroying the foundations of the EC.[33] What bothered Carrington, Howe and others, however, were not the insults and accusations of selfishness *per se*. Britain's past efforts to uphold the international economic and political order had always elicited doubts about its motives. What was different here, and what really disturbed them, was Thatcher's willingness to place a narrow version of Britain's national interest above the deep-rooted great power instinct to pay a price, even a modest price, to help maintain the international order or some part of it. British governments had been willing to relinquish, and even abandon, some of their responsibilities to the international order during the previous forty years, as their exits from Greece, Palestine and Aden had shown. What they had not done for a much longer period, however, was to threaten the operation of that order, or part of it, to gain their way.

Thatcher's attempt to do so on the Community budget was the beginning of her contribution to British statecraft, for by it, she began to nudge the country away from two axioms of its diplomatic culture. The first was that Britain was a necessary beneficiary of most forms of regulated international order, no matter how imperfectly expressed, and, hence, should always seek to contribute to their maintenance. The second was that, should it fail to do so, then grave consequences would follow for Britain's substantive interests and its reputation as a responsible great power of considerable influence. The budget episode proved both axioms to be no longer true. Once upon a time, it might have made sense for Britain to pay an unfair share of the costs of a particular regime, like the Community's finances, because it obtained a great benefit from the bigger system which that regime helped underwrite. Now, not only was that not the case, but also Britain had relatively little to lose from the regime failing and could use this to secure rewards for its participation and acquiescence in the regime's continued existence.

Thus, when Thatcher insisted that Britain obstruct the operations of the EC in the absence of a budget agreement, nothing particularly bad happened to it or, at least, nothing which a more *communautaire* approach to the budget could have plausibly staved off. Possibly, Carrington would have enjoyed an easier and more profitable European presidency in 1981 had Britain been in better standing with its fellows. Whether one views the disappointing results of his efforts to improve European Political Cooperation as evidence of Carrington's own limitations or the ineffectiveness of the instrument at his disposal, however, there is little to suggest that a different approach to the budget would have made his task any easier. There were enough organizational and policy obstacles to an effective EPC process to explain its shortcomings without having to draw on any 'spillover' effects from differences between the members on internal Community policy.

To be fair, one of the reasons why the budget policy did not have major unfortunate consequences for Britain was that, notwithstanding the images presented of her by her strongest supporters and critics alike, Thatcher pursued it with considerable caution and restraint. She did not hold the EC hostage by threatening to wreck it. At no point did she openly threaten Britain's departure – quite the reverse. Time and again, especially when the Labour party's opponents of the EC invited her to make such a threat, she responded by emphasizing her own and the country's commitment to staying in because of the Community's international importance. However, she did express this importance in political and security terms rather than economic ones. Leaving, she said in 1979, would not be in the interests of ' . . . Britain or the wider world'. The EC was one of the world's 'areas of stability', Thatcher told Schmidt in 1980, which, she added, prefiguring a later debate, ' . . . we must try to enlarge.'[34] Nor did she take the measure which many called for of withholding all or a portion of Britain's contributions. Blocking the conduct of Community business on other matters was one thing. Several members had pursued this linkage strategy in the past, and there was a well-defined place for it in the EC's bargaining culture. To withhold, however, made sense only if one had given up hope of receiving rebates, was prepared to deny oneself the influence of a shareholder and to engage in conduct of questionable legality. Ultimately, Thatcher appeared unwilling to place herself and the country in any of these positions.

A final factor in the success of her budget policy was, as so often seemed to be the case with Thatcher, her own good luck. Thatcher's stubbornness, patiently conveyed by those who usually executed her diplomacy, kept Britain in the field, while other pressures on her opponents contributed to their making the concessions they eventually did. The most obvious of these pressures was that, precisely as the British had maintained, the existing budget mechanism was driving the Community into bankruptcy. Even many of the principal beneficiaries began to concede this when they found, like

France, that they were becoming net contributors with the prospect of only paying more once the Spanish and Portuguese had joined. If this development was lucky for Thatcher, however, it was so because she happened to be right.

She was also lucky in that the attentions of many of her opponents began to shift to other issues. Deadlocked on the details of financing the Community which currently existed, the Germans, Italians and French in particular began to sketch out plans for the future of the Community as an economic and political union. Good fortune this time, however, came at a price. Thatcher was wrong, not in the substance of her response to her colleagues' plans for European union, but in her initial judgement of their willingness and capacity to try and realize them. Her own emphasis on winning the budget fight contributed to this miscalculation, and it may be claimed that Thatcher was more distracted than any of her rivals from effectively addressing what proved to be the lasting issue of significance. If this is so, however, it must be added that many of those who urged restraint on the budget fight and found the whole issue distasteful were among the strongest voices urging Thatcher to ignore her own tendency, mistaken in their view, to assume that her European colleagues meant what they said when they indulged in the rhetoric of European union. A less 'Thatcherite' policy on the budget, therefore, would not have resulted in British foreign policy being better prepared for the fight to come over the future of Europe.

9 Thatcher's European Policy II: Sovereignty and Nationalism

It is remarkable, in retrospect, that the British government saw the 1983 Stuttgart summit as significant for establishing the principles of a final budget settlement, and not for the Solemn Declaration on European Union. The Solemn Declaration committed members of the European Council to '... broad action to ensure the relaunch of the Community', and to providing '... a general political impetus for the construction of Europe'. As such, it took its place in a long line of similar calls for European unity stretching back to the Treaty of Rome and beyond. Economic integration, according to key figures like Paul-Henri Spaak and Walter Hallstein, was the means to eventual political union, and the Paris summits of 1972 and 1974 had committed the Community to achieving this goal by 1980. To facilitate this, they had commissioned a report by the Belgian Prime Minister, Leo Tindemans, which called for: the establishment of economic and monetary union; reform of Community institutions; and the implementation of common foreign, regional and social policies.[1] The Solemn Declaration was itself a response to an initiative launched by the foreign minister of the Federal Republic, Hans-Dietrich Genscher, with the assistance of his Italian counterpart, Emilio Colombo, two years previously. This called for more policy coordination, more majority voting on matters of common policy, and a clearer relationship between the European Council and the Parliament.

These calls for European Union all had three things in common. They were all vague about precisely what a political union entailed and how its was to be achieved. None of them had enjoyed a great deal of success except, perhaps, in providing an impetus to more effective intergovernmental collaboration, a process which could be viewed as antithetical to political union rather than as one of its building blocks. The member governments simply kept on finding too many issues in the proposals of their fellows on which they, at least, were not prepared to surrender their sovereignty. This explains, and partly excuses, the Thatcher government's reluctance to take the most recent burst of activity on this front sufficiently seriously. Finally, however, unsuccessful or not, proposals for European Union kept on coming. By the mid-1980s, therefore, it should have been clear that a policy of waiting for this particular storm to blow over as it had in the past was not going to be successful. The issue was not going to go away.

This is not to say that Britain did not have a position on European Union. It did; from the start, British governments had been so sceptical about its feasibility that they had barely bothered to engage the question of its desirability. Instead, they had been contented to warn how disappointment at the failure of overly-ambitious collaborative schemes could leave the participants worse off than if they had never tried. Britain was for the idea of European Union so long as, in practice, it could be watered down, as the Genscher–Colombo proposals were, to an affirmation of more and better practical collaboration between governments where and when it was both possible and desirable. Thatcher made her own version of this position clear in her report to Parliament on the London summit at the end of 1981. The Community was certainly about '...a lot more than economics'. However, the Genscher–Colombo plan did not, in her view, point the way to 'a federal European state' which is why she did not '...kill the proposals stone dead.' She added, however, that she did not think that such an idea '...would have a ghost's chance of getting anywhere.'[2]

For a time, it seemed as if Thatcher was right. The budget question and its various ramifications for other areas of policy like enlargement, the CAP and institutional reform continued to dominate EC politics, even after Stuttgart. However, France's diplomacy, on assuming the Presidency at the beginning of 1984, skilfully combined flexibility on the budget question with renewed pressure for movement towards European Union on the basis of, or more properly in reaction to, a draft treaty authored by Altiero Spinelli and endorsed by his colleagues in the European Parliament in February 1984. At Fontainebleau, two committees were set up, one to consider the problem of creating a sense of common European identity for citizens of the Community, the other to explore the question of institutional reform. The second, under the chairmanship of an Irish senator, Professor Dooge, presented a preliminary report to the Dublin summit at the end of 1984. This reaffirmed essentially that progress towards effective political union would be achieved only by shifting the balance of power within the Community towards the Commission and Parliament and away from the Council of Ministers, the European Council and the individual member states represented on both.

Anticipating the thrust of the Dooge report, however, British policy had already begun to shift. In October, on a visit to the Federal Republic, Howe had responded to an earlier and general challenge from Kohl about who would be willing to follow the West Germans into a United States of Europe, by saying that Britain's commitment to Europe was now 'profound and irreversible'. Britain was helping to '...build the common European identity to which we all aspire.' As practical testimony to the common identity he had in mind, however, he pointed to the British troops already in the Federal Republic and the recent success of Operation Lionheart, the annual exercise by which the British rehearsed an emergency reinforcement of the British Army on the Rhine. Thatcher was more direct. In an address to the Franco-British Council in Avignon, just before the Dublin summit, she declared that she did not believe there could be a United States of Europe like the United States of America, because their histories were 'too different'. Strengthening cooperation between the nations of the EC was just as worthy a purpose, but to submerge their identities would be '...contrary to the instincts of our people and therefore could not bear fruit.' Thatcher went on to identify areas for cooperation: more unity on the common market, more unity of action in world affairs and more unity of action on economic problems. 'There have been so many reports telling us what to do, so many theoretical models,' she concluded, and 'another report' would be no substitute for 'practical progress.'[3]

THE SINGLE EUROPEAN ACT

By the end of 1984, therefore, the British government's objections to the principle of European Union in its strong form, at least, had been revealed by the pace of events. However, it still hoped some of the other EC members shared its reservations about anything more than closer, practical cooperation. After Dublin, therefore, a scramble followed to define what should happen next before the Milan summit in the summer of 1985. In addition to the final version of the Dooge Report which was due at that time, the Community was confronted with both British and joint Franco-German proposals. The former suggested more foreign policy coordination and a streamlining of the EC's decision-making processes, by more majority voting where the Rome Treaty permitted it and by allowing abstentions where it did not. It was, in effect, an attempt to reconfirm that European Union would mean nothing more than a better system of intergovernmental collaboration animated by the spirit of what Thatcher was to call agreements among gentlemen.

The Franco-German 'draft treaty on European Union' which followed the British initiative by a couple of weeks focused upon security cooperation and strengthening the Western European Union (WEU).[4] The British took heart from this emphasis. Together with a recent West German invocation of the Luxembourg compromise on lowering cereal prices, it seemed to indicate that business as usual, or what Howe called 'political reality', was the order of the day in EC politics. Thatcher claimed that the two proposals were similar, and noting that '. . . imitation is the sincerest form of flattery,' she said that nothing in either necessitated revisions in the original Rome treaty or an intergovernmental conference (IGC) to consider so doing. Its modest character aside, however, the British were worried about what the Franco-German initiative might portend. It had been constructed without their formal knowledge and, according to Howe's memoirs, Thatcher had received a non-committal response from Kohl when she had invited German comments on the British draft at their most recent meeting with one another.[5]

The Milan summit confirmed that the British had been right to be uneasy. Its substantive achievements were uncontroversial, but the same could not be said regarding its decision on how to proceed in the future. Over the objections of Britain, Denmark and Greece, the others agreed to an IGC to discuss, or negotiate, a treaty on foreign and security policy and amendments to the Treaty of Rome to be ready for the next Council in Luxembourg at the end of 1985. This, according to Mitterrand, would help distinguish those who were in favour of '. . . a strong united Europe from those who are hanging back', even though it did not commit the EC to proceeding by treaty amendment or by any other particular course to whatever each member thought the final goal of European Union might be.[6]

At Milan, the possibility of a 'two-speed' or 'two-tier' Europe was openly considered by those who espoused moving towards union as quickly as possible, and the question was raised of whether Britain or the other dissenters would participate in the IGC. Both were, perhaps, measures of the ill-will which was beginning to attend the process rather than genuine threats. The idea of separating to proceed to union would have been hard for other members besides the dissenters to swallow, and an IGC boycott by the dissenters would be the quickest way of assuring their second-tier status, a possibility which not even Thatcher was prepared to consider at this stage. In the months before Luxembourg, however, and in the midst of the IGC, Howe was at pains to signal that Britain believed '... the Treaty of Rome is not immutable,' that it was '... not afraid of "European Union",' and that it had always favoured making 'practical improvements'. The question, he said, was how this 'organic process of ever-closer union' was to be '... taken forward' so Europe could enjoy '... the real power and influence that its unity alone can bring.'[7]

The result of the conference was the Single European Act (SEA) agreed to at the Luxembourg summit and signed in February 1986. Its preamble reiterated '... the broad objective – creation of a European Union', before laying down the 'detailed legal framework' for 'practical progress' on Community institutions, the internal market, economic and monetary cooperation, social policy, research and technological development, and the environment. Changes would be implemented by amendments to existing treaties, and a separate section dealt with the legal framework for European Political Cooperation. However, at the 'heart' of the SEA, to use Derek Unwin's phrase, '... was the commitment to a fully integrated internal market by the end of 1992.' It was this which explained Thatcher's willingness to accept both the substance of the agreement reached at Luxembourg and the decision to implement it by treaty amendments. However, the commitment to a single market brought to the fore the issue on which Thatcher was to find herself in direct confrontation with most of the other members of the Community and, it later transpired, at least two of her senior ministers – Howe and Lawson – who exercised responsibilities for Britain's external policy. How much 'harmonization', if any, of national laws, regulations and policies was required to sustain a genuine single market, and could there be harmonization without a single political authority to oversee and enforce its operation?[8]

The British answer to the first question had long been very little at all, and so the second question scarcely arose. Before Milan, Malcolm Rifkind had declared that Britain '... did not believe in harmonization for its own sake,' and this sentiment was echoed by Thatcher in her report on Milan to the House of Commons. She did not believe it was necessary '. . . for the completion of the internal market' and, she declared, 'We' would resist it '. . . with all the power and strength at our command.' Accordingly, before and after Luxembourg, the British government sought to play down the significance of the measures under consideration or, at least, present them as consistent with their own preferred 'practical' approach. British officials were reported as expecting 'modest progress', and the IGC was initially portrayed as a triumph for 'the pragmatists' and 'the minimalists' and, as such, an 'airy fairy' exercise, according to Thatcher, no more of which would be necessary. Britain, she claimed, had obtained a commitment from the others on the single market, had successfully defended (with Ireland) the retention of certain border controls which were effective because they were islands, and had preserved the Luxembourg Compromise. As to the rest, Thatcher returned to the theme of 'the enormous gap', as she called it, from which other countries suffered '. . . between their rhetoric about what they want to do and what they do in practice.' Part of Britain's task, 'the whole time', was to '. . . diminish their expectations and draw them down from the clouds to practical matters.'[9]

DELORS AND HARMONIZATION

If Thatcher was the champion of bringing the Community down from the clouds of European rhetoric, then Jacques Delors, the President of the Commission since 1985, was the champion of keeping them out of the cellar of practical politics. Both sides of the argument over the future of European Union had been disappointed by the outcome of the Luxembourg summit. Those who wanted harmonization to facilitate the transfer of authority away from the Council of Ministers and towards the Commission, the Parliament and the Court were convinced it had not done enough. Delors himself called the Act 'a compromise for progress'. On the other hand, people like William Cash, the Conservative MP who later became a leading figure in the British opposition to further integration, maintained the Act amounted to a direct threat to British sovereignty being smuggled through Parliament with insufficient debate. Indeed, Lord Denning, who was responsible for steering the European Communities (Amendment) Bill past wrecking amendments in the House of Lords and a supporter of the SEA, argued that as a binding treaty which subordinated British law to Community law in many areas, the Act did spell the end of British sovereignty.[10]

Nevertheless, for at least two years after the SEA, it appeared that Thatcher's view of its consequences, or lack of them, was broadly accurate. Greatly helped by a British presidency of the Council in the second half of 1986 which doggedly stuck to the practicalities of lowering everything from air fares, farm prices and food surpluses to the levels of hostility towards the US in the EC, the Community seemed to return to the pattern of budget wrangles and the 'make-or-break years', as the journalists used to call each one, of the early 1980s. After the London summit at the end of 1986, for example, Howe pointed to decisions on cutting beef and dairy production, as well as agreements with the US on avoiding confrontations over pasta, lemons and steel as measures of Britain's and hence the Community's success. In contrast, Bettino Craxi, the Italian prime minister, suggested that the British were merely avoiding the difficult issues.[11] At the end of the Belgian presidency in June 1987, which Tindemans said would focus on foreign affairs, Thatcher told the rest of the EC that getting its finances right was merely a matter of 'good housekeeping', while the French prime minister, Jacques Chirac, accused her of being 'housewifely'. Small wonder then that Michael Binyon could claim to have detected a 'gradually warming Europeanism' on Thatcher's part. The fights were familiar and appeared to impart no particular direction to the Community's future other than one in which spending was better controlled and farm policy reformed.[12]

Appearances were deceptive, however. An increasingly personal confrontation developed between Thatcher and Delors, in which the latter enjoyed a number of advantages, in addition to his own talent and that of his Commissioner with responsibility for creating the single market, Lord Cockfield. The first of these was that the SEA had confirmed 1992 as a target date for the single market which Britain, perhaps more than other members of the EC wanted, and so everyone including Britain was operating under a specific time constraint. To fail to meet it would conceivably be a greater loss to Britain than anyone else. The second was that the Act had also linked the achievement of a single market with the achievement of harmonization. Perhaps, as per the British view, the former could be achieved without the latter, but it could not be achieved without discussing the latter. And finally, on the question of some form of monetary union, one of Delors' major objectives, the British government was itself badly, and increasingly, divided. Thus, even the distractions created by the mainly positive but glacially paced initiatives in Political Cooperation on South African economic sanctions, Syrian links with terrorism and establishing a naval presence in the Persian Gulf under WEU auspices could not forestall the momentum engendered by these three.

At the beginning of 1988, therefore, as the Council of Ministers argued over whether farm production might be best controlled by financial stabilizers – penalties on overproduction – or set-asides – financial incentives or compensations for not growing crops – the Commission began to elaborate its vision of what the single market should look like after 1992. National taxation systems, Delors and Cockfield had argued, needed to be brought closer into line with one another, principally by a uniform rate of Value Added Tax (VAT) on the same goods. In addition, the social policies of the member states needed to be increasingly coordinated, both to create a uniform environment for potential investment and to advance the cause of social justice by, for example, establishing Community-wide standards for industrial safety, the length of the working week, and the length and number of vacations to which people would be entitled. Finally, the Commission and several member states began to call for strengthening the existing European Monetary System (EMS), or Exchange Rate Mechanism (ERM) as it was to become known.

Eventually, in the Commission's vision, a European Union (EU) would emerge with a single currency and financial authority, common economic, social, external and defence policies, reformed central institutions with legal authority and political power over those below them, and finally the free internal movement of goods, services, capital and labour. The EU would not constitute a federal state or supranational authority for, under the principle of 'subsidiarity', affairs would be handled at the level – Community, regional, national or local – which could do so most effectively. However, Delors himself professed no doubt as to where the balance of power would, and ought to, eventually lie. National parliaments, he told the members of their European counterpart in the summer of 1988, might be gone within seven years of 1992, and within ten years 80 per cent of economic legislation would certainly be passed at the

European level, where an embryo government would be taking shape.[13]

BRUGES

It was Delors' vision more than anything else which prompted Thatcher's famous address to the College of Europe in Bruges two months later. It had been widely expected that Thatcher would take this opportunity to strengthen the less conflictual image she had been presenting at recent summits by saying something reassuring about Britain's commitment to the Community. Instead, however, Thatcher provided the fullest exposition to date of why she thought a move towards a European Union incorporating stronger federalist and supranationalist elements was wrong, and for this reason the Bruges address warrants a close examination.

She began by reasserting the British position on the way forward. The EC, she declared, was 'the practical means' by which Europe could ensure the prosperity and security of its people in a world of '... many other powerful nations and groups of nations'. Rather than arguing, therefore, each member needed to cooperate with the others and pull its own weight, pursuing prosperity by encouraging individual initiative and prosperity. Thatcher then set out the principles upon which, in her view, successful cooperation would be based. 'My first guiding principle is this...' she declared:

> ... willing and active co-operation between independent sovereign states is the best way to build a successful European Community. To try to suppress nationhood and concentrate power at the centre of a European conglomerate would be highly damaging and would jeopardize the objectives we seek to achieve. Europe will be stronger precisely because it has France as France, Spain as Spain, Britain as Britain, each with its own customs, traditions and identity. It would be folly to fit them into some sort of Identikit European personality.[14]

Then she returned to her point about why the US could not serve as a model for Europe. Their histories were so different. People had originally gone to America to escape European intolerance, and out of that they had created a pride in being American, just as Europeans experienced pride at being, for example, British, Belgian, Dutch or German. Europe should seek to become more united in a common purpose, for sure, but in a way which '... preserves the different traditions, parliamentary powers, and a sense of national pride in one's own country.' It was these which had '... been the source of Europe's vitality through the centuries.'

After this preamble, Thatcher began to sharpen the focus of her argument. Working together, she asserted, did not '... require power to be centralized in Brussels or decisions to be taken by an appointed bureaucracy,' and it was ironic, she added, that some in Europe were advocating this direction when even the USSR had seen the need to go the other way. Centralism and bureaucracy might be acceptable to some members of the Community, Thatcher accepted, and that was all very well; '... what people wished to do in their own countries is a matter for them.' However, she continued, '... we in Britain would fight attempts to introduce collectivism and corporatism at the European level...' for:

> ... We have not successfully rolled back the frontiers of the state in Britain only to see them reimposed at a European level with a European superstate exercising a new dominance from Brussels.

This was a ringing declaration of intent, but the rest of the Bruges speech was unremarkable in terms of developing the point. Thatcher returned to the theme of reforming common policies which, in her view, did not work. She stressed the importance of encouraging personal enterprise and avoiding intervention and planning by the state. She pointed out the contradiction between the liberalization of the Community's internal market and its use of protectionist measures against outsiders and, finally, she declared that nothing the Community attempted in the field of security policy should be allowed to undermine Nato or America's commitment to Europe's defence.

Nevertheless, the Bruges speech succeeded in creating an uproar. For many, the substance of what she said was not the problem. As one unnamed European official said, 'It's her tone I can't stand... Not all what she says is objectionable. It's the way she says it.'[15] He might have added that the context in which Thatcher chose to make her claims was equally troubling. The rhetoric, as some saw it, about rolling back the frontiers of the state belonged in Conservative party conferences, the knockabout of British politics or even the knockabout into which some European Council sessions appeared to descend if they ran on too long. It had no place, they argued, in a public and widely publicized setting with considerable diplomatic significance. Besides, supporters of the idea of a stronger union claimed, the 'nightmare', as Thatcher called it, of a 'centralized European government' was hers alone. No one wanted that and in tilting at it, she was effectively tilting at a windmill for unworthy reasons. Party politics and personal power, the real reasons for what she said in this view, destroyed her claim to be speaking from a national position above politics.

There was, however, much more going on than this. Thatcher believed that European Union, in the form in which it was presently being discussed, was both unattainable and undesirable. Until now, however, she had been unable to do much beyond simply react against it. This approach was facilitated by her own misplaced confidence, and that of her advisors, that no one would seriously pursue an idea which was so bad very far. It was now clear that British diplomacy was as mistaken on this, and that Thatcher's diplomacy, in particular, had failed to get the other EC members to concentrate on correcting the obvious shortcomings of its existing common policies before moving on to the larger questions of political and economic union. Accordingly, Bruges marked the beginning of Thatcher's attempt to work out a more coherent position with which to bolster her nationalist instincts. To do so, she forced herself into what was for her the increasingly unfamiliar territory of political and cultural identity. In so far as she did, it may be said that she made a more sustained and perhaps more honest attempt than her opponents to reconcile the national political facts of post-Cold War Europe with the integrating imperatives of the quest for market-driven growth and prosperity.

THATCHER'S CULTURAL AND IDEOLOGICAL NATIONALISM

She did so, however, only with considerable difficulty. It was one thing to point out, as Thatcher did at Bruges, that European countries were not only different from the US, but from each other. This was a commonplace observed by nearly everybody on all sides of the debate. Much harder for her to acknowledge, however, was the idea of these differences ('France as France, Spain as Spain', etc.) being a source of Europe's strength. Indeed, cultural nationalism, the emotional commitment to a particular collective identity and way of life, was usually used by the supporters of a stronger union to *finesse* the nationalist objection and reassure those who were scared of losing their identity. Internal cultural diversity would be a source of strength for the whole. Perhaps, but little in Thatcher's record suggests she would have been greatly attracted to this formulation, and if she was, she did not make it clear at Bruges.

She did not for a number of reasons. Cultural nationalism was a difficult phenomenon for any British prime minister, let alone Thatcher, to acknowledge with ease for the simple reason that, in these terms, Britain is not a nation. It is a union of nations – English, Scots, Welsh and some Irish – each of which might be said to enjoy its own identity and distinctive way of life to which its members are emotionally committed. 'Britishness' in cultural terms alone is a problematic concept. Indeed, it has been suggested, usually by Celtic nationalists or social theorists who think that other identities like class and gender are more important or real than nationality, that 'Britishness' is really a cover for 'English' domination and that 'Englishness' is a cover for something else. In this view, Thatcher was merely an English nationalist in a more severe and obvious version of the traditional dominant mode. However, one does not have to accept this extreme position, and its refusal to see in Britishness anything more than an instrument of dominance, to acknowledge that problems with the idea have important consequences.

The most important of these is that cultural nationalism is less likely to provide the driving force behind British prime ministers than behind most of their Community colleagues or, indeed, US presidents. It is also, in a more cynical vein, less likely to be an easy card to play. This goes doubly for Thatcher, whose background, training and fundamental outlook all pointed to her having a deeply sceptical and unsympathetic attitude to the idea of nationalism as an expression of culture. Her indifference to claims about the destruction of British coalminers' 'way of life', for example, is far more indicative of her attitude in this regard than was her commitment to defending the 'way of life' of the Falkland Islanders. What was important to Thatcher, then, was not blood, soil and songs, but pride in the achievements of one's forebears and being their heir, and in Britain this meant pride in their discovery and development of the practical arrangements by which people could live in liberty and, through enterprise, secure their individual welfare and, thus, the welfare of all.

When she acknowledged the importance of cultural nationalism, therefore, Thatcher was not really recasting herself as a German

romantic revelling in the sheer diversity of human culture as evidence of God in the world. Hers was, in essence, an ideological
nationalism which linked the right ideas about how all people
should live with the history and the genius of a particular people.
In this, Thatcher's nationalism had much in common with that of
the Americans she so admired, although in her case it was more
tempered by the realization that even a universal truth does not
imply the universal imposition of its consequences. Others might
live in error if they wished, she acknowledged at Bruges; all she was
saying was that she would oppose this error at the European level
and not allow it to be imposed upon Britain.

MONEY, POLITICS AND BRITISH SOVEREIGNTY

But how was this to be prevented? While Thatcher had given her
cultural and ideological nationalism their first explicit airing at
Bruges, she had said next to nothing about the political nationalism
and sovereignty which it sustained as the precondition of all else.
Against all expectations based on her previous record, it transpired
that Thatcher found political nationalism nearly as difficult to deal
with as its cultural counterpart, albeit for very different reasons.
Cultural nationalism she found difficult because she suspected that
culture was, as often as not, an excuse for acting unwisely or
unjustly. Her problems with political nationalism, however, were
caused by the specific circumstances in which the Community's
challenge to British sovereignty emerged over monetary policy.

A common monetary policy in some shape or form had been one
of the aspirations of the Community since its foundation, justified
by a combination of political and economic arguments. Politically, it
was claimed that without common economic and monetary policies, it would be impossible to establish a real common market.
Growing interdependence might reduce the ability of states to
pursue their own economic and monetary objectives, but at the
same time, it would magnify the impact of those measures they did
attempt on the well-being of their fellows.[16] The economic argument led to similar conclusions, but starting from theoretical pre-
mises, it had the advantage of simplicity. Economic transactions
would be more efficiently conducted in a system with a single
medium of exchange rather than one with many, and investments
would be higher and growth rates greater in conditions of more,

rather than less, monetary stability. Accordingly, various efforts had been made to create some sort of common monetary policy for the Community, culminating in the decision to establish the European Monetary System (EMS) in 1978.

The most important part of this was an exchange rate mechanism (ERM) which was designed to restrict the amount by which the value of a member's currency could fluctuate against the values of the others. If it did so by more than the specified amount, then the central bank of member country in question was pledged to intervene with measures which would appreciate or depreciate its currency as appropriate. Other central banks might help, and if currencies persistently failed to stay within the proscribed rates, then a general realignment of currencies might be made. The system was designed to create greater monetary stability within the EC, but it was also conceivable that at some point in the future the bands through which currencies were permitted to fluctuate would be reduced to nothing as a step towards creating a single European currency which would replace all the national ones. In its early years, however, the EMS had problems enough even in its circumscribed form. Italy and Ireland joined only after the former had been allowed to participate within a wider band than the rest and the latter had been promised help with the transition costs with financial assistance from the Community and the Federal Republic. Britain refused to join.

It did so for a variety of reasons. In the past, Britain had effectively underwritten the world monetary system and, more recently, the sterling area, experiences which, perhaps, heightened its sensitivity to any compromise of its own financial independence by a monetary system in which it would not be the dominant force. By the time the EMS was established, however, Callaghan's government simply was reluctant to surrender its ability to offset Britain's lack of economic competitiveness and the resulting unemployment by devaluing sterling. Sometimes Thatcher echoed these arguments. In 1986, for example, she declared that Britain had no intention of joining the EMS 'at present' because within such a system one could only deal with speculation against sterling by either using up 'precious reserves' or '...sharply putting up the interest rate'. She wished to retain the option of, as she put it, '...taking the strain on the interest rate'. Nicholas Ridley put the argument more bluntly, however, when he declared that Britain could never match German rates of productivity. Hence, if it surrendered control of the exchange rate, it could only compete with Germany by cutting wages, and this was impossible because Britain would not receive the subventions which smaller states obtained to make up its losses.[17]

Needless to say, Thatcher neither could nor wished to espouse such pessimism about Britain's long-term economic prospects – quite the reverse. Indeed, on other occasions she presented keeping Britain out of the EMS as a policy which flowed from the country's economic confidence and strength. One of the proudest achievements of her government, she maintained, was its early abolition of exchange controls, for without them, British economic policy would be exposed to the judgements of the international money markets. This was the discipline it needed, she argued, and the value of currencies should be set simply by the price at which those who held them were prepared to trade. In addition, Thatcher's purely economic attitude to the EMS was shaped by the monetarist convictions which she retained throughout her term of office. The money supply, no matter how hard this might be to measure in practice, was the best and only guide to monetary policy. One could not, as she told Peter Jenkins in her last month of office, '...have two masters'. There would come a time when the exchange rate and monetary measures provided conflicting signals about whether to reduce or increase interest rates. To be guided, as she maintained her Chancellor of the Exchequer was in 1988, by a sense that the pound was 'over-valued' in relation to the deutschmark had led him to lower interest rates when monetary indicators suggested that this would have unacceptable inflationary consequences.[18]

Difficult and highly technical arguments were at stake here about whether Britain would have enjoyed faster growth and lower inflation inside or outside the EMS. In retrospect, it may be seen that the arguments were greatly complicated by even greater feelings of mutual ill-will among the principal protagonists than were suspected at the time. Accordingly, for many years the formal British position on membership of the EMS remained stuck between outright rejection and outright acceptance. Britain, the government maintained, would enter when conditions were right. What precisely this meant was not made clear, however, until the Madrid summit in the summer of 1989, when Thatcher said that Britain would join only when its rate of inflation had been brought down from 8.3 per cent to less than the Community's average of 4.5 per cent, and when others, notably France, had liberalized their monetary policies by abandoning exchange controls.[19] By then, however, a great deal had happened both at home and abroad to greatly complicate both Thatcher's and Britain's position.

To begin with, two of Thatcher's senior ministers, Lawson and Howe, had become convinced that Britain should respond more positively to the pressure from the rest of the EC to join the ERM, as it was increasingly called in the latter half of the 1980s to distinguish it from European monetary union (EMU). Inflation had begun to worsen sharply in the second half of 1987 because of a combination of tax reductions and pay increases not justified by increases in productivity. As a result, Lawson began to argue that only by participating in the ERM and linking sterling to the deutschmark, could Britain reduce the damagingly high value of the former, as he saw it, by non-inflationary methods. Howe had become convinced that whatever benefits had accrued to Britain from keeping out in the past, it obtained them no longer. Now that the hard work of his own chancellorship had been completed, the choice lay between trusting the anti-inflationary self-discipline of the Thatcher government and its successors or binding oneself to a system which, with all its faults, enjoyed the advantage of being policed by a Bundesbank with an as yet unsullied reputation. Britain should enter when the time was right, he said in 1988, but it could not '. . . go on forever adding that qualification to the underlying commitment.'[20]

Initially, Thatcher refused to yield to either this pressure or the pressure from most of the rest of the Community to which it was coupled. She had never liked the EMS, of course, but much more importantly now the stakes had been raised by its incorporation into Delors's much more ambitious plan for a three-phased progression towards full economic and monetary union underwritten by a European central bank presiding over exchange rates which were 'unequivocally fixed' and eventually over a single European currency. From the moment that the call for a European central bank was renewed at the Hannover summit in the summer of 1988, Thatcher's position became much more difficult. It did so, because she was now presented with a stark choice between her economic and her political convictions, exposed by, as much as anything else, her own attempts to demonstrate the impossibility of a European Bank ever being established.

While she had acquiesced to a West German proposal for a study of the idea of a central bank while at Hannover, Thatcher had added that she saw '...no possibility of a European Central Bank in my life time and possibly never'. A few days before Bruges, she was to explain why on Spanish television:

> Each country would have to give up control over the future of its own economy, over its own currency, so that neither Parliament, nor government, nor the Commission would have a say in what happened, in what steps had to be taken to uphold the value of the currency.

The problem, she said a month later, was that '...A central bank has a total and absolute duty to protect the value of currency,' and to do that, she continued, '...it has to be capable of determining without contradiction, economic policy'.[21] This was true, but for someone who avowedly put 'getting the economics right' before considering other things, and berated those politicians who lacked the courage to do so, these were strange points to make as criticism of the idea of a central bank. Arguably, an independent monetary authority with bankers' values would have been ideal precisely because it removed the ability to make monetary policy from politically accountable centres of decision like governments and legislatures. For Thatcher, however, surrendering political independence to enjoy the benefits of a well-policed monetary union, even if that were attainable, was too high a price to pay.

Under that kind of pressure, it was her instincts as a political nationalist which were foremost because a classical liberal view of the state provided no arguments as to why it should continue to exist if a more efficient provider of its services was available. Thus, her own economic arguments and the Foreign Office-inspired homilies on practical cooperation were abandoned in favour of a defence of British sovereignty and sovereignty in general. Britain, Thatcher told Scottish Conservatives at the start of 1989, was not '...some flimsy or recent creation...' but rather

> ...a great and ancient citadel within whose walls the peoples of these islands have sheltered for almost four centuries. Within those walls, liberty, justice and human progress have flourished in a manner unsurpassed anywhere else in the world.

And, as she told Parliament before the Madrid summit that summer, the ability '...to run an independent monetary, economic and fiscal policy lies at the heart of what constitutes a sovereign state.' Every time a treaty was signed with the EC, she continued, '...a little sovereignty was voluntarily surrendered.' In this regard, the agricultural policy was one thing, but sovereignty over '...taxation, fiscal and monetary matters went to the heart of the control of the executive...' and 'In my view...', she told Parliament a year later, '...we have surrendered enough.'[22]

After Madrid, Thatcher was forced to conduct her defence of British sovereignty from a position of increasing isolation in her own cabinet and the European Council. In Madrid, under the pressure of threats of resignation from both Howe and Lawson, she had accepted the first stage of the Delors proposals and said that Britain would attend another IGC, although it did not accept that further amendments to the Rome Treaty were necessary. The British also secured agreement that the Delors plan was not the only basis for moving forward and began working on their own proposal for monetary reform which later produced John Major's 'hard' European currency unit (ecu) idea. Instead of a single currency for all Europe, an ecu would be created which circulated alongside national currencies and might, one day, replace all or some of them. Shortly after, Thatcher transferred Howe from the Foreign Office and Lawson resigned after one of Thatcher's advisors, the economist Alan Walters, called the ERM 'half-baked' and implied the same of those, like Lawson, who were increasingly advocating membership of it for Britain. The following December in Luxembourg, after the politics of German unification had momentarily caused Kohl to hesitate about the Delors timetable for an IGC, the Community, less Britain, endorsed EMU, the Social Charter and moving ahead on Delors.

By the spring of 1990, and despite Thatcher's best efforts, it became clear that events in eastern Europe and Germany would not be allowed to slow down the process of creating a European Union – quite the reverse. In January, Ireland took over the presidency and its foreign minister, Gerry Collins, said the Community had no choice but to quicken the pace of integration. This was confirmed by Kohl in March when he declared that a united Germany would '...accelerate, not constrain...' further integration, and in April, France and Germany announced their joint determination to push for European economic and political union by 1 January 1993. At the Dublin summit in April, Thatcher again accepted the establishment of IGCs on political and monetary union, but on condition that those in favour spelt out in detail what they meant by such a union before the rest endorsed any general principles. In October, Britain finally joined the ERM without Thatcher's longstanding conditions being particularly satisfied, and sterling promptly sank to the bottom of its band.

Just under three weeks later at the Rome summit, Britain found itself isolated again when the other members agreed with a decision of the Italian presidency to move to the second stage of economic and monetary union according to Delors, beginning on 1 January 1994 and achieving a single currency by the end of the decade. Thatcher declared that anyone who thought a single currency could be established by imposition was living in 'cloud cuckoo land', and she declared that the discussion on political union had produced only a '... rat bag of proposals'. Her tone on this occasion, together with a combative performance in her report to the House of Commons on Rome, persuaded Howe, by his own account, to resign, and this, plus the damaging manner in which he made his departure with a direct attack on both the style and substance of Thatcher's policymaking, precipitated the leadership contest which ended her political career.[23]

THE DIPLOMACY OF SOVEREIGNTY

Both the style and the substance of Thatcher's European policy have been heavily criticized, the style for contributing to her fall and the substance for being completely wrong. The former may be briefly dealt with here for it receives a fuller treatment in the final chapter. Just conceivably, a government which did not convey the impression of being at war with itself also might have steeled the country better to the prospect of not participating in all aspects of the proposed European Union. And, by so doing, it might also have presented Britain as a more credible threat to those who wished to proceed regardless and a more credible leader and ally of those who shared its doubts. However, this is unlikely, and not merely because of the way Thatcher dealt with her European colleagues on occasions. Being rude to foreigners, even foolish and mendacious foreigners, is, of course, unforgivable. There is nothing to be gained by it abroad, and a great deal less than some of Thatcher's advisors evidently believed to be gained by it at home. There is little to suggest, however, that it hurt British interests a great deal. Certainly memoirs, interviews and newspaper reports abound with claims that if Thatcher had not been so stubborn on this particular percentage point, if she had paid attention to her officials and had not kept the heads of government up all night negotiating a deal they had already settled in the background with the European presidency team, if she had not forced them by her contempt into actually making good on their rhetoric, then Britain would have done a great deal better. Perhaps this was so on the small change of EC negotiations, the side-payments, derogations and let-offs which seem indispensable to the implementation of any new common policy. On the big questions, however, this seems extremely unlikely precisely because they were big questions. To suggest that the prime minister of country *x* would have sided with Thatcher on the sovereignty issue, but because she was so rude and abrasive he decided to commit his country to full economic and monetary union is counter-intuitive to say the least.

Thatcher's problem was, however, that the questions at stake were very big questions, the biggest you can get by any classical understanding of foreign policy priorities, for they concerned the goal of preserving independence, and Britain kept finding itself in a minority of one on most of the arguments. The question was, therefore, what should it do when confronted by such a difficult situation? The diplomats' answer is never put oneself into a position of sustained opposition in arguments one cannot win or, finding oneself in one, get out of it as quickly as possible. The problem with the negotiations on sovereignty and, indeed, on many other Community matters, however, was that they were not normal diplomacy, the conduct of relations between countries in an effort to seek the resolution of disputes by negotiation. They were rule-making exercises which purported to change the status of the participants and, as such, they were extremely difficult to break off. However, if one did not break Community negotiations because of a failure to agree, one found oneself trapped in talks to establish rules which would make agreement either compulsory or unnecessary.

Most of Thatcher's colleagues and opponents responded to this problem by claiming that the challenge posed by the EC to national sovereignty was not real, that sovereignty no longer mattered, or that a new kind of pooled sovereignty was in operation and had, in fact, been so for some time. The claim that the Community does not pose a challenge to national sovereignty is hard to deal with, for it is not clear whether it is based on a reading of the 'real' character of EC rhetoric or on a judgement that the national facts of Europe will subvert and destroy any federal enterprise which seeks to ignore them. The 'reading' is almost undoubtedly wrong. When people like Pierre Bergevoy, then the French foreign minister, said as he did in the spring of 1989 that a 'European political authority' was the price of monetary union, they clearly meant it, even if what they meant was not clear and might be subsequently modified.[24] The judgement about national facts is, of course, almost certainly correct, but while it might provide solace to those who fought and temporarily lost the sovereignty battle, it was hardly a reason for not fighting it. Even if a European Union is unattainable because there is no corresponding sense of political community to sustain it, this does not mean that the effort to create it should not be opposed as damaging, wasteful and wrong.

The weight of opposition to Thatcher's European diplomacy, however, was concentrated on the concept of sovereignty itself. Thatcher's view of it was charged with being false, historically out of date, rooted in a frozen misinterpretation of British constitutionalism and, in so far as she saw sovereignty as immutable, un-British in its dogmatism. To say her view was false involved confusing the concepts of independence, meaning one was free to do what one wanted, and sovereignty, meaning one had the right to do what one wanted. In an age of interdependence, the argument ran, neither Britain nor anyone else was independent anymore and, therefore, were no longer sovereign. As Lord Plumb, the leader of the European Parliament, expressed it, Thatcher was fighting a lost battle because the EC had 'long since gone beyond the stage' of '...merely sovereign states cooperating with each other'. She was so, according to other critics like William Wallace, because she was too influenced by those like A.V. Dicey who had begun stressing the 'illimitable' sovereignty of Parliament in the nineteenth century. According to Leon Brittan, this involved turning it from a pragmatic instrument for solving problems into 'a semi-religious creed'. To do so was to echo the absolutists of continental thought who saw sovereignty as an end, rather than as a means, of policy and, in Lord Cockfield's view, such 'absolute sovereignty' was '...the attribute of the caveman...'[25]

There was no such thing as absolute sovereignty according to Howe, either in the sense that one could attain complete independence or in the sense that, if one did not enjoy complete sovereignty, then one had none at all. Sovereignty, he argued, '...is not like virginity, which you either have or you don't,' and it was wrong and damaging to present the issue in these terms. Instead of the old-fashioned, either–or concept of sovereignty, most of these critics offered some notion of it as a power or capacity which could be pooled or partnered with the sovereignty of others to make both the sum of the parts and the parts themselves stronger without destroying the latters' identity. This, they argued, was the only way forward, at once historical opportunity and historical necessity, and as the Italian prime minister, Giulio Andreotti, declared at the Rome summit '. . . when history is accelerating, you have to accelerate with it.' If you did not, then you would be left behind, a threat which was much illustrated by the overworked metaphor of a train leaving the station with Britain variously in the guard's van or on the platform instead of the driver's cab where it ought to be.

Thatcher herself accepted the idea of divided sovereignty on occasions. She had spoken in 1989, for example, about the sovereignty of the EC over some areas of policy being agreed to by its members, and the following year, her new foreign minister, Douglas Hurd, talked of 'pooling' Community diplomats and embassies. In so doing, however, everybody, including Thatcher, begged the important questions which she habitually asked at European Councils but to which she received no answer. Where was pooling leading, and what sort of union was envisaged?[26] For behind the avowedly pragmatic, but for people like Howe and Denning surprisingly postmodernist, rearticulations of sovereignty as a poolable resource, there lay two difficult issues. The first concerned the point at which the transfer of powers to the Community would leave the members with only what Geoffrey Marshall called 'residual sovereignty', for while sovereignty was a formal concept, sovereignty with no power to back it would be meaningless. Some, like Denning, argued that Britain had already subordinated itself to Community law, and where it had, there was no legal way back. Even if Britain enjoyed the right to pull back, however, Marshall asked, would it be practically possible in the face of established and sanctioning Community institutions. People on both sides of the argument considered this question unanswerable, but whereas Thatcher saw this as grounds for hesitation, her Community colleagues and their supporters at home did not. Some, indeed, regarded the novelty and uncertainty of the project as part of its attractiveness and, as such, evidence of Europe's vitality and innovative energy.[27] The second, and far more pressing problem as it turned out, concerned the EC's own failures. As Thatcher said about her partners at the start of the Gulf War, 'They are always talking about political union, talking,

talking, talking... and what happens?'[28] The collapse of even the proto-monetary union established by the Maastricht treaty and the European Union's (EU) divided response to the disintegration of Yugoslavia demonstrated that even a successful transfer of responsibilities is not much use if the actor to which they are transferred is incapable of effective action.

These, however, were not part of Thatcher's story for she had been forced to resign by then. Had she remained in office, she would have conducted the resistance to political, economic and monetary union more vigorously than her successor, although whether she would have gained more than the derogations and suspensions he obtained is difficult to say. Even before her defeat, however, it was becoming clear that the fundamental character of international politics, and European politics along with them, was changing. As a result of the end of the Cold War, the Europe against which Thatcher fought was not the Europe which emerged post-Maastricht. It was a much more uncertain state of affairs in which the European great powers wavered perilously between the bourgeois preoccupations of the Hansa and resuming their responsibilities in a classical sense.

Thatcher's foreign policy failed, but the end of the Cold War was to prove her right. Without its certainties and disciplines, the weaknesses of European Union were exposed. In the meantime, it is to her credit that she did not contribute to the confusion of European politics by joining the general attack on that most successful of European political principles, sovereignty and the system of states maintained by it. Instead, she pointed out the folly of so doing and, by her own efforts to work out a coherent nationalism to bolster her case for why British sovereignty was worth defending, Thatcher also pointed to the only practical cure for the European immobilism which followed.

10 Thatcher's Soviet Policy: Diplomacy at the Summit

The events which overtook Thatcher's defence of British sovereignty in Europe were the end of the Cold War, the collapse of the USSR and the resulting merger of East and West Germany into a single German state. She played a considerable part in bringing about the first of these and resisted, unsuccessfully, the other two. However, and notwithstanding her early reputation as 'the Iron Lady' and the eventual prominence she was to achieve in East–West relations, Thatcher's government began by pursuing an almost entirely orthodox Soviet policy under the guidance of Lord Carrington. The broad outlines of this had been established after the great powers had failed, in their half-hearted way, to strangle the Bolshevik revolution at birth. The USSR, like the Russian Empire before it, was to be kept out of western Europe unless its strength was needed to deal with forces there which were even more hostile to British interests and values than was Russia. Then, by the concerted action of the other great powers, it was to be shepherded out again and left alone to its affairs, provided that these did not impinge on British interests elsewhere, for example in the eastern Mediterranean or the North West Frontier of the Indian Empire.

These axioms remained in force after the Cold War had begun, modified only by the realization that the USSR was now so strong that no European coalition acting without US support could control it. Thus, British Cold War diplomacy had concentrated on two objectives: maintaining a common military and political front to deter Soviet expansion; and maintaining contacts with the USSR to reduce tensions or, at least, to keep them to a tolerable level. The first was achieved by Britain's own practical contribution to European security and by helping American administrations to keep the US engaged in Europe by countering the neutralist and anti-American sentiments at home. The second objective, maintaining contacts, involved striking a fine balance between those who believed that the ideological character of the USSR was such that no accommodation between East and West was possible, and those who hoped that a final diplomatic settlement lay just around the corner and, with goodwill on both sides, was achievable. On occasions, it also involved trying to manage those, like Reagan, who seemed to oscillate between both positions on the basis of judgements about the current diplomatic situation, the personal qualities of Soviet leaders and the requirements of domestic politics.

To the end of maintaining contacts, the British were usually strong supporters of conference diplomacy between the great powers on particular issues, for example regional settlements like the Geneva agreements on South East Asia in 1954 or arms control agreements like those designed to regulate chemical weapons in the 1980s. They also contrived to be enthusiastic about summitry between the superpowers, provided adequate consultation had taken place between the US and its allies beforehand. In addition, however, several British prime ministers – Churchill, Eden, Macmillan and Wilson, for example – had sought roles for themselves and their country in bilateral negotiations with the USSR when the opportunity presented itself and necessity, in their judgement, dictated that they should take it. The circumstances of these interventions were similar. In each case, relations between the superpowers had stalled with both sides apparently willing, but unable, to get negotiations moving again, and in each case, British prime ministers had convinced themselves, or had been convinced by others, that they might provide what George Walden called 'a catalyst of common sense'.[1] This common sense told them that the threat posed by the USSR to western Europe was rooted in Russian national interests and insecurities rather than revolutionary Communist ambitions and, thus, it was neither necessary nor possible to crush the USSR. The power which made it a threat also made it a fact of international life.

Of course, the accuracy of this view, widely regarded as sensible in many circles, has been cast into doubt by subsequent events, at least in the medium term. And in so far as British governments believed that such a view of the USSR played no part in the shaping of America's Soviet policy, they deluded themselves. It was not for these reasons, however, that the success enjoyed by British initiatives in East–West relations had ranged from modest to disappointing. The main reason for this was that the superpowers were effective duopolists when they chose to be so. Successes, like Macmillan's worthy effort to restore momentum to arms control negotiations, were swiftly appropriated by the superpowers. Initiatives, however, were much more likely to fail, either because both superpowers might prefer no progress to letting in a third party, or because one or the other of them would see the initiative as pressure upon it in particular. Wilson's Vietnam initiative, for example, was regarded by both superpowers in this light with the result that it succeeded only in exposing the limits of Britain's international influence.

Disappointing though Britain's record on East–West initiatives was, however, it was sufficiently successful to tempt successive British governments to keep trying them when the opportunities arose. Thatcher's government was no exception, although until the Soviet intervention in Afghanistan at the end of 1979, it experienced difficulty in positioning itself. Should it encourage Carter to adopt a tougher approach to the USSR, providing ammunition for the domestic critics of his weakness, lend support to his defence of *détente* and signing the SALT II arms control agreement, or, despairing of effective leadership in any particular direction emerging from the Carter administration, carve out its own course? There was evidence of all three. On her first trip to Washington, Thatcher had called for tough American leadership which she pledged Britain would follow. However, she had also defended *détente*, as she did in her first meeting with Chancellor Schmidt when both leaders asked the Senate to ratify Salt II. On her way to her first G7 meeting in Tokyo, Thatcher's plane had stopped briefly in Moscow and, while there, accepted an invitation from Kosygin to visit the USSR. However, within two months of coming into office, Thatcher had also sent a letter of protest to the Czechoslovakian government concerning its treatment of dissidents and, at a conference in Geneva on Vietnam's treatment of its refugees, Britain had sponsored so strong a condemnation of Hanoi that only China supported it.[2]

The Soviet intervention in Afghanistan, however, allowed Carrington to give more shape to Britain's Soviet policy. His neutralization proposal was unsuccessful but, on the table in various forms for over a year, it represented a sustained effort to keep the lines of communication open, even if only to tell the USSR how unacceptable its conduct had been and to warn it of the possible costs. Thatcher's involvement in East–West relations, by contrast, was fragmentary and of secondary importance. Even after Reagan was elected at the end of 1980, her support for a tougher US policy remained balanced by a commitment to *détente*, and the deepening Polish crisis of the following year found Thatcher looking for a man who would actually make the cuts she wanted in defence spending. Paradoxically, given that the main cuts were eventually to fall upon the Royal Navy, Thatcher's own concern with defence policy, as opposed to defence spending, seemed focused on missions outside Nato's sphere of operations. The '. . . balance of deterrence or the balance of terror', she told *Time*, '. . . is holding the line across Europe.' The problem now was '. . . troubles almost girdling the world below the Nato belt.'[3]

In the light of the war between Iran and Iraq which had broken out the previous year, this was a reasonable claim. The sense of stability on the central front which Thatcher conveyed, however, was scarcely consistent with the main thrust of Anglo-American security policy which was about to develop. Quite clearly, Thatcher had by this stage no set policy of her own towards the USSR, but rather sets of tough and reassuring responses which were made as the context required. Thus, it was others who took the lead in trying to shape East–West relations although, it must be said, with no more discernible effect than Carrington. Giscard d'Estaing, the French president, for example, travelled to Warsaw to meet Brezhnev, breaching an agreement by Nato leaders to suspend high-level contacts with the USSR, and the leaders of the Labour party, Foot and Healey, met Brezhnev in Moscow to secure a 'breakthrough' on the withdrawal, but not the destruction, of medium-ranged missiles. By the spring of 1982, in contrast, Thatcher's own forays into East–West relations consisted of a two-day visit to Yugoslavia, where she praised Tito's legacy and stressed the importance of respecting the rights of small states, and a declaration of support for US arms to Pakistan which she bravely gave on a visit to India.

FUNERALS AND FALSE STARTS

After the Falklands War and Carrington's departure in the spring of 1982, it was widely expected, not least by the prime minister herself, that Thatcher would become more interested in foreign policy, and that a more confrontational approach following the tone set by the superpowers themselves would result. In October 1982, for example, she visited West Berlin declaring that its inhabitants had a 'special need' to know that Britain honoured her obligations. 'I come before you . . .', she continued, '. . . as Prime Minister of a country which has so recently proved that.' And, just before the general election in the spring of the following year, she asked for a large majority, not merely to counter the doubts expressed by one of her ministers about the effects of unrestrained power, but also because '... there is so much at stake internationally.' 'Already', she claimed, '... one feels oneself taking a more forceful leadership role because of the combination of one's own style and one's own experience.'[4]

What was at stake, in fact, was Britain's own defence policy, for the Labour party was advocating the unilateral abandonment of Britain's nuclear deterrent and the withdrawal of American military bases from the country. Thatcher threw herself into providing strong support for Reagan's approach to the USSR in Washington, European capitals and at home. As far as Britain's Soviet policy was concerned, however, her claims of a new level of involvement amounted to very little. She had not attended Brezhnev's funeral in November 1982, agreeing with those leaders who believed that their absence would more eloquently convey their view of Soviet conduct than anything they could say if they went to Moscow. Although Geoffrey Howe, the new foreign secretary, visited Hungary after the 1983 election, Thatcher's own contribution amounted to the harsh judgements she had made on Soviet morality in Washington the following September. It was not surprising, therefore, that, as Jim Callaghan was told on a visit to Moscow, in its view, the chances of a summit between Andropov, the new Soviet leader, and Thatcher were remote.[5]

They were so quite simply because Britain and the USSR had very little to say to each other at this stage. Throughout 1983, as the superpowers argued over intermediate-range nuclear forces (INF), the British government remained committed to the deployment of the Cruise and Pershing systems if the USSR could not accept the US zero option. All the Soviet government wished to talk about with Britain, however, was how many of its own missiles it would withdraw or destroy if the British declined to accept the new American missiles and abandoned their own deterrent, a position which Sir Ian Sutherland, the British ambassador to the USSR, told the Russians was '... totally unacceptable'. Nevertheless, as the superpowers traded offer and counter-offer regarding the numbers and locations of systems to be deployed in an interim agreement short of zero without success, concern grew about the increased tension which accompanied their failure to agree. The Peace Movements in each country exploited this unease by suggesting that if the new missiles were deployed, then a nuclear war would likely follow. They advocated a policy of neutrality for Nato's European mem-

bers if US policy could not be changed. Others were more sanguine. In 1981, for example, Carrington rejected the suggestion of a
rift between the US and its European allies. 'It isn't so much
neutralism...', he argued, '...as worry.' In his view, once the arms
control talks got '...going and hopefully we have some success,
then a good deal of that worry will disappear.'[6]

This was both a truism and, on the time scale with which diplomats wish they would be left alone to work, eventually proved to be
true. In the short term, however, there was no progress on arms
control, and even people like Carrington (now temporarily retired
from international affairs) began to wonder about the ability of the
superpowers to reach an agreement. In April 1983, he had decried
the Soviet use of 'megaphone diplomacy', but by the following
August he was faulting both sides for conducting what he called a
Leninist 'war of nerves' and 'one-dimensional moral crusades'.
Even Henry Kissinger was quoted by Nicholas Ashford as saying
that the US lacked the psychological, as well as physical, resources
to be '...the sole or even principal centre of initiative and responsibility in the non-Communist world.'[7] Thatcher did not share this
concern, but there were those in the British government, the foreign
secretary among them, who did, or, at least, saw in it the possible
opportunity for a British initiative. The problem was how to seize
the opportunity, if such it was, without undermining the Americans
or seeming to criticize them.

Part of the solution was provided by the USSR when, in November 1983, after the Bundestag voted in favour of accepting the new
missiles, it broke off the negotiations on them in Geneva and
refused to resume parallel talks on strategic forces and conventional
weapons. In the new year, there were reports that the USSR was
asking for British help in resuming the talks, and the British were
rumoured to be receptive. This, it seemed, was their opportunity,
for they could no longer be plausibly charged with aiding and
abetting a Soviet attempt to put pressure on the US. The USSR
had broken off the talks in a situation where no agreement entailed
its least favoured outcome. Now it was in the humiliating position of
looking for a way to restart them. The other part of the solution was
to proceed by indirect diplomacy. In February of 1984, the Foreign
Office and the USSR Foreign Ministry exchanged telegrams recognizing 60 years of full Anglo-Soviet diplomatic relations, but as they
did so, Thatcher herself paid a visit to Hungary. According to
Howe, this reflected a shift in British policy towards treating the

governments of eastern Europe as genuine entities rather than mere instruments of Soviet policy. While she was in Budapest, however, Thatcher made a speech echoing an earlier effort by Howe in Stockholm in which he had called on the USSR to return to the talks in Geneva on balanced reductions. Less than two weeks later, Andropov was dead, and Thatcher was in Moscow for his funeral. It seemed as if her moment had come and, indeed, several sources have subsequently suggested that the trip to Hungary, and Howe's preparatory work for it, opened the door which led eventually to a major improvement in East–West relations.

For several reasons, however, it is unlikely that this is the case. Even before Thatcher's trip to Hungary, George Shultz, the American secretary of state, and Andrei Gromyko, his Soviet counterpart, had conducted a lengthy meeting the previous January, demonstrating that the superpowers were maintaining high-level contacts with one another, even if they seemed to agree about very little during them. As Thatcher herself acknowledged on her return from Andropov's funeral, the themes of her own pronouncements in Budapest and Moscow, 'realistic dialogue' with agreements based on 'respect' not 'rhetoric', had been signalled in a major speech by Reagan back in January.[8] Besides, the British were still not sure what they wanted to do with this 'small opening', as the Foreign Office had described one of Andropov's offers the previous year. If she could make the Russians see sense, then well and good, but Thatcher had no intention of implying that Reagan was a source of the present deadlock by playing the middleman. The diplomats also rejected the role of an intermediary, although for somewhat different reasons. In another context, US–European relations, George Walden, a former member of the Foreign Office, had described the role of a 'middleman' as being 'vulgar' and this was a view shared by many of his former colleagues. Sutherland in Moscow, for example, insisted that Britain would not be a 'postbox' for the superpowers.[9] If Britain was to play a part, then it would be its own part, but how could this be done without implying criticism of the Americans?

Their answer was that, at the present time, it could not, and they knew this because the Americans, in the person of Vice-President Bush, had explicitly warned them off trying. Bush had always been less tolerant than his master of advice from the European allies. In a calculated outburst in 1982, for example, he had declared that '...We have heard a lot of protests from our European allies. I'm sorry...', he had continued, the US was '...the leader of the free world and under this Administration, we are beginning to act like it.' On his way to Andropov's funeral in 1984, Bush visited London for consultations with Thatcher. Speaking with the press afterwards, he noted her high standing with the American people and described her recent visit to Hungary as 'extraordinarily interesting'. She had a useful part to play, but, Bush added that he '...did not want to leave the impression that...the whole United States–Soviet relationship can be brokered or solved by an intermediary.' 'That', he continued, '...has to be by contact between the United States and the Soviet Union themselves.'[10]

The British government took the warning to heart, with the result that the evolution of Thatcher's Soviet policy was reduced to a snail's pace. As she had declared in her 'realism' and 'respect' speech of March, '...this is the stuff of steady, unspectacular diplomacy, not political theatre.' There would be summits, but they were usually 'the keystone, not the foundation' of diplomatic settlements. These were wise words, but even Thatcher, perhaps, had not counted on the extent of the ensuing paralysis. By July 1984, Howe in Moscow was having to endure Russian proverbs from Gromyko about the wind from the east being 'cold and dry', while he himself was reduced to retorting with platitudes about the world being unable to afford '...the politics of the empty chair', and claiming afterwards that he had gone to Moscow with no expectations of 'rapid results'. Talks without preconditions were being offered. He said he had checked this first with the Americans before saying it, and he added that the USSR risked being seen as the country which '...would not take yes for an answer.' In October, Gromyko accepted an invitation to visit Britain the following year and, a month later, the indirect approach was resumed when Malcolm Rifkind visited Poland, his contribution to ending Warsaw's diplomatic isolation balanced by a visit to the grave of the famous, murdered, dissident priest, Father Jerzy Popieluszko.[11]

To what end, it remained hard to say. With an American block and with Soviet diplomacy apparently incapable of imagining anything beyond restoring the appearances of the *détente* partnership, it looked as though Thatcher's Soviet policy would go the way of the less distinguished of its predecessors. Without encouragement from one or other of the superpowers, the British could offer nothing more than the long haul of patient diplomacy to restart negotiations in which their own involvement would be peripheral. This was a worthy goal, no doubt, but scarcely one to hold the attention of a prime minister who had her hands full with Europe, a new initiative on Ireland in the making and an agreement with China over the future of Hong Kong – the problems of which were just becoming apparent. What Thatcher's Soviet policy needed, if it were to survive, was a more receptive audience in Moscow or Washington. In Mikhail Gorbachev, this is what they got and much more, for not only did he grant Britain's Soviet policy the significance which its authors sought, he succeeded in tempting them into taking more imaginative steps than they had previously thought possible.

GORBACHEV

Gorbachev had visited London at the end of 1984 and established himself, in Thatcher's celebrated phrase, as a man with whom one could do business. Despite the attention which Thatcher's relationship with Reagan has attracted, her relationship with Gorbachev was just as puzzling and, arguably, more important given the eventual impact it was to have on her international career. If Reagan was an unlikely friend in personal terms, then Gorbachev was even more so. Certainly, he possessed the agile mind and combative personality which Thatcher was reputed to value. She might be 'close' with Reagan, as she said in 1987, but with Gorbachev she found it easy to talk and argue.[12] Nor was the fact that he always maintained, and she always accepted, that he was a Communist the problem. Professional respect between politicians of widely different views who do not have to compete with one another is not unusual. What is odd is how seriously Thatcher continued to take Gorbachev even after he had begun to elaborate the details of the 'new political thinking' with which he eventually succeeded in undermining the legitimacy of the Soviet state and his own political position. Any British politician who proclaimed a new era in world affairs which required a post-national, post-class, collective effort on the part of humanity to solve its problems, whether he was lying, hopelessly naive or obfuscating in the contemporary rhetorical style which she so despised in the EC, would have received very short shrift from Thatcher indeed.

Certainly, any British prime minister who aspired to an international role would have made it their business to establish a personal relationship with the leaders of either superpower if this was at all possible. This would be so, both as a matter of duty and because these men were powerful, and all politicians are in some measure attracted to power. However, there are numerous cases of politicians not pursuing relationships with colleagues simply because they are powerful. Thatcher herself, for example, assiduous though she may have been in her cultivation of Reagan and Gorbachev, refused to put herself about for Chancellor Kohl, even as he became the most powerful leader in Europe and, more importantly, refused to modify her support for Gorbachev as his position weakened. In fact, she did the reverse. And, of course, power-seeking provides an unsatisfactory explanation of both Reagan's and Gorbachev's willingness to conduct close political relationships with Thatcher. The tentative conclusion must be, therefore, that the Thatcher–Gorbachev relationship was a success in great part because they liked and admired each other.

However, neither Thatcher's successful meeting with Gorbachev at the end of 1984, nor Chernenko's timely death three months later, were, in themselves, sufficient to establish her, as *The Times* put it, 'At The High Table' of international affairs. Progress in this regard remained dependent on the Reagan administration' ability and need to tolerate independent *démarches* on the part of its allies. For the best part of two years following 1985, very little happened which did not emphasize just how narrow the margins were for this kind of diplomacy. Thatcher's attempt to keep SDI research and deployment within the bounds of existing arms control agreements as they were conventionally understood received some praise from the Soviet government at the end of 1984. It had moved the barometer of East–West relations, they said, '. . . a little bit towards realism'. However, when Howe made a speech the following year which, while noting that research into ballistic missile defence was both permissible under the 1972 treaty and prudent, expressed great scepticism about both the feasibility and the desirability of the idea, the US response was swift.

Richard Perle, an undersecretary in the Pentagon, made some well-publicized and highly critical remarks and Charles Price, the American ambassador to London, met with Howe, although they both maintained the meeting had been arranged in advance. Less noticed at the time, but perhaps of more significance, it appears that the Americans were also distressed by Thatcher's performance in Moscow at Chernenko's funeral where she reputedly assured the

Russians that Reagan fully shared her view that anything beyond research into missile defences would have to be a matter for further arms control negotiations.[13] As a result, the British were keen to publicize their support for the US rejection of Gorbachev's proposal for a freeze on the deployment of new missiles in April 1985. By the end of the month they were casting out Soviet spies, and while the USSR and the US edged towards the first summit of the Reagan presidency in Geneva the following November, Anglo-Soviet relations deteriorated. Following the mutual ejections of diplomats and others, Gromyko was alleged to have snubbed Sutherland, the departing British ambassador by not saying farewell to him. Two months later, after the British secured the escape of Oleg Gordievsky, a senior KGB official whom they maintained had been working for them for over 19 years, a further and escalatory casting out of those accused of espionage took place.

Thus, the post-summit world might, as Gorbachev maintained in Geneva, be '... a safer place', but one would have scarcely known it from the state of Anglo-Soviet relations at the end of 1985. Howe continued his visits to eastern Europe to 'broaden the dialogue' beyond arms control and the two superpowers, but the mission had the air of William Rogers being sent to the Middle East by Henry Kissinger to keep him busy, and the return visit of the Hungarian premier, Kadar, attracted little attention. Thatcher, on the other hand, unable to develop her own policy, fluctuated between expressing concern that Reagan should not surrender the arms control initiative to Gorbachev and the usual rhetoric of firmness and resolve. The West, she told Parliament just before the summit, sought balanced and verifiable reductions of nuclear weapons but, she asked, 'Does anyone who has witnessed Mr Gorbachev's performance think he respects weakness?' She had made her own view of the USSR clear less than three months earlier. It was engaged, she had said, in a 'massive propaganda offensive', for '... the reality and the nature of Communism had not changed, even if its image has been touched up.'[14]

If Thatcher was seeking a special relationship with Gorbachev, this seemed an unpromising place from which to start. Following the Geneva summit, however, British diplomacy continued to signal differences between its position and that of the Americans not just on SDI, but also on whether the limits on nuclear forces imposed by SALT II should be broken. The treaty had been signed by the superpowers but never ratified because of the collapse of *détente* in

the late 1970s. Both sides had more or less respected their understandings of the agreement in succeeding years. Now, however,
the US wanted to deploy new forces which would place it in
violation of SALT II's ceilings on delivery systems unless it scrapped
older ones. This the Reagan administration was reluctant to do, for
it had always believed that SALT II was a poor agreement for the
US and maintained that the USSR had already violated it by
deploying more new systems than were allowed and by taking
measures to make it difficult for the US to monitor Soviet missile
tests.

Throughout 1986, hints and signals continued between Britain
and the USSR. Gromyko reportedly asked Whitelaw and Healey in
Moscow if the British government could exercise a modifying influence on the Americans over SALT, to which Whitelaw replied that
provided the USSR stuck to the treaty, the US would have no
reason for breaking it. This seemed to place the burden of responsibility squarely on Soviet shoulders but, given that it was the US
which was considering the possibility of a serious 'breakout' from
the constraints of the treaty, this was not so. The point was confirmed more obviously by Thatcher a day after the Moscow meeting, when she declared that both sides should keep to the provisions
of SALT II and expressed the opinion that she was sure that the
Americans were '... anxious that both sides should continue...' to
do so.[15]

There remained very little to show, however, for all the
patient signalling. The Russians responded more favourably
than the Americans to a British proposal for eliminating chemical
weapons at Geneva. A trade agreement had been signed at the
beginning of the year incorporating encouraging projections
about the future growth of Anglo-Soviet commerce, and the following July, Shevardnadze, the new Soviet foreign minister, paid a
visit to Britain which had twice been cancelled since the original
invitation to Gromyko because of the diplomatic expulsions.
During his visit, the two countries reached a number of agreements,
among them the settlement of a 69-year dispute over the Bolshevik
seizure of British assets, and it was also rumoured that Britain
would play a part in setting up the next Soviet-American meeting
because, as a result of their own espionage ructions, the two superpowers were finding it difficult to communicate with each other. A
visit by Thatcher to Moscow the following spring was also confirmed.

REYKJAVIK AND THE RUSSIANS

Whether this diplomatic manoeuvring and the invitation to which it led would have succeeded by themselves in raising the tempo of Anglo-Soviet relations is difficult to say, for by the time Thatcher went to Moscow her value to Soviet diplomacy had been transformed. It was so by two unforeseen events in October 1986: the summit between Reagan and Gorbachev in Reykjavik and the revelations of the Iran–Contra scandal. In a paradoxical manner, both confirmed Thatcher's earlier rhetoric about Gorbachev respecting strength as containing more truth than even she expected. Gorbachev's offer of an end to all nuclear weapons in two five-year phases was one of the first fruits of his 'international *perestroika*' announced earlier in the year. However, more surprising in narrowly diplomatic terms was his response to Thatcher's predictable rush to remind Reagan that Nato's strategy rested on its ability to use nuclear weapons.

Gorbachev had taken care to provide Thatcher with a prompt briefing of the discussions in Iceland. The chief Soviet negotiator, Viktor Karpov, had come to London (before going on to Paris) and, following his talks with her, had even suggested the possibility of decoupling proposed cuts in intermediate range missiles from a commitment to abandon SDI. How frank Soviet diplomacy was being with the British at this stage is unclear. Karpov's suggestion of decoupling, genuine or not, was possibly unauthorized for he was subsequently removed from his position, and it is also not clear whether he gave Thatcher details of Gorbachev's final proposal to Reagan. The special treatment continued, however, when, on the eve of Thatcher's US trip, Gorbachev sent her a letter, although whether to get her to lobby the president on SDI or to moderate her own anti-denuclearizing stance is again unclear.[16] Soviet diplomacy was beginning to attach great importance to Thatcher's role, but just how important was not revealed until she replied to Gorbachev following her meeting with Reagan. It might be supposed that, on the basis of the tough line she took in steering Reagan back towards nuclear orthodoxy, the USSR would have excoriated Thatcher as an obstacle to progress or worse (from her point of view), simply cut her out of the process. Instead, according to the British ambassador, Sir Brian Cartledge, Gorbachev used the opportunity of the letter's delivery to tell him that he regarded Thatcher as the strongest leader in the West after Reagan. It was she who had clarified the West's position post-Reykjavik, and her views on nuclear disarmament had prevailed over those of the American president.[17]

How is this gift to be explained? It is improbable that Gorbachev's purpose was to separate Thatcher from Reagan in an attempt to weaken the latter's position. On the issue of complete nuclear disarmament, the differences between her and Gorbachev were greater than those between the two presidents. It would have been a deep and Machiavellian *finesse*, more appropriate to the world of espionage and espionage fiction than to diplomacy, which sought to weaken Reagan by encouraging Thatcher to adopt an independent position even if it was diametrically opposed to the interests of Soviet policy at this point. The more likely explanation, therefore, is that Gorbachev actually meant what he said to Cartledge, and for two reasons. Possibly, he realized that Reagan had violated the parameters within which US strategic policy was formulated when he flirted with Gorbachev's proposal for a total ban in ten years. Like Tsar Nicholas in the Baltic, he had shown an interest in a proposal to which his government could not let him agree (it remains a matter of conjecture as to whether Gorbachev would have found himself in the position of Kaiser Wilhelm had he returned to Moscow with an agreement).[18] Secondly, Gorbachev may have judged that Reagan was going to be crippled by the revelation that the US government had secretly sold arms to Iran in an attempt to free American hostages in the Lebanon, using the proceeds to support the activities of the Nicaraguan Contras.

For Gorbachev, the first of these was more important, for the full extent of the arms scandal was not known for several weeks. The person for whom the scandal was a more important gift was Thatcher herself. At last, not only did she possess a clear opening from the USSR, she could also be reasonably confident that Washington would not, for the moment, be well placed to rein her in. The Reagan administration's reputation for not dealing with terrorists and their sponsors had been shattered, and precisely at the moment when the British had frustrated an attempt to blow up an Israeli airliner in London and were trying to convince the international community to adopt strong measures against Syria for its role in the affair. Thatcher was swift to act. In December, when Shultz, Meese and Weinberger arrived in London for what the former called 'a rebuilding job', she went before the European Parliament to share her concern at the high levels of anti-Americanism in

Europe and called on its members to help '... build up the Atlantic relationship'. A month later, at the start of 1987, she staked out a leadership role for herself and Britain in the upcoming arms talks. 'I hope...', she ventured, '... that we will be the nation that has the continuity in government and the continuity in leadership that I think is really necessary at the moment to the western world, when you face a time when, by their constitution, the US has to change presidents.'[19] She did not have to add that Britain, too, was due an election.

A TROIKA?

Thatcher's open bid for leadership immediately provoked an American response in the form of a more public airing of some of the differences between Britain and the US. At the beginning of 1987, Richard Perle expressed dissatisfaction with the verification procedures in Britain's proposals for a chemical weapons ban, and he accused Howe, their architect, of 'mealy-mouthed evasion' when the latter had been invited to criticize the USSR. In February, when Thatcher and Craxi, the Italian prime minister, made a joint appeal to the US to consult with its allies before permitting its SDI research to violate their understanding of the ABM treaty, Kenneth Adelman, the chief American arms negotiator, was similarly blunt. 'It's nice', he said, '... to have the views of the allies... but it's nicer to have the views of the allies on issues they know more about.'[20] For the time being, however, such criticisms lacked their former weight because of Reagan's domestic difficulties and also, more importantly, because Thatcher had secured her invitation to visit Moscow in March 1987, the same month in which the Geneva talks between the superpowers to secure an INF treaty were convened. She had just met one president, and now she was off to see the other, while they had no plans for a meeting until a treaty had been negotiated. As Mitterrand, with whom she had consulted before leaving for Moscow, observed, Thatcher might not speak for the Community, but she possessed 'sufficient authority' for France '... to attach great interest to what she will say there.'[21]

   If there was to be a challenge to Thatcher's Soviet diplomacy, therefore, it could only come from Gorbachev himself. The obvious area of disagreement between them was on nuclear weapons, but over precisely what aspect of them became very unclear as a result of the accelerating pace of Gorbachev's 'international *perestroika*'. Thatcher, it had been widely expected, would use her visit to Moscow to pressure Gorbachev into reducing the Soviet nuclear arsenal or, more accurately, into removing preconditions he had set for reductions which he professed the USSR was otherwise ready to make. Before she had even left Britain, however, the particular concessions which were supposed to give substance to Thatcher's visit had already been made. As far as Gorbachev was concerned, an INF treaty was no longer conditional on either commitments to reduce British and French nuclear forces or American undertakings about its SDI programme. Without this mission, the old fears about being merely a middleman were revived. What would Thatcher do in Moscow, and how would she avoid appearing, in Robin Oakley's phrase, as a '... nitpicker, the mere messenger-girl of a tarnished American president'?[22]

As events transpired, the evaporation of Thatcher's arms control mission was not a problem. Indeed, in terms of the concerns voiced by Oakley it was a great advantage, for it is difficult to see how the role of a go-between could have been avoided if extracting Soviet nuclear weapons concessions had been the primary item of business. Great differences existed between Thatcher and Gorbachev on nuclear weapons, but they were not the differences which most people, even at this late stage, believed them to be. Gorbachev had always argued that the political value of nuclear weapons as, what US arms control negotiators called, 'bargaining chips' far outweighed any military significance they might have, and he was rapidly becoming convinced that their political value resided only in their being negotiated away. Thatcher, in contrast, had been one of those who had adhered to the strategy of the 'zero option' as a way of getting the USSR to reduce the number of its nuclear weapons or, failing that, as way of exposing the hollowness of its professed desire to get rid of them. In all the types of missiles subject to the INF negotiations, the USSR enjoyed a great numerical superiority, and it was widely assumed that the assymetry of sacrifice entailed by any zero agreement would prevent the USSR from accepting it.

It was this sort of thinking which led Thatcher to accept the perverse tactic, from the point of view of her own desire to keep nuclear weapons in Europe, of responding to Soviet concessions on particular classes of missiles by linking them to reductions in other types. Thus, when an agreement on long-range (between 1120 and

3100 miles) theatre nuclear forces (LRTNFs) seemed in prospect, it was linked to progress on reducing short-range (between 300 and 600 miles) systems (SRTNFs), which in turn was linked to reductions in battlefield systems and conventional force levels. What Thatcher feared was that success at each level would deliver a nuclear-free Europe dominated by a conventional imbalance in the USSR's favour, the very circumstances which had led Nato to build nuclear weapons into its strategy in the first place. Her preference, therefore, was to reach agreements short of zero in each class of weapons, and as this was overtaken by the pace of events which culminated in the INF treaty agreed to by the superpowers in September 1987, to draw the line at battlefield nuclear systems. 'A few' of these, she argued, should be retained and modernized as per earlier Nato agreements, and increased where necessary to compensate for any erosion of security resulting from the loss of theatre forces.

The extent to which this preference was clear at the time of Thatcher's Moscow visit in March is hard to say. Certainly, her general conservatism on arms control and her particular commitment to retaining the British deterrent received hostile attention from the Soviet press. What is clear, however, is that right up until the Moscow meeting, both sides were adhering to their established positions, the British advocating and the Russians resisting the extension of the scope of negotiations to cover systems in which the USSR possessed a numerical advantage. Earlier in that month, for example, Yevgenniy Primakov, one of Gorbachev's closest advisors on foreign policy had expressed the opinion that any European attempt to include short-range systems would prejudice the prospects for an INF treaty, and Thatcher had stated that while there was no explicit link between INF and shorter-ranged systems, she expected progress on them both '...at the same time'.[23] What is also clear, however, is that even if both sides were aware of the new differences between them resulting from the realignment of their countries' basic positions on arms control, neither was prepared to allow them to prevent a successful summit.

While in Moscow, Thatcher was treated as a visitor of the first rank. A private dinner with the Gorbachevs and informal discussions were allowed to disrupt the formal schedule. She was provided with uncensored time on Soviet television and permitted to meet leading Soviet dissidents. Thatcher reciprocated, of course. Afterwards, she described the meeting as 'historic' and professed that she would 'unhesitatingly' accept Gorbachev's word on any specific promise he made. She 'firmly believed', she declared, that it was in the West's interest '. . . to encourage and welcome the course on which Mr Gorbachev has embarked,' and a month later, she told a deputy Soviet foreign minister, Alexandr Bessmertnykh, that Britain would accept a global INF agreement rather than the proposal which the Americans still supported which allowed both sides to retain 100 launchers each. The success of the meeting was confirmed in December, when it was announced that Gorbachev would visit Thatcher on the way to his summit in Washington with Reagan to finalize the INF agreement. Originally it had been reported that he would be coming to London, but in the event his entourage only made a brief stop at Brize Norton, a Royal Air Force base, where they met leading members of the British government. Despite the abbreviated nature of the visit and the Europeans' refusal once again to give Thatcher a mandate to speak for the whole Community, the British regarded it as both a coup and a success.

Gennadiy Gerasimov declared the visit proof that as far as the USSR was concerned superpower relations were not '. . . the end of the story. We value relations with other countries.' As far as Thatcher was concerned, however, the point was that Gorbachev had come to Britain, rather than elsewhere, and it was she, rather than anyone else, who was able to greet him with the news that the EC supported the INF agreement. Notwithstanding the lower key treatment the meeting has received in subsequent memoirs (Thatcher's included), British ministers were reported as being euphoric with the meeting's success. Anglo-Soviet relations, one of them maintained, were now on 'a completely new plane', as a result of which one could not imagine Gorbachev 'cooking something up' upon returning to Moscow. As for Gorbachev, he had called Britain 'the third force' responsible for bringing about the INF agreement, with the result that there was speculation at least in the sections of the press which were favourable to Thatcher that, in the words of Andrew McEwan and Michael Evans, an international 'troika' was emerging of which Europe, or perhaps even Britain, was the third member.[24]

For the moment, at least, Thatcher's Soviet policy had succeeded where Churchill's, Eden's and Macmillan's policies had all failed in enhancing Britain's international standing and influence. Her success had been made possible largely by Gorbachev's belief that international recognition could help arrest the decline of the USSR and the erosion of his political position within it, but it was a tribute to Thatcher's own statecraft that he valued Britain so highly in this regard. On the basis of her relationship with Gorbachev, Thatcher could claim both a place at the superpower table and a major role in moderating the sources of Soviet conduct. These were both established objectives of postwar British policy towards the USSR, but if influence and status were not to be merely the ends of Thatcher's own diplomacy, then the question arose of how the new relationship might be exploited to serve specifically British interests.

Speculation in the press to the effect that Thatcher had succeeded in restoring a semblance of the Big Three partnership of the Second World War pointed to an increasingly obvious but radical and risky answer. The alliance of the Big Three had been held together by the common German enemy. The Federal Republic in 1987, of course, posed no threat to the international order comparable to those which Germany had posed in 1939 or even 1914. In Thatcher's view, however, its commercial strength and policy on European Union already directly threatened both British interests and British independence. Her problem was that, as long as the Cold War order existed, she could do little more than attempt to mobilize anti-German alliances with other members of the Community, and Britain's most likely partner, France, was very reluctant to be drawn. German and British diplomatic successes alike posed problems for France. The Germans, however, had the advantage of being undeniably European while, for France, a British success always contained within it the potential of an Anglo-Saxon or worse, wholly American triumph. As the Cold War order collapsed, therefore, the possibility of encouraging the USSR to perform Russia's traditional role as a counter to any bids for the mastery of Europe re-emerged. The only questions were, would Thatcher have the nerve to attempt it, and, if so, could she execute the *démarche* quickly enough, for the decline which had made Gorbachev so receptive to a partnership with the British soon threatened to make it not worth having from their point of view.

11 Thatcher's German Policy: The 'Unambiguous Failure'[1]

The German problem, as Thatcher called it by the end of her political career, was as it had always been since 1871. How should British foreign policy deal with a country which was both larger and wealthier than Britain, and had been prepared to use its advantages to achieve predominance in Europe? The answers given by successive British governments were that it should be countered, contained and, once American power established itself in Europe, converted. Countering Germany had entailed the construction of global alliances to conduct two world wars, but after 1945 containment and conversion predominated. Containment of the country was achieved by occupying and partitioning it into two German states, the Federal Republic (FRG) in the west and the Democratic Republic (GDR) in the east. These were admitted into regional military and commercial organizations which severely circumscribed their autonomy, and then their conversions were attempted by the imposition of social systems shaped by the ideological priorities of their respective occupiers and patrons. Comprehensive though this settlement might sound, however, it had not resulted from some grand plan of the victorious allies but rather from their failure to agree and the ensuing Cold War.

In the West, at least, this had important consequences. While many people might regard partition as an acceptable way of dealing with the problems resulting from Germany's size and wealth, no one could say that it was other than a temporary and unsatisfactory state of affairs brought about by Soviet intransigence. With the West Germans, they had to agree that at some point in the future, the two German states would be united if this was their wish. Further, the policy of containing Germany by enmeshing it in a series of regional organizations was modified in the western zones of occupation by the decision to use its resources to make a major contribution to the defence of western Europe. As a consequence, the FRG was encouraged to recover its former economic strength and allowed to develop its own powerful armed forces. Finally, the Cold War, together with the extent of the catastrophe which had preceded it, made the policy of conversion more successful than it might otherwise have been. The belief that a national identity could be substantially rebuilt and reformed with outside help appeared validated by West Germans who were content to do nothing which might upset the security arrangements within which they pursued their recovery and prosperity.

This was clearly confirmed by the contrast between the first really autonomous foreign policy initiatives of the Weimar regime in the 1920s and those taken by the newly-prosperous Federal Republic at the end of the 1960s. While the Stresemann government had sought to outflank the Versailles settlement by establishing a relationship with its fellow outcast, the USSR, Chancellor Brandt's *Ostpolitik* sought to stabilize the FRG's existing external circumstances by assuring its neighbours that it accepted the 1945 settlement. This is not to say that the penitent Republic presented its neighbours with no problems during its period of rehabilitation. Even in its truncated state, the FRG had become the most powerful economic force in the EC some 10 years before Thatcher became prime minister in 1979, and had put forward its views on the future of the Community with increasing confidence. Its governments consistently argued for a higher level of integration than that favoured by the other great power members of the Community, Britain and France, on the grounds of economic efficiency – the political and economic practices which had worked well in the Federal Republic should work in western Europe too – and on the grounds of security. If one wished the German problem to remain solved, they argued, create strong European institutions to keep the Germans under a form of control which they would find acceptable, and give them secure market access to keep them busy. As a result, both German preferences about the future of the EC and the ability of the FRG's people to exploit them posed problems for British commercial and political interests.

In addition, the FRG's membership of Nato in 1955 resulted in a new set of tensions over the alliance's strategies and, particularly, the place of nuclear weapons in them. The arguments were complex at times, but at their heart was the fact that the principal battles in any war with the Warsaw Pact would take place on German territory. The result was a division of opinion in the FRG between those who wanted nothing to do with nuclear weapons, and those who, accepting the need for them, argued that Nato could best deter by threatening to use them early and massively. The USSR should entertain no illusions that an act of aggression would not result in a major response, and if the worst came to the worst, an early response would entail most of the weapons being used on the territory of the GDR or further east. The FRG just might be spared the worst. This was unrealistic, but it was politically necessary because no FRG government could afford to appear as if it was willingly accepting that the country should bear a disproportionate share of the burden of Nato's nuclear risk. This possibility, of course, was precisely what the FRG's principal allies found far more easy to entertain, not merely for the selfish reason of trying to spare their own national territories but also, they argued, because the capacity to conduct extensive military operations on German territory before resorting to nuclear strikes against the USSR by systems based in the US or on submarines made America's commitment to the defence of Europe both easier and more credible.

Differences on security policy between the FRG and its allies were usually resolved by a combination of German accommodation to US military requirements and political compromises designed to sooth German sensibilities. Cruise missiles, for example, were located in several Nato countries to spread the nuclear burden, while Pershing II missiles were able to strike quickly deep into the territories of the Warsaw Pact, yet both were evidence of the US determination to deter by being able to fight a nuclear war in Germany. In these arguments, Britain usually sided with the US, and since the FRG could be relied upon to give way, they were a source of considerable diplomatic and political satisfaction. Like the British Army of the Rhine on permanent station in north Germany, they provided a reminder of the security arrangements upon which the FRG's prosperity continued to depend, and although troops and missiles alike were there to protect the FRG, their presence was also a reminder of the circumstances in which British forces had gone into Germany in the first place, as conquerors and occupiers.

During the Cold War, of course, this victors' sentiment was expunged from official consciousness. Arguments were between allies over policy and not over the rights which one country enjoyed within the other. Only in the most ignorant and ill-informed expressions of British popular culture was it explicitly retained, and then usually in the guise of lampooning those who had remained anti-German because of the war and the FRG's subsequent commercial success. When Anglo-German tensions emerged in 1987 over the INF treaty and what was to follow, therefore, the force with which these sentiments returned into official British circles surprised everybody, not least many of the officials themselves. Only when it became clear that the FRG was capable of mounting a challenge to its postwar probationary status, and unclear whether the US would meet that challenge, did the British begin to realize how important the Cold War German settlement had been to their own sense of security.

BRITAIN, GERMANY AND NATO'S POST-INF DEBATE

The German dimension to the INF treaty had posed problems for British interests even before it was signed, although through no fault of the FRG. From 1964 onwards, the US had provided the West Germans with a number of Pershing I missiles, while retaining control of the nuclear warheads which might be fitted to them in an emergency. The political significance of, in effect, allowing the Federal Republic a finger on a nuclear button, albeit a button which was not yet activated, was far clearer than its military rationale. Nevertheless, for several months in 1987, the USSR sought the inclusion of the German Pershings in the INF agreement. The Americans refused on the grounds that they were third-country systems and, hence, not part of the negotiations. Britain and France had a direct stake in this principle being maintained, for the inclusion of the German Pershings in INF would conceivably strengthen the Soviet case for bringing their own systems under consideration. Eventually, the impasse was broken by Nato offering parallel commitments to INF. After the agreement, the Germans would destroy the missiles and the Americans would then destroy the warheads, and this the USSR regarded as acceptable.

For the British, the doubtful precedent which this contrived arrangement still implied was offset by the advantages of removing the missiles. Gone, the German Pershings' aberrant arms control properties would pose less risk to Britain's refusal to include its own nuclear weapons in negotiations than if they were still in place to be talked about. However, in heading off the threat to one British interest, the FRG's eventual willingness (the decision had not been free from controversy there) to remove them presaged a threat to another. This was the retention of what the British called a 'sensible

mix' of nuclear and conventional weapons, including US nuclear
forces for the defence of Europe. To this end, it was clear in
Thatcher's mind that the retirement of Cruise and Pershing missiles
should not lead inexorably to the removal of other nuclear systems.
Indeed, even as the superpowers were finalizing the treaty, she
began to stress the importance of the modernizations to which Nato
had been previously committed, increasing, for example, the range
of the Lance battlefield missiles and equipping planes with air-
launched Cruise missiles instead of free-fall bombs. The FRG's
response to this was swift, if not yet as decisive as it was to become.
Kohl asked Thatcher for 'more sensitivity' to German needs
because, as sources pointed out, the vast majority of the 4000
warheads remaining post-INF would be used, if used at all, on
German territory.[2]

Neither Thatcher nor the Reagan administration were very sympathetic to this argument because of their shared assumptions about
how best to deter an aggressor, and because the German claim
reflected nothing new about the military realities of the situation.
Whether Nato strategy was based on the use of nuclear firepower in
tactical or theatre settings, and even if the new doctrines incorporating non-nuclear munitions were ever adopted, there could be little
doubt that if a war broke out, Germany would suffer terribly. What
was beginning to change, of course, was the FRG's sense that it was
beyond its power to do anything about this state of affairs, although,
for the time being, it was. In February 1988, the American Defense
Secretary, Frank Carlucci, confirmed that it remained the intention
of the US to modernize the Lance missile by extending its range. It
was also rumoured that Thatcher would accept 60 more nuclear-
equipped F111 aircraft in Britain and, on a visit to Nato, she called
on the alliance to stand by a decision taken five years ago to
modernize its short range weapons, for 'You do not deter', she said,
'with anything obsolescent.'[3]

Thatcher was not isolated in this position at this stage. The
following month, Nato was treated to the spectacle of a French
president and a French prime minister disagreeing with each other
in public over the issue. Mitterrand declared discussion of modernization at this time to be 'paradoxical' and 'inopportune', but
Chirac objected to the president's calling into question what, in his
judgement, was an integrated command matter. In October, Carlucci announced the US was developing a short-range attack missile
to replace free-fall bombs and Nato's Nuclear Planning Group was

reported as proceeding with its force modernization plans. Indeed, as late as January of the following year (1989), even West Germans were still arguing about the merits of modernization. Rupert Scholz, the defence minister, was in favour while, Genscher, the foreign minister and leader of the junior party in the governing coalition, remained opposed.[4]

However, the impetus for modernization steadily slackened throughout 1988. The Nato summit in early March maintained consensus only by a textual agility which allowed everyone to maintain that their position was the position of the alliance. References to force modernization were dropped in favour of a declaration that they would be kept 'up to date...where necessary'. The British claimed authorship, but the adjustments reflected sensibilities of the FRG. A year later, in April 1989, Kohl succeeding in getting Nato to postpone a decision on the modernization of the missiles until 1991–2, and less than a week after this decision, he sent Genscher and the new defence minister, Stoltenburg, to Washington for consultations about a new missile reduction initiative which the FRG wished to take up directly with the USSR. Both the Americans and the British called on the West Germans not to break ranks with Nato, the British, in particular, insisting that the FRG initiative would not become Nato policy because there was '...no question of us agreeing to negotiations'. As Thatcher told Parliament, Nato strategy could not '...be determined by one country', and presumably this was her message to Kohl when she visited him a few days later.

The meeting was not a success. The Chancellor maintained that the FRG remained committed to Nato's retaining some nuclear weapons deployed under the doctrine of flexible response. Indeed, the following year, he made it clear that he, like Thatcher, did not believe that a world without nuclear weapons was attainable. All he wanted to do was to satisfy the expectation of the German people that negotiations about the weapons which most threatened Germany should get under way as soon as possible, and this objective, the West Germans maintained, was entirely consistent with early Nato declarations about reducing the short-range, land-based nuclear systems of both sides to 'equal ceilings' in conjunction with conventional cuts and the elimination of chemical weapons. Should he fail to take this initiative, Kohl warned Thatcher, she might shortly have to deal with a Chancellor whose position on nuclear weapons was far more radical than his own. In Thatcher's under-

standing, however, any such talks could only raise expectations of a
new zero on battlefield nuclear weapons, achieved in a manner
which was completely at odds with Britain's interpretation of the
earlier Nato understandings. According to Howe, this was that
symmetry between the conventional forces of the two alliances
should be reached before talks began on reducing the USSR's
12:1 advantage in systems like Lance.[5]

Again, what were rapidly becoming Anglo-German differences
were papered over during the next Nato summit at the end of May
1989 by a careful formulation, drafted this time by the Americans.
The agreed statement essentially accepted the substantive points of
the British position that no missile cuts should take place until a
conventional agreement was fully implemented. In Thatcher's view,
however, it did concede the principle of negotiations on short-range
missiles, and by making proposals for major conventional arms cuts
at the same time, the Americans also held out the prospect to the
FRG that these talks might take place in the near future. Thatcher
tried to link the new position to a commitment to modernize the
Lance missiles, but without success.[6] Indeed, a year later at their
summit in Bermuda, President Bush told Thatcher that the US was
no longer interested in modernizing the Lance missile and at a Nato
meeting in Canada the following month, the British were reduced
to conducting a rearguard action with only modest American support. The West Germans suggested that all non-strategic nuclear
weapons should be negotiated away. The Italians and Belgians
agreed as far as missiles were concerned, while the Dutch argued
that at least nuclear artillery shells should go.

With only British support, the new American Secretary of
Defense, Richard Cheney, argued that the doctrine of 'flexible
response' must remain. There should be a mix of nuclear and
conventional weapons, and Nato should continue to be deliberately
vague about at what point they might be used in the event of a war.
By July 1990, however, even this position had been abandoned by
the Americans. 'Flexible response', President Bush suggested to his
Nato partners, might be replaced by an approach in which the use
of weapons was clearly envisaged as a 'last resort'. This clearly
accorded with the preferences of most of the Nato governments
and the sentiment then prevailing among their publics (if the truth
be known, most of the latter had probably always assumed that
flexible response meant using nuclear weapons as a last resort). The
British claimed Bush's letter showed the American nuclear guaran-

tee to Europe still existed by arguing that 'last resort' did not mean 'no first use.' This was probably so and, as subsequent events were to show, it probably did not matter for the foreseeable future. Even so, the Bush initiative represented a major defeat for Thatcher's foreign policy, for by the time it was made, it signalled far more than the fate of a hundred or so missile systems and many more obsolescent nuclear charges. It also confirmed the defeat of Thatcher's bold attempt to define both Britain's and Germany's places in the post-Cold War European order.

FROM REAGAN TO BUSH

In retrospect, it is possible to argue that Thatcher's attempt to become a member of a troika with the superpowers was never likely to succeed for long. The success of her approach was very much dependent on the personalities and circumstances of those with whom she aspired to work, and once George Bush secured the Republican nomination and succeeded President Reagan at the start of 1989, Thatcher was in trouble. Bush had already cast doubts on her ability to serve as a middleman between the superpowers when he was vice-president and, as president-elect, he had undoubtedly been unfavourably impressed by Reagan's attempts the previous November to present Thatcher as the representative of continuity and steady hand on the helm in a time of transition.[7] Upon his assuming office, therefore, the press detected a discernable tilt in American policy away from Britain and towards the Federal Republic, which the new administration denied only in the most pro forma way.

It was reported, for example, that Thatcher's call to congratulate Bush was not the first from a European leader to which he made a courtesy reply (Thatcher's staff countered by saying she had been unavailable to receive his call earlier). His first European speech was made in June in the Federal Republic, not Britain, and members of his staff were quoted as saying that the British portion of his visit was, by comparison, '...just a little pit stop'. Responding to events in Germany at the end of 1989, Bush caused the British discomfort by suggesting that '...the events of our time call for a continued, and perhaps intensified, effort by the Twelve to integrate...' This was precisely the opposite of Thatcher's position, and Bush called her to make clear that his comments represented

neither a change in US policy on the EC nor a snub to her.[8] If the
tilt was clear, however, the reasons for it were less so. The Americans may have been worried that Thatcher had become a victim of
her own version of the so-called 'Gorby-mania' which occurred
when ever Gorbachev visited the West in the late 1980s, and that
this was affecting her judgement when it came to Soviet policy.
Elements in the Bush administration subscribed to this view when it
was applied to their own former president, and two intelligence
assessments recommended that the tempo at which US–Soviet
relations were improving be slowed down. It was no longer certain,
they argued, that Gorbachev could remain in power, and for all the
talk of 'international *perestroika*', there was no reduction in the
resources the USSR was committing to its military effort.

Many people in Britain, in contrast, including Thatcher, believed
that the American tilt was driven by budget constraints and the
hope that a strong relationship with the FRG would permit the US
to withdraw some of its own forces from Europe. This interpretation of US motives seems the more accurate of the two for, after a
pause of several months, America's Soviet policy resumed, and
indeed accelerated the Reagan line of seeking to improve relations
with the USSR, not just because this was important in itself, but to
help Gorbachev survive. It is likely, therefore, that Bush's British
policy was not driven by fears that Thatcher had 'gone soft' on
Gorbachev so much as by the need to curb the expectations which
Thatcher and others had developed that her own involvement as an
independent, authoritative and possibly senior participant was
indispensable to the successful conduct of East–West relations.
Whatever the motives driving the new American approach, however, its most important consequence for the British was the decision, in effect, not to resist the FRG's calls for negotiations on the
short-range nuclear missiles. Without US support, Thatcher's German policy, so long as it was about missiles only, was effectively
blocked.

There was no one else to whom she could turn for effective
support. The smaller European members of Nato agreed with the
West German position and, while Mitterrand supported the British
conditions on negotiations over the short-range systems, France was
not prepared to align itself openly and strongly with Britain against
the FRG and the US. Most important of all, Thatcher's new relationship with the USSR was of no use on this issue. Indeed, her
post-INF policy, with its insistence on deploying what the USSR

called 'compensatory' systems, had become a major obstacle to the deepening of the new Anglo-Soviet relationship. Speaking at a dinner in honour of Oskar Fischer, the GDR's foreign minister, at the start of 1988, Shevardnadze accused Thatcher of seeking an arms build-up. A year later, and a month before the FRG's request to Nato for talks on short-range weapons, he offered unilateral cuts, communicated first to Genscher, in return for Nato restraint, and he repeated his offer at the Conventional Forces Europe (CFE) talks which began in Vienna the following March.

By the summer of 1989, Soviet diplomacy on arms control at least was firmly focused on the FRG and maintaining that the British position was damaging Anglo-Soviet relations. In June, for example, when Gorbachev negotiated an agreement on principles to guide Soviet-FRG relations, Gerasimov said that the USSR wanted positive relations like these with all European countries, '...but some countries are more willing than others.' 'In this sense,' he continued, '...West Germany is more willing than Britain.' Asked what Britain needed to do to be a better partner, Gerasimov replied that it was important not just to make agreements, but to follow them up. When he was asked whether a similar agreement to the one just negotiated between Gorbachev and Kohl was likely with Britain, he replied '...I don't think so. France is on the cards. Paris is the next stop.' As another Soviet spokesman had declared a few days earlier, he had to agree with the 'sad fact' that, because of 'rash moves' by the British, they were becoming marginalized.[9]

Both assessments were overly pessimistic. They were prompted by disappointment with the British and designed to pressure London into moving more quickly on its Soviet opportunity by suggesting that it might not always be there. Only two months earlier, Gorbachev had been in Britain visiting Thatcher. However, the April summit had been an awkward affair, rearranged because of the Armenian earthquake and, therefore, squeezed into an itinerary which included visits to Cuba and Ireland which the British found unflattering. The personal discussions between the two leaders were reported as satisfying, but in public Gorbachev launched no new initiatives and altered the content of his Guildhall speech to such an extent that Thatcher's response was misdirected. As such, the visit was a microcosm of all that had failed to happen in Anglo-Soviet relations since the INF agreement two years before in 1987.

The two leaders had continued to offer one another strong personal support. The following summer, for example, in a broadcast on the Russian service of the BBC, Thatcher had used Britain as an example of how peoples of different cultures could live together in a single political unit. We, she claimed, '. . . all owe our patriotism to the United Kingdom.' Accordingly, she told her listeners that when they obtained their '. . . freedom of culture and you are more confident of it', she thought it would 'strengthen' their sense of being a part of the USSR. In another broadcast in December 1988, after Gorbachev had cancelled the first date for his visit, she again called on Soviet citizens to support him for she was sure that living standards would rise once less was being spent on armaments. Gorbachev, for his part, reciprocated as best he could, expressing his desire to rearrange his visit to Britain as soon as was possible, inviting Thatcher to Kiev the following summer and, after another row about spies and expulsions had blown over, bringing the date of her visit forward to September 1989. However, the clearest expression of why Gorbachev attached so much importance to his relationship with Thatcher came in a letter to *The Times* from Nikolai Uspensky, who was Director of the Second European Department at the USSR Ministry of Foreign Affairs, two months before Gorbachev's visit in 1989. Thatcher, Uspensky wrote, had been the first in the West to grasp the significance of Gorbachev, *perestroika* and the changes occurring in the USSR.[10]

Personal loyalty based on feelings of gratitude and admiration which were mutual was keeping the new Anglo-Soviet relationship alive, but little else. As long as arms control and their differences on that dominated the relationship, there was nowhere for it to go. Lively arguments about how life, liberty and happiness might best be secured were all very well. In the absence of another major issue of mutual concern and interest, however, all Thatcher's Soviet policy could do, and did, was focus on keeping Gorbachev in office and on what she judged to be the straight and narrow road of reform. All he could do was endure what was, in effect, a condition of permanent probation, in the hope that something else might materialize. The September 1989 summit in Moscow seemed to fit the established pattern. Thatcher and Gorbachev were reported as having the customary frank, but mutually satisfying, exchanges. She praised his courage and wisdom while sticking to her own position on nuclear weapons. Meanwhile, the important and substantive developments on arms control were being negotiated in Wyoming by Shevardnadze and Baker. By her own account, however, and largely unreported at the time, Thatcher had asked for the early summit and during it had raised the question of Germany's future with Gorbachev, establishing that neither of them had an interest in a swift unification of the two German states.[11] At last, a major issue on which Anglo-Soviet interests might coincide had emerged.

FROM 'DAS VOLK' TO 'EIN VOLK'[12]

Even now, it is hard to grasp the pace of events which transformed German unification from a remote possibility to a virtual certainty in the space of a year. Until 1989, 'one nation, two states' within the 1945 framework had been accepted as a geopolitical reality in the West and had been required as a geopolitical necessity by the East. Even most Germans seemed to accept the situation. In 1985, for example, Kohl had told his countrymen that the return of Silesia, while he did not rule it out, had to be regarded as 'distant dream'. In Moscow, in the autumn of 1988, his suggestion that the 'unnatural' division of Germany might be brought to an end with the consent of the great powers received a brusque response from Gorbachev. The 'so-called German question', as he termed it, had been the result of 'historical development', and any attempt '...to upset what has been created...or push through unrealistic policies' was, in Gorbachev's view, '...an unpredictable and even dangerous business'. The following January, when Fischer declared that the Berlin Wall remained 'an element of stability in Europe', the architects of 'international *perestroika*' did not demur. As Shevardnadze argued, '...Each state has a right to build its frontiers as it wishes, so we must proceed from that and respect the sovereignty of the state.'[13]

This statement crystallized the confusion of aspirations and assumptions upon which Soviet diplomacy was by now being conducted. Gorbachev and Shevardnadze wished to grant their allies in eastern Europe full autonomy, hoped that the Communist leaderships were sufficiently representative of their peoples for a complete collapse not to ensue, and yet still professed to regard the Berlin Wall as a legitimate instrument of state security policy. However, the changes reflected in Shevardnadze's statement that, in effect, the Wall was a matter for the East Germans, together with his similar signals about the rustiness of the Iron Curtain and the mild Soviet response to political reforms in Poland produced swift and unanticipated results. In May, Hungary announced that it would remove the fences along its borders. At the beginning of June, Bush, on his German visit which had left the British feeling so uneasy, made the customary call for the USSR to take down the Wall, and Kohl declared that German unity was not a 'distant vision'. He wished to see it by the end of the century.[14]

All we want for East Germany, one West German diplomat was quoted as saying, '... is what the rest of Europe has enjoyed: self-determination.' As far as the question of unity was concerned, this was an ambiguous formulation, for the demonstrations which followed in major cities of the GDR were not led by people who sought unity. The following month, however, the Bavarian politician, Theo Vagel, raised the question of the rights of the one million ethnic Germans living in the 40 000 square miles of eastern territories allocated to Poland in 1945. Kohl's response was that, while the FRG renounced all territorial claims and was bound by the 1970 Treaty of Warsaw to this effect, the German question remained '... legally and politically unresolved'. In August, an exodus of GDR citizens developed which created crises at the Hungarian border with Austria and in the FRG's missions all over eastern Europe. In September, Hungary opened its border with Austria and, a week before Thatcher left for Moscow, Kohl travelled to the FRG's border with Austria to greet the 16 000 East Germans who entered that day.[15]

Like many other non-Germans, Thatcher probably wished that Germany might be kept divided permanently. The very best one could hope for from a successful unification was the emergence of a dominant commercial power in the EC, while a variety of nightmares centred alternately on Berlin and Moscow competed for the worst case imaginable. There was, however, no moral, political or legal justification for denying the Germans their right to national self-determination, only one conceived in terms of *realpolitik*. Accordingly, Thatcher adopted a policy of trying to slow down the process of unification which, it was becoming clear to everyone, would amount to the FRG absorbing the GDR. To begin with, this was an instinctive response to the problem on her part, although no more so than the response of those, like Leon Brittan, who argued that unification should be welcomed because opposing it would '... make it more likely to occur in the form which we would least want.'

Quickly, however, Thatcher developed a powerful argument in support of her calls for caution. Nothing, she said at the EC's

November 1989 summit in Paris, should be done which complicated Gorbachev's task in the USSR for, as she had said in London
a few days before, '. . . the very pace of change could put the goal of
democracy in jeopardy.' Therefore, there should be no discussion of
border changes or unification at this time, for the Cold War was not
over. Indeed, she was quoted as saying at Camp David a week later,
it would '. . . last until 2000.'[16] Instead, Thatcher argued, a multi-
party democracy should first be given a chance to develop and
flourish in the GDR. By her own record, she claims that she made
this particular proposal to Gorbachev at their September summit. It
does not appear to have been given a clear public airing in Britain,
however, for nearly another two months, indeed until the day after
the Berlin Wall was opened. Clearly, Thatcher did not relish the
position of supporting the continued existence of the GDR, a policy
which was sure to generate both internal and external opposition,
but just as clearly, the pace of events forced her hand. No one else
in the West, it appeared, was prepared to make the argument, and
so at the same meeting of Nato's North Atlantic Council at which
Bush had suggested intensifying the pace of European integration,
Thatcher declared that there should be no border changes for ten
years until democracy had taken root in eastern Europe.[17]

By arguing that German unification should be delayed to avoid
complicating the USSR's problems, Thatcher had placed Britain on
the brink of very deep waters. To enlist the support of the country
against whom an alliance is directed to shape the fundamental
policy of that alliance courted a diplomatic revolution in the fundamental alignment of the great powers. In the absence of support
from her other allies for her German policy, this, it seemed, was
what Thatcher was prepared to do, or at least threaten. The vital
question, however, was would, or could, the USSR respond. Until
the end of 1989, at least, her German policy was supported by the
actions of Soviet diplomacy. In October, Gorbachev had taken the
opportunity of his visit to the GDR on its fortieth anniversary to tell
the local leadership that it could expect neither political nor military
support from the USSR if it used force to resist change. As a
sovereign state, the GDR would have to find its own solutions to
its problems by pursuing reform. This was confirmed at a meeting
of the Warsaw Pact which adopted a declaration on non-interven-
tion in Bucharest at the end of the month. However, the Bucharest
meeting also declared that any discussion of Europe's postwar frontiers would be 'destabilizing' at this time. More to the point, Gor-

bachev and Egon Krenz, the new leader of the GDR, made it clear that German unification '...was simply not on the table.'[18]

There were, however, no similarly encouraging signs from her allies. Thatcher had, she claimed, obtained the agreement of the EC in Paris and the US at Camp David that international borders should not be altered for several years. The great ambiguity, however, was whether the intra-German boundary qualified as such a border. In international law, there was a strong case for saying it did, for the two German states had recognized each other, and the GDR had been accepted by the international community as a fully sovereign state when it became a member of the UN. Until the breaching of the Berlin Wall, at least, the French appeared to accept this view. Unification, Mitterrand had declared at the beginning of October, should not come for ten years, but this reservation vanished only to re-emerge briefly in December to secure Kohl's wavering adherence to the Delors Plan. The West Germans were more reticent. If events in the east made a swift unification possible, it seems clear that Kohl's government neither wished, nor considered it politically possible, to avoid seizing the moment. Nevertheless, Kohl still proceeded with caution. During the great events in Berlin he was in Poland and could be drawn only into declaring that a united Germany and a united Europe went hand in hand, a bromide, but one which rankled nevertheless with the British. Even upon his return home, Kohl declared that he did not think it would be possible for the GDR to join the EC before 1992. Not until over a month had passed did he finally declare: '...My goal, when the historical hour allows it, is the unity of the nation.'[19]

Silent (for once) were the Americans. Both at the Malta summit with Gorbachev in December 1989 and the subsequent Nato meeting, Bush's public attention was firmly focused on the big issue of the end of the Cold War and its implications for the American position in Europe. US policy on German unity was expressed in a set of principles after Malta. Any settlement, these declared, must respect all Germans' right of self-determination, take into account the FRG's existing commitments to Nato and the EC, involve peaceful and gradual means and respect the Helsinki Final Act's position on present borders. Given the tempo of events in the GDR, these principles shed very little light on American policy and especially how the US would react to a dash for unity. In retrospect, however, it is possible to see that they did clearly signal the chief US interest in the process. Unlike the British, who were convinced that the simple fact of a united Germany would have major implications for the European balance of power and their own influence, the Americans were concerned only that a united Germany, whenever this might emerge, should stay within Nato and the EC. In the meantime, the Bush administration appeared content to see how events would unfold, not least because throughout December it was absorbed with its plans to oust Noriega from Panama.[20]

GORBACHEV'S GERMAN GAMBLE

By the new year, it was clear that neither Gorbachev's nor Thatcher's policies were working, principally because, left to itself, the GDR continued to disintegrate. What Thatcher's policy badly needed was some sort of signal from the USSR that events were moving too quickly. Only this could have rallied European and North American support for her thesis that nothing should be done to make Gorbachev's situation more difficult. No such help was forthcoming, however, and not because the USSR already lacked the means or the will to risk signalling its displeasure at what was happening. Instead of trying to slow the process of unification, Gorbachev and Shevardnadze began to echo the calls of the left in both German states for a 'unified Fatherland' separate from either Nato or the Warsaw Pact.[21] Where Stalin and Khrushchev had both failed at the height of Soviet power, they hoped to succeed in decisively shaping the geopolitical future of a unified Germany. This was not the diplomacy of despair. It was a gamble premised on Gorbachev's tendencies to overestimate the extent of Soviet diplomatic influence and to believe the transformational rhetoric of his own new political thinking.

The gamble failed, not least because it destroyed the possibility of effective Anglo-Soviet cooperation on the German question. Thatcher could have worked with Gorbachev to slow the unification process down, but the last thing she wanted was a unified Germany unconstrained by Nato and the US. Within two weeks, the USSR had pulled back from requiring that a unified Germany be either neutral or a member of a new pan-European security organization which would both replace Nato and the Warsaw Pact. In early February 1990, Kohl obtained assurances from Gorbachev that the future of Germany was a matter for the Germans to decide. The only conditions he put forward were that any new German state or states which emerged should sign peace treaties with all the countries the Germans had fought during the Second World War, that German external borders should remain unchanged and that the prevailing military balance between East and West should be kept intact. The latter, should a single German state emerge, might be interpreted as requiring that it be neutral, but neutrality, as events were to show, was not the only way of preserving the semblance, at least, of a balance.

The initiative on the German question now resided entirely with the US and the FRG itself. Prior to Kohl's Moscow visit, the two countries had collaborated on creating a framework for negotiating German unification, the 'Two Plus Four' arrangements by which the two German states would work out the details and timetable under the supervision of the four occupying powers from 1945, the US, the USSR, Britain and France. The initial response of the British and French had been to prefer a 'Four Plus None' or, as Thatcher called it, a 'Four Plus Two' arrangement that put authority clearly in the hands of the occupying powers. Neither the FRG nor, more importantly, the Americans, were interested in this, however, and under considerable pressure from the latter, Britain and France accepted their formula.

As a consequence, when Shevardnadze travelled to Ottawa in mid-February 1990 for the 'Open Skies' conference on arms control verification, he found himself on the receiving end of what was, in effect, a *fait accompli* from his Four Powers colleagues regarding the details and directions of the unification talks. The USSR still preferred a neutral Germany, but this was no longer a condition of Soviet cooperation. Instead, it was reduced to hoping that a similar preference would be expressed by the citizens of the GDR through the ballot box, and that this would result in some arrangement, perhaps a confederation, in which the two German states retained considerable autonomy. The possibility of this, if the Germans so desired, was allowed to Shevardnadze in Ottawa, and on this basis the USSR accepted the 'Two Plus Four' arrangements. Towards the end of the month, Kohl and Bush, meeting at Camp David, presented a plan put forward earlier by Genscher for a unified Germany in Nato, but with 'special military status' for the territory of the former GDR as it soon would be. The eventual agreement, accepted by Gorbachev in July, specified that Nato forces would not operate there, while the Red Army could remain for a period of three to four years. To obtain the agreement, the FRG also accepted limitations on the size of its own armed forces and made cash payments to the USSR, avowedly to pay for the upkeep and eventual rehousing of the Russian forces in Germany, and on this basis German unification was completed the following October.[22]

POLISH QUESTIONS

For the British, at least, the heat should have gone out of the German question after Ottawa and Camp David. Thatcher's policy had been defeated by a German-American combination which no one else was prepared to challenge, and which the glimmer of a partnership with the USSR came nowhere near matching. Surely now, the challenge before British diplomacy was to prepare for life with the new Germany at the heart of Europe. British conduct at the 'Open Skies' conference suggested this to be so. Far better was it to be in the group making the demands, even demands with which they might not fully agree, than to be their isolated subject like Shevardnadze or, worse, like Italy and other Nato countries which had suffered at the hands of Nazi Germany, simply left out of the final talks altogether. Camp David, after all, with its troop ceilings and recognition of the Soviet desire to keep forces on German territory for some time (a desire Thatcher called 'quite reasonable') represented an attempt to limit the power of the new Germany.[23] As the five months between Ottawa and the final Soviet acceptance of its terms suggests, however, this was not so, nor was it the case that the responsibility for this delay was the USSR's alone. British diplomacy, and Thatcher in particular, for whom by now the prospect of isolation no longer held even the faintest terror, also played a part in keeping attention fixed on issues raised by German unification.

As late as the end of January 1990, Thatcher had told the *Wall Street Journal* that she still hoped that unification was still 10 to 15 years away, and the following month, while Kohl was in Moscow, she had told the Polish prime minister, Tadeusz Mazowiecki, that 'massive consultations' would be necessary before there could be unification talks. After Ottawa, she relaxed her position. Now, Thatcher said, there was '...no doubt that this coming together of the two parts of Germany is going to happen,' although she still reiterated her preference that it happen slowly in a call to Bush at Camp David before Kohl's visit.[24] Thatcher's acceptance of the inevitable, however, did not diminish the intensity with which she pursued the other major issue raised in her meeting with Mazoweiki, the need for guarantees of the Polish–German border. Poland had acquired territory from Germany at the end of the war from which much of the German population had been expelled. Most Germans regarded this as a painful loss, but the FRG, along with its Nato allies, had accepted the postwar boundaries in the 1970s as the price of *détente* and expanded relations with the East. By international law, therefore, and on the basis of the formal positions of all the concerned parties, there was no issue.

However, the progressive disintegration of the Soviet position in eastern Europe made it possible to question the validity of all the agreements which, while enjoying technical legality perhaps, had been imposed by the diktat of the allies to satisfy Stalin's security concerns. In these circumstances, some Germans began to ask under what obligations were they to maintain arrangements to which they had agreed when there was no choice, and people like Thatcher and Mazoweiki wanted to know what would be the consequences of such questions for the conduct of German foreign policy. They wanted a new set of guarantees, but this was precisely what Kohl found it very difficult to give. In February 1990, the most he would offer was a 'full understanding' of the proposal that the two German parliaments should issue a joint declaration acknowledging the border along the Oder–Neisse line, and a few days later he declared that German unification could not wait on the successful conclusion of talks with the Poles about frontiers. Then, in a major escalation of the dispute, he declared that any final settlement of the border would have to be linked to Polish compensation for the Germans removed from the eastern territories at the end of the war. It would, Kohl declared, be 'criminally negligent' of him not to link the question of the frontier to obtaining a promise from Poland to drop its claims on Germany and guarantees for the rights of the ethnic Germans in Poland. More of these, it seemed, had remained in Poland after 1945 than had previously been realized.[25]

For a short time, Kohl's requests created a diplomatic furore. The Poles had responded to his first attempt at linkage by threatening to renew their claims against Germany on behalf of Poles conscripted into slave labour there during the war. Now they fiercely lobbied the French and British governments to support their claim to a place in the 'Two Plus Four' talks. Gorbachev was reported as declaring that a united Germany in Nato was now '...absolutely out of the question', while Sir Ewan Ferguson, the British ambassador to France, called for strong Anglo-French cooperation as '...our interests coincide as never before.' From the start, Thatcher in particular offered strong support to the Polish government. Both their countries, she had said, during the Mazoweiki visit, had suffered experiences this century which had '...left their mark and which we are determined should not happen again,' and she again offered her full support and understanding of Poland's wish to see its border guaranteed just before Kohl's meeting with Bush at Camp David.

The Poles did obtain the right to a place at sessions of the 'Two Plus Four' talks which dealt with border questions, but not before Mitterrand had thrown France's weight behind them, deeming Kohl's undertakings 'insufficient'.[26] Thatcher had made the running on behalf of Poland, but, it appeared, Mitterrand's influence was needed before Kohl would yield to Polish pressure. However, this was not the case. The crisis was not ended by the operation of a reconstituted balance of power exerting diplomatic pressure on the Germans. Whatever front Thatcher may have aspired to create on the Polish question, little actually materialized. France's involvement was constrained by its need for German cooperation in its EC policy. The US was not interested and, interested or not, the USSR was unable to perform because of its own emerging problems in the Baltic states and because the Poles placed no more worth on Soviet guarantees than they had in 1939.

In fact, the crisis was ended for much the same reasons as it was started, German domestic political considerations. There is no reason to supposed that Kohl, as a German nationalist, did not wish that what had been German might be German again. There is no evidence to suggest, however, that Kohl, the practical and responsible politician, sought to translate those wishes into a policy of confrontation. As a politician, nevertheless, he was concerned to retain the support in the coming elections of both those on the German right who took this aspiration more seriously than he, and those across the political spectrum who believed that the request for Polish guarantees was nothing more than an attempt to humiliate Germany by maintaining its probationary status. Once Kohl had made his stand on the national question, therefore, he promptly jettisoned his counter-claims on the Poles in return for support from the Free Democrats, the junior and liberal partner in his coalition, for a swift unification. In mid-March, the coalition won the elections in both German states providing him with a mandate for this course. The following June, at the ratification of the unification agreements by both German parliaments, Kohl declared that '...Poland's border with Germany, as it stands today, is final' and the following November, he confirmed this when Mazowiecki made the first visit by a foreign head of government to the newly united Germany.

Mazowiecki's visit capped the first foray of a new German diplomacy which, while it did not jettison the 'good citizen' imperatives of the old FRG, was much less reticent about the price others must pay if German governments were to maintain the line. Kohl's March manoeuvre had been especially successful and, indeed, in the way he had exploited the interplay of domestic and international politics, there were echoes which were positively Bismarckian. Like Bismarck, however, Kohl was unable to execute his *finesses* without cost. The Polish dispute was swiftly resolved, but not in time to prevent a damaging series of revelations which appeared in an interview given by Thatcher to the German magazine, *Der Spiegel*, at the end of March and on the eve of a banquet at Saint Catherine's College, Cambridge which both she and Kohl were to address. In the interview, Thatcher quoted Kohl as telling her the previous December, 'I can guarantee nothing. I do not recognize the present borders.' Kohl denied this and Thatcher's claim that the FRG's constitutional court had overturned earlier assurances about the Polish border. As a result, he made no direct response to her call at Cambridge for 'a great alliance for democracy' and the continued presence of 'sizeable' American, British and French forces in Europe, as well as nuclear weapons. Those who wanted a united Germany '...to be firmly integrated into European structures', he replied, '...must logically support further progress in European integration.'[27]

Now it was Thatcher's turn to exploit a strong stand against foreigners for essentially domestic purposes, although, it must be said, with far less success than the German Chancellor. A depressing pattern of Anglo-German relations was allowed to emerge. Kohl, it transpired, had not consulted with Thatcher before the German elections as he had with other European leaders. The two governments experienced difficulties in settling the terms under which Royal Air Force training flights and British army manoeuvres were conducted in Germany and, after Nicholas Ridley, a senior minister, was forced to resign in July for expressing the opinion that the ERM was a 'German racket', the Prime Minister's Office signalled that Ridley's views were not without favour at the heart of the government. A seminar had been held at Chequers, the prime minister's official residence, at which a number of academics had presented an unflattering historical review of the Germans. They had been bad, the seminar concluded, but as Norman Stone argued, the West had civilized them.

There was nothing substantially inaccurate in this, but it was scarcely diplomatic to allow these points to surface, and it was poor diplomacy to let them surface as part of no policy.[28] For by then, Thatcher had no German policy, merely an anti-German disposition, and with this, Britain's allies were increasingly reluctant to be associated. Poland's sense of insecurity had been addressed on terms consistent with the requirements of both her honour and her need for German credits. France remained almost immobilized by the calculation that the costs of Franco-German enmity would be high and certain, whereas in comparison the benefits of Anglo-French cooperation were modest and their value difficult to discern. Thatcher's Soviet counterweight, after lurching alarmingly towards advocating her personal nightmare, an independent Germany free from all formal external constraints, had proceeded to disintegrate. She remained loyal to Gorbachev in his confrontation with Yeltsin, supported him in the battle of the laws, and on her final visit to Moscow in June 1990 predicted that the USSR would end the century on a high note.[29] Perhaps the new dimension to the empathy in their relationship provided by the trials of beleaguered leadership best explains this, however, for while, in the time remaining to it, the USSR was still to prove of use to the US, as an asset of British diplomacy in Europe it was already finished.

So too, it appeared, was Thatcher's diplomacy. By the summer of 1990, she had been driven from the field of international statesmanship, and it seemed as though her German failure had confirmed the arguments of those who believed she had become fundamentally unsound on international affairs. The whole policy, it could be argued, had been founded on her prejudice against the Germans, hence the petty and purposeless insults into which it disintegrated. It had depended on a series of miscalculations about the balance of power. Thatcher had overestimated the capacity of the USSR to shape events in Europe, her own capacity to shape American policy there and Britain's ability to compete with the FRG for influence over the other European great powers. Finally, her policy had been undone by her persistent failure to understand the nature of diplomatic influence. One of the reasons why she had failed to mobilize support from the other Europeans great powers, it could be claimed, was because she completely lacked any diplomatic capital with them. No one, in the end, was disposed to help Thatcher, even if she might be right, when the costs of cooperating with her would be high and the memories of her previous treatment of them remained fresh. Her critics had always maintained that Thatcher was rooted in her own particular sense of the past, and that she had aspired to conduct the diplomacy of Palmerston on the resources of Charles II. With US support, the illusion had been sustainable, but with the Cold War ending, her critics claimed, the illusion had been exposed and Thatcher's Britain was being left behind.

12 Thatcher's Statesmanship

Thatcher's German policy was not the high point of her international career. It was premised on miscalculations about Britain's capacity to influence the European balance of power and, even after it had clearly failed, was kept alive for domestic political purposes. Mitigating circumstances might be pleaded for this latter development. By the middle of 1990, Thatcher's position within the Conservative party had become very difficult, primarily because her commitment to a new system of local revenue-raising, the Community Charge or Poll Tax, was alienating many Conservative supporters. This had provided her rivals, former colleagues who had suffered at her hands and those who were convinced that Thatcher was past her best with the chance to rally support against her. Playing the German card and, thereby, drawing attention to her credentials as a patriot was part of Thatcher's response to this pressure. Had she been merely a domestic leader, this would have been understandable, if unwise. For someone who aspired to the status of an international statesman and who took the great power politics of sovereign states seriously, however, it was a major error. Thatcher's willingness to provoke Germany with no greater purpose than winning a fight within the Conservative party undermined her own claims about the importance of international politics and their emerging character now that the Cold War was coming to an end.

It was a low moment, but it was only a moment. Her opponents' claim that Thatcher's German policy demonstrated the extent to which she had lost touch with events proved false, as did the expectation that her failure in this regard would end her international career. Both were based on misreading the fluid character of post-Cold War international relations and the opportunities for leadership which they were beginning to provide. German–American cooperation had overwhelmed her on the question of unification, but this, in itself, provided dramatic confirmation of Thatcher's claim that Britain and other European states ought to be concerned about the new and expanded extent of German influence. Unbeatable though the combination turned out to be, however, it did not presage a new axis which would be opposed to British interests and influence on all issues.

Indeed, even before Germany was finally united in October,

Thatcher was provided with another opportunity for restoring her old security partnership with the Americans by Iraq's invasion of Kuwait. Her strongly voiced expectations throughout the summer and autumn of 1990 that the crisis would result in a war did not always help the efforts of President Bush to convince Congress that his military build-up was accompanied by a sustained effort to find a peaceful solution. No one, however, least of all the new Germany, could provide the Americans with the level of diplomatic and military support which the British were prepared to offer. Thatcher's domestic decline allowed her role in the Gulf crisis to be presented as a final encore recalling happier times for her, but there is no reason to suppose that her energetic response to this and other international problems would not have been maintained had she remained in office. Far from being a statesman grounded in the axioms of Cold War and World War, Thatcher appeared to have an appetite far stronger than that of her successors for responding vigorously to the challenges of a world no longer disciplined by the superpowers.

This appetite was partly a function of her personality. One suspects that had Thatcher been the prime minister of a smaller and less influential country than Britain, she would still have sought a role on the international stage, exploiting the opportunities provided by international organizations to build her own and her country's reputation. However, it was also a product of the positive reinforcement which Thatcher obtained when she applied her principles about what governments ought and ought not to be doing to the realm of international affairs. As in domestic policy, it was her sense of what governments ought not to be doing which was strongest. Whereas in domestic affairs, however, this sense was derived primarily from the economic liberalism Thatcher espoused, in foreign policy it was rooted in her instincts about society, and especially the nebulous character, as she saw it, of social pressure. Thatcher set little store by the idea of the social and this, as she discovered, was a very powerful and liberating assumption when one had to respond to demands from the outside world made by those purporting to speak for international society.

SOUTH AFRICA, THE COMMONWEALTH AND THE BRITAIN THAT CAN SAY NO[1]

In this regard, Thatcher's predisposition and its consequences were no more in evidence than on the question of the part international society should attempt to play in ending apartheid in South Africa. The former British colony and dominion of South Africa had been developed under the leadership of its white minority along explicitly racist lines. The non-white majority of the population had been denied basic political and economic rights for racist and religious reasons which secured the economic prosperity and attendant privileges of the white minority. The members of both the UN and the Commonwealth (the latter an organization South Africa had left in 1961 anticipating increasing criticism of its policies) had condemned these developments and had sought to punish South Africa for violating international standards by imposing economic and other sanctions upon it. These measures were most strongly advocated by those who were most offended by white racism and those who either did not care about, or would be least affected by, their immediate consequences. In contrast, those with most to lose from sanctions, among them Britain under successive governments of both parties, were the most reluctant to impose measures which, they argued, would probably not work or, by precipitating South Africa towards extremes of either right or left, would make matters worse.

Without British support, however, a system of mandatory and comprehensive sanctions could not be imposed on South Africa. Accordingly, when Thatcher came into office in 1979, no such system was in place. All that had been agreed to were some restrictions on the export of military goods and the exclusion of South Africa's citizens from the cultural and sporting life of the international community. Sanctions were seen as a judgement and as a supplement to the increasing internal pressures on the apartheid system which, from the point of view of the western great powers, often complicated a patient diplomacy they had been conducting to get South Africa to cease its interventions in neighbouring states and disengage from Namibia. Nevertheless, as the internal pressure increased upon the South African government, so too did the demand that Britain and countries like it should impose stronger sanctions to support the opposition to apartheid. It was these demands which Thatcher resisted, usually successfully and always controversially, throughout the 1980s.

There is no evidence to suggest that Thatcher sympathized with either apartheid or the racist assumptions which were made to justify it. She publicly opposed it on numerous occasions although, characteristically, not in terms of opprobrium at its perpetrators but

rather the fury she would feel at being treated differently or denied
her right simply because of the colour of her skin. 'Apartheid', she
said after the 1985 Commonwealth conference in Nassau, '...is
wrong, and it must go.' Her credentials in this regard were confirmed by no less a person than Nelson Mandela after he met her
in the summer of 1990. 'There is no doubt', he said '...that she is
an enemy of apartheid.'[2] It is equally clear, however, that Thatcher
saw this as no reason for severing all contacts with South Africa.
This was justified on diplomatic grounds. The world was full of
odious regimes pursuing policies of which Britain could not approve
but with whom it was in Britain's interests to conduct relations. We
talk to those with whom we disagree, she told Neil Kinnock after
President Botha visited Britain in 1984, and, as Malcolm Rifkind
pointed out the following year, if Britain could conduct a dialogue
with the USSR, it could certainly conduct one with South Africa.[3]

It seems likely, however, that Thatcher also did not regard apartheid as one of the worst evils in the world. The evidence for this is
circumstantial but compelling. Under pressure at the 1990 Commonwealth conference in Kuala Lumpur, for example, she suggested that some member states were '...jolly lucky it was us who
colonized them and not other people,' and throughout the period
she expressed sympathy for what under F.W. de Klerk became
known as 'group rights' for protecting minorities, the white one
especially. This was, Thatcher said, a 'perfectly normal idea'
although, as she stressed on other occasions, any such arrangements
would have to meet with the approval of the majority.[4] The precise
reasoning for her sympathy in this instance for collective rights is
not clear. Thatcher simply may have believed that, under its white
minority regime, South Africa had recorded achievements which
were superior to those of its neighbours, worth defending and
vulnerable if the abolition of apartheid was pursued to the exclusion
of all else. People who are right, in this view, should not be sub-
jected to the democratic tyranny of those whose beliefs are demonstrably wrong. It is more likely, however, that Thatcher accepted
the argument that politically illiberal states with liberal economies
would, sooner rather than later, be forced to reform by the requirements of intellectual-moral consistency and their own economic
success.

Thatcher's determination to maintain contacts with the South
African government and, indeed, to enter into a personal cor-
respondence with the country's last two presidents before reform

did not translate into tolerance of their policies. She frequently added her own personal condemnations, for example, to protests lodged by the British government about the way in which dissent was dealt with in South Africa. She also intervened to help secure a reprieve for six black Africans sentenced to death after they had been seized from a mob which had lynched alleged collaborators with the security services, and added her voice to the campaign for the release of Nelson Mandela, saying she would not visit the country while he remained in prison. Thatcher condemned the raids which the South Africans conducted upon the offices and camps of the African National Congress (ANC) in neighbouring states. In June 1986, for example, a series of such attacks was carried out just as a team of representatives of the Commonwealth known as the 'Eminent Persons Group' (EPG) were about to arrive in Cape Town from Lusaka. Speaking later in the month, Thatcher condemned the raids and said they had prevented a 'successful conclusion' to the EPG visit. When invited by Julian Amery to accept that, while the timing of the raids had been poor, they were no different in principle to Israeli attacks on Arab terrorists and US raids on Libya, Thatcher had refused. 'I hope', she had replied to Amery, he would agree that '...the South African case is different from any other, different in its apartheid, different in its degree of violence on all sides.'[5]

If she had little tolerance for the conduct of the South African regime, however, Thatcher had even less for the idea of imposing more sanctions on it and none at all for pressure on her to do so. The case against sanctions was simply made. Their likelihood of bringing about a positive change in the policy of the South African government was doubtful at best. 'Sanctions', Thatcher told Parliament in 1986, '...have never been known to bring about internal changes.' They were in place on military transfers, she said, but South Africa experienced little difficulty in procuring the weapons it needed. It manufactured what it could and smuggled in the rest. The idea, she declared on a visit to Nigeria in 1988, that the collapse of South Africa could be achieved by '...a concerted push from outside to destroy [its] economy was...an illusion.'[6]

In contrast, the costs of sanctions to Britain and to the South African people (the non-white majority, in particular) were all too clear. According to the Anti-Apartheid movement in 1986, 10 per cent of Britain's direct overseas investment went to South Africa. It was the principal foreign investor there and a major source of credit. Britain was also one of South Africa's most important trading partners, although less important than the US. Suspending commercial contacts would affect between 150 000 and 250 000 British jobs according to those who did not wish to see these links broken and, according to the government, 800 000 people there enjoyed residency rights in Britain. Should things go badly wrong in South Africa, they argued, Britain could expect to have to make arrangements for these people in addition to those who might come from Hong Kong before it reverted to China.[7]

Within Britain, the government's emphasis on the possible economic costs of sanctions was generally successful in preventing the demands for tougher measures gaining broad support. Therefore, sympathy for the predicament of the non-white majority translated into accepting the need for gestures of disapproval designed to isolate South Africa from the international community. However, claims such as the one made by David Owen after the failure of the EPG mission in 1986 that there was now '...a desperate need' for Britain to show it was '...prepared to pay a price to live up to its feelings of moral repugnance' resonated only with the most committed opponents of apartheid.[8]

Much harder to sustain and, therefore, much less successful was the claim that tighter sanctions would primarily hurt those whom the international community was seeking to help in South Africa. The problem with this was that it depended on seeing the operations of the market economy as the principal engine of social change in South Africa, rather than as the principal beneficiary of racial oppression. Economic growth, in this view, was creating a black middle class with rising expectations about its place in South African society and, if it were to be sustained, this growth would require expanding markets and, hence, new consumers who could only come from the non-white majority. Foreign businesses, in particular, were agents of change because they imported more enlightened business practices into the country. Sooner, rather than later, therefore, South Africa would reform, not because it was faced by threats, but because it was confronted, in Geoffrey Howe's phrase, by 'the overwhelming weight of commonsense...'[9]

This was not a claim with which many of Britain's partners in the Commonwealth and the EC were disposed openly to associate themselves, and their reluctance to do so was fuelled by the call of most of the non-white political leaders in South Africa for tougher sanctions to be applied. Some of these, particularly in the ANC, were quite simply hostile to the operations of the market, and sought its destruction as the precondition of freedom. Others, whether they agreed with Thatcher's claims about who would suffer and who would not, were convinced that the white minority's capacity to suffer at all and capital's ability to tolerate uncertainty were both extremely fragile. Therefore, pressure of this nature would precipitate reform, they argued, while any reluctance to apply it would encourage the South African government to drag its feet. The campaign against apartheid was waged by a coalition of countries and organizations in the UN, the Commonwealth and the EC. Since Britain's willingness to implement any measures adopted would be critical to their success, however, and that agreement, under Thatcher, was not forthcoming, the campaign was, in practice, directed not at South Africa but at Britain and, to a lesser extent, the US.

The call for stronger sanctions at the UN was customarily defeated by both countries' use of the veto in the Security Council. However, the same call within the Commonwealth and the EC was not so easily deflected. Within both, after 1983, a pattern of diplomatic activity was established in which everyone, including Britain, would agree to make representations to the South Africans about changing their policies, and in which everyone except Britain would agree that these representations should be accompanied by threats of further actions should the South Africans fail to comply before a certain amount of time expired.

The 1985 Commonwealth Heads of Government Conference (CHOGC) in Nassau, for example, agreed to new economic measures and decided to send the EPG to South Africa to engage in a dialogue and warn that further sanctions could be expected if there was no progress after six months. The British were party to the agreement, but Thatcher minimized both the extent of the new measures agreed to and the likelihood of further measures being adopted. A year later in June, the EC, under the British presidency, agreed to send Howe on another mission and listed a set of measures it was prepared to take should the mission not succeed. In August, however, a Commonwealth meeting in London deemed these steps to be so inadequate and Britain's commitment to them so weak that it was decided to establish a committee for sanctions policy on which the British were not represented. At the 1987 CHOGC in Vancouver, the final communiqué recorded Britain's dissent from five of its provisions, and at Kuala Lumpur in 1989,

Britain's assent to the final communiqué was undermined by a press release issued shortly afterwards in which Thatcher outlined the differences between her South African policy and the rest of the Commonwealth's.

In addition to the dominant pattern of British isolation and dissent, the dispute was also characterized by both its acerbic character and the sense of outrage expressed by Thatcher's principal opponents at British policy. At Nassau, for example, the Malaysian prime minister, Mahathir Mohammed, had claimed that a failure on the part of countries with 'the biggest economic clout' to impose sanctions would constitute an act of hypocrisy, and just before the conference, Gandhi had asked Thatcher to examine just where Britain stood on the issues of freedom and human rights. During Howe's visit to southern Africa on behalf of the EC, Kaunda of Zambia accused Britain and the US of 'kissing apartheid', and at Vancouver the Zimbabwean president suggested that Thatcher was guided by 'racial and financial motives'.[10] Thatcher, it must be said, replied in kind to such charges. Apartheid, she told Parliament upon returning from Nassau, would not be ended by '...creating unemployment in this country in order to create more unemployment in South Africa.' To Mugabe's jibe about her allegedly racist and financial motives, she pointed out that he would not have been at Vancouver at all but for the help that Zimbabwe had received from Britain under her prime ministership. And she countered the charge of hypocrisy on a visit to Australia in 1988 by asserting that South Africa's problems would not be helped by deciding '...from a comfortable luncheon or parliament building or international conference at a five star hotel...that there should be poverty and starvation on the part of a large number of black people.'[11]

Thatcher's opponents justified the degree of their hostility towards her in terms of moral outrage, for they shared the prevailing international sentiment that discrimination and exploitation on grounds of race were worse than discrimination and exploitation on other grounds. It was this which made it possible for South Africa to receive so much attention in a world replete with odious regimes and, indeed, made it possible for several of these regimes, which mistreated their own people on a no less discriminatory basis, to assume a position of moral ascendancy in the campaign for sanctions. As the dispute continued, however, it became clear that much of its intensity derived from the frustration which the two sides shared at their inability to get the other to budge.

The strategy of the states in favour of sanctions was to obtain British consent to a joint agreement which offered dialogue with South Africa now in return for a commitment to taking further measures at some point in the future should Pretoria continue to prove obdurate. After each meeting, however, the British challenged both the extent and the significance of the commitments to which they had agreed and attempted to insert their own reservation on the claim that sanctions would bring about a change in South African policy. The manner in which this was done, as much as the fact of it, contributed to the frustration of those opposed to Thatcher's position. After the Nassau meeting, for example, where, according to Lange, the New Zealand prime minister, arguments had taken place over whether the term 'sanctions' or the term 'measures' should be used, Thatcher called the measures agreed to tiny, signifying the point to journalists with her fingers. At Vancouver, her aides presented statistics from an earlier period to convey the impression that Canadian trade with South Africa was currently increasing. And at Kuala Lumpur, the press statement stressing Britain's differences with the rest of the Commonwealth was released just when the foreign secretary, John Major, and Sir Patrick Wright, the head of the Diplomatic Service, were celebrating the apparently successful creation of a new consensus with Chief Emeka Anyaoku, the Commonwealth Secretary-General.[12]

The problem as Ivor Stanbrook, one of her own backbenchers, saw it was that Thatcher appeared '...to condemn sanctions more than she condemned apartheid.' To be fair to Thatcher, it appeared that her opponents became more absorbed with condemning her than seeking another way forward once it was clear that Britain would not accept strong measures against South Africa. Nevertheless, it was she who was in the minority and, after the EC decided to send Howe to southern Africa in 1986, members of the diplomatic service, including the foreign secretary, became increasingly worried about the consequences of diplomatic isolation for Britain. It was Howe's opinion, for example, that should his mission fail, then some action would have to be taken, not because he had any great confidence in its effectiveness, but to deflect charges that Britain was neither seeking consensus nor acting in good faith. To this end, and in his capacity as President of the European Council, Howe began to support some measures against South Africa with which his government did not agree. Thatcher's response was to assume a tighter grip on South African policy by cutting the Foreign Office

from her deliberations, the better to maintain her line of no substantive concessions to the pressure for sanctions. The threat of
diplomatic isolation was, for her at least, an empty one.[13]

Whether the sanctions sought by the rest of the Commonwealth
would have had a major influence on events in South Africa is
difficult to say. As it happened, events there unfolded at their own
pace, both at the general level of the struggle between broad social
movements and the particular level of individual human strengths
and weaknesses. President Botha, whose own commitment to real
change in South Africa was questionable to say the least, suffered a
stroke and was levered out of his positions of power. About his
successor, *The Times* saw fit to comment that 'Nothing in Mr de
Klerk's background suggests that he is tomorrow's man' but, of
course, he was. And as Thatcher herself was fond of pointing out,
the economy which he and, eventually, Mr Mandela inherited, was
in better shape for its not having been exposed to comprehensive
sanctions.[14]

Opinions differ as to whether this was one of the more elevated
episodes in postwar British diplomacy. Thatcher's opposition to
sanctions on the grounds that they would not work was partially
undermined, at least, by her strong support of them in other circumstances, most obviously when Iraq invaded Kuwait in the summer of 1990. All she could argue then was that Iraq's actions were
more wicked and more dangerous than those of South Africa and,
she could have pointed out, economic sanctions were only one
aspect of the UN's response to Iraq's aggression.[15] Elevated or not,
however, it was an important episode for postwar British diplomacy.
It demonstrated the hollowness of the axiom that British influence
depended upon the country being seen as one of the principal
supporters and shapers of collective action undertaken by the international organizations of which it was a member. The other members of organizations like the EC and the Commonwealth were
either unable or unwilling to force Britain to conform and its refusal
to do so had few lasting consequences. Britain was not asked to
leave the Commonwealth and, *pace* those thinkers on the political
right who thought it would have to anyway, the government also
came under little internal pressure to quit. Indeed, if influence
means having a concrete effect on outcomes rather than just participating and being seen to participate, then British influence in the
postwar Commonwealth was never greater than under Thatcher's
prime ministership.

THE POSITIVE CONTRIBUTION

Rediscovering that one could say 'no' openly and clearly in the Commonwealth, the EC and even to the Americans without the ceiling falling in was an important achievement of Thatcher's statecraft for British foreign policy. However, it could constitute no more than the foundation of a claim to international statesmanship. On its own, the diplomacy of resistance, even successful resistance, is the diplomacy of weakness, and international statesmanship is not usually associated with defending the interests and sensibilities of weak states. It involves playing a creative role in the great international events of one's time and, less certainly, having a lasting and positive impact on the conduct of international affairs. With regard to the first criterion, there can be little doubt that Thatcher qualifies as an international statesman of the first rank. Britain's international reputation and still considerable strength made it possible for her to be involved in the major international questions of the 1980s, but it was her own personality and ideas which enabled her to exploit the opportunity provided to her by her country with a degree of success not enjoyed by any other recent British prime minister.

To be sure, there were lots of issues of importance to British interests in which Thatcher was only peripherally involved and which the Foreign Office handled with considerable success. She played no part, for example, in the negotiations over Hong Kong and with Ireland until it came time to provide Britain's minimalist interpretations of what the treaty drafters in both cases had been constrained to leave opaque. Thatcher also played little part in the British efforts to achieve an international agreement on the control of chemical and biological weapons at Geneva or to achieve a ceasefire in the first Gulf War between Iran and Iraq undertaken at the UN. Her involvement in Britain's Middle East policy was, if entertaining and effective on occasions, essentially episodic.

However, on the traditional big questions of war and peace between the superpowers, as well as the new big questions about Europe's future political and economic arrangements, she was nearly always at the centre. Thatcher played a critical, if supporting, role in encouraging the American decision to confront the USSR, and a leading role in ensuring that the confrontation was conducted on essentially British and European terms. When American diplomacy lost its direction during Reagan's second term, it was Thatcher who provided the Western response for which

Gorbachev was looking with such success that she, briefly, appeared to become a third force whose involvement would be essential to the successful conduct of East–West relations. However, Reagan and Gorbachev had provided her with that opportunity and, with the former's replacement by Bush and the latter's increasing decline, it quickly disappeared. All the diplomatic talent in the world could not recreate the role on British influence and power alone, and the Europeans were no more willing to confer their authority upon Thatcher in this regard than they were to confer it upon each other.

With regard to the second criterion of statesmanship, having a lasting and positive impact on the conduct of international affairs, Thatcher's claim is more problematic. So too, however, is the criterion. Metternich and Bismarck, for example, arguably had no lasting diplomatic legacy. Metternich was swept away with the international order he created and Bismarck's disintegrated when he left office because, it is alleged, no one else was capable of running it. However, both are rightly regarded as international statesmen because of the central roles they played in the great international questions of their respective times. Indeed, since the idea of statesmanship presupposes that certain individuals are capable of making a major impact on international affairs, it may reasonably be claimed that the subsequent collapse of everything a statesman worked for confirms their centrality to what was achieved just as much as it does the limitations of their achievements.

Even taking these reservations about the legacy criterion into account, however, it must be concluded that Thatcher's achievements in this regard were more limited. They were so because, by philosophy, instinct and inclination, Thatcher was not a political builder – quite the reverse. For her, ideals and interests in the world were not to be realized by the patient construction of virtuous restraints upon the impulses of human weakness, but by removing the constraints imposed upon those whom she regarded as the virtuous and strong. Accordingly, where she left her most lasting imprint on the conduct of international relations, within the EC, it was a negative one. Thatcher blocked the emergence of a more integrated policy process committed to the increasingly centralized regulation of civil society in the Community and, while she often acted alone in this, her colleagues and successors in Europe have been willing to accept the arrested process which was her legacy, at least for now. However, her success in torpedoing the Maastricht treaty from her political grave, as it were, was not just a negative triumph, for it and the European policy from which it resulted were the fruits of an orientation which was remarkably suited to the conduct of post-Cold War international relations.

If Thatcher left no international or regional order of which she was a primary architect as her legacy, then she did leave a way of conducting oneself in the economically liberal, but politically nationalist, world which was beginning to emerge. One of the great successes of America's Cold War diplomacy had been to convince the European great powers of their powerlessness while nearly every other type of actor from transnational corporations to mobilized small states and guerrilla movements was being acclaimed as the newly influential. The consequences of the world war for Europe, the Soviet threat and the attractions of free-ridership all played their part in making the British, Germans, French and Italians receptive to the news of their own emasculation as great powers. However, the ideological authority conveyed upon the superpowers, and particularly the US, by their own success was of critical importance.

Collaboration through denationalized and depoliticized institutions was the dominant theme of US diplomacy in Europe during the Cold War. With the fading of the imperatives to listen to this message, it is not surprising that older patterns of behaviour began to reassert themselves among the European great powers. The most spectacular example of this was West Germany's dash, after forty years as a sober, bourgeois trading republic, for unification at the first opportunity, whatever the cost. However, it was Thatcher, for all she was the Americans' most faithful ally and admirer, who, much to their chagrin, led the attack on their preferences about how European great powers ought to conduct themselves. For her, a world of national states committed to liberal economic and political principles, free, within the context of general rules about promises, violence and the place of governments in economic affairs, to pursue their own interests as they saw fit, was neither a half-way house to a better institutionalized world order nor the best to be hoped for, given human capacities for laziness and self-delusion. It was a desirable state of affairs for people who sought to prosper liberally but live nationally. There was no reason, in Thatcher's mind, why 56 million people who regarded themselves as British, should not trade and invest freely, yet retain the political independence to regulate their own common affairs and define their interests and preferences in the outside world. In contrast, there were many reasons, both moral and practical, why they should not be prevented from doing so.

This rediscovery of what it was possible to do was the legacy of Thatcher's statesmanship to Britain and the other European great powers. One needed neither the fragile national sensibilities nor the mercantilism priorities of *le Gaullisme* to pursue *les politiques de la patrie et de l'indépendance*. Legacies are bequeathed, however, but they can also be rejected and, while it is unwise to make an assessment on the basis of a single successor, it is difficult to ignore the extent to which Thatcher has failed to leave her stamp on the conduct of British foreign policy. The latter, while not reassuming its pre-Thatcher preoccupation with preserving status and influence through responsible conformity, has been conducted with less energy and vigour, at least at the level of the political leadership. It is possible to explain this in terms of the domestic and party political problems confronting her successor, as well as the general uncertainties which quickly overtook the initial widespread hubris about a New World Order being within reach and the End of History being in sight. It is also possible to claim that Thatcher accomplished what she did because of who she was and that people like herself are few and far between. If no one but Bismarck could operate Bismarck's system, then perhaps no one but Thatcher could conduct Thatcher's foreign policy.

THATCHER'S DIPLOMACY

There is, however, a reverse side to the great person argument which suggests that, whatever the essential soundness of her core principles, Thatcher's own personality was the primary obstacle to their successful implementation. She never developed, in this view, a feel for international relations or, more importantly, for the requirements of diplomacy, and because she insisted on dominating the process, the damage Thatcher inflicted on the actual conduct of Britain's foreign relations was a far greater legacy than what she attempted to achieve and, thus, her approach was one which no subsequent British prime minister should seek to emulate.

In so far as international relations conform to Churchill's powerful image of a mysterious and subtle chess-like game of opaque stratagems and whispered outcomes, then there is some substance to the claim that Thatcher was not a natural player and never became wholly proficient at it. International relations made her impatient, and on military affairs in particular, perhaps because she was a woman, she sometimes sounded uncertain and unconvincing. The impression of uncertainty was strengthened by the fact that on foreign affairs, where great speeches are at a premium, Thatcher made few even good ones. Her record in declaratory foreign policy rests on a few great phrases, not great speeches. There is little evidence to suggest, however, that her uncertainties, such as they were, ever damaged British policy or interests. No record exists of the sort of gaffes which President Reagan was capable of making, for example about recalling missiles or the end of apartheid in South Africa, nor of claims like those made by her predecessor, Harold Wilson, about Britain's world power status and frontiers on the Himalayas (although she did manage to refer to the Pakistan–Afghanistan border as the frontier of freedom on one memorable occasion).

Thatcher's impatience with international relations, however, is another matter. Howe's criticisms of her in connection with EC negotiations have already been noted.[16] Episodes like the press conference in which Thatcher suggested the tiny character of the concessions on South African sanctions which she had made to the rest of the Commonwealth, or allegedly spoke to her European colleagues in direct and unflattering terms, were unfortunate. Over the sanctions, for example, she robbed herself of any personal gains she might have obtained from her concessions. Certainly, the requirements of diplomacy, indeed of simple civility, dictate that one should not be rude to other people, both because it is wrong to give way to one's emotions and because it is likely to be counter-productive. This said, however, there is no evidence to suggest that Thatcher's conduct, even when it irritated people like Howe and made them work harder, had a substantive impact on British inter-ests.

In fairness to Thatcher, it must be added that she was right to be impatient with much that happened or, more often, failed to hap-pen because of the requirements of diplomacy. And in this regard, it is also worth recalling that foreign policy and diplomacy, while overlapping activities, are not exactly congruent. It is the job of diplomacy, as the management of international relations by nego-tiation, to avoid or blunt the differences which may give rise to conflict between states if at all possible, but this is not a priority of policy. The latter is concerned, first and foremost, with advancing interests. Where differences existed, therefore, it was not Thatcher's job to be polite, and there is little evidence to suggest that other leaders felt unfairly constrained by this consideration in their dealings with her or each other.

This distinction between the priorities of diplomacy and foreign policy, however, implies that there exists an important relationship between the two which needs to be taken care of within the foreign policy process of a country. It is here, and not in her relations with foreigners, that the worst problems with British foreign policy under Thatcher are to be found. A powerful impetus to Howe's remarks about Thatcher's dealings with foreigners was that he too had suffered from what he judged to be her directness and rudeness.[17] He did so, not just because of political or personal differences, but also because, whatever its professional merits in the conduct of diplomacy, Thatcher did not trust the Foreign Office's instincts over policy and interests. This suspicion long pre-dated her falling out with Howe, for she was convinced it remained a bastion of defeatism and appeasement, and the loss of the Falkland Islands confirmed this view, so much so that Thatcher determined to have her own foreign policy advisor.

If the purpose was to improve the relationship between the political direction of policy and its execution by diplomacy, however, then this practice was not a success. Thatcher saw special advisors like Sir Anthony Parsons and Sir Percy Craddock as being more inclined to curb her instincts from a Foreign Office perspective than to ensure that the political direction of policy was more effectively implemented by their former colleagues. Charles Powell, also seconded from the Foreign Office, prospered as Thatcher's Private Secretary and foreign policy advisor, but largely because he came to share her views, and this did nothing to improve the relationship between policy and diplomacy. Indeed, Powell was one of the principal agents of Thatcher's eventual attempts to circumvent the Foreign Office on matters of foreign policy about which she had strong preferences. Thus, on visits to Moscow, for example, and, most notoriously, at the CHOGM in Kuala Lumpur in 1989, Foreign Office officials and experts were virtually excluded from participation. And when Thatcher supporters had campaigned for the creation of a foreign affairs unit in Downing Street the previous year, it was Howe who had led the counter-attack. There was no need, he had argued in a letter to *The Times*, for an American-style National Security Council because there was no

Foreign Office bureaucracy pursuing its own line at odds with the government.[18]

It is impossible to distinguish clearly the extent to which these arguments were driven by genuine differences over the substance of foreign policy, concerns about Thatcher's style and the struggle for power and influence within the Conservative party which dominated the final years of her prime ministership. What is clear, however, is that throughout her tenure, Thatcher never established firm control of the practical execution of British foreign policy. To begin with, of course, she did not care to and was content to leave the Foreign Office to itself and those in the Conservative party who were least in sympathy with her while she attempted to preside over the revival of the British economy and society. The war for the Falkland Islands changed all that, partly by making Thatcher realize the importance of foreign affairs to her agenda, but also because she caught David Watt's 'foreign bug'.[19] Being successful abroad was both personally stimulating and electorally advantageous.

It is this combination, perhaps, which encouraged her to appoint Howe to be foreign secretary after the 1983 election. He was a close ally, having, as Chancellor of the Exchequer, presided over the most important and most politically difficult policies in the Thatcher government's strategy for reviving Britain. Howe was also, however, someone whose personal, political impact was never likely to overshadow hers. By temperament and training, he was well suited to the demands of diplomacy while Thatcher directed policy and executed the big *démarches*. Unfortunately for Thatcher, the qualities which made Howe attractive as a foreign secretary also made it very likely that he would succumb to the errors, in her view, of the Foreign Office outlook. It was one thing to persuade the Treasury to accept a new orthodoxy built on tight money and balanced books. That was preaching to the converted. It was another to ask the Foreign Office to place Britain's influence at risk and its relationships under strain for the sake of a new conception of British interests.

This, as it turned out, was never particularly to Howe's liking, and by the end, Thatcher had become convinced that the foreign secretary had not only been 'captured' by his Department of State, but also aspired to use its doubts about British foreign policy as one of the planks in his own campaign to replace her. Why Thatcher did not dismiss him sooner, and why, to judge by the extent of the differences which Howe subsequently maintained existed between them, he did not resign, remain unclear. She may have underestimated the extent of their differences, or she may have calculated that even the nature of his opposition would merely add to the grey background against which she aspired to shine. Howe, clearly, liked being foreign secretary, probably lived in hope of even better things, and there was no evidence to suggest that one's prospects of leading the Conservative party were enhanced by resigning from a Conservative government.

Thatcher, of course, was in a difficult position. If she kept appointing people as foreign secretary whom she judged were unlikely to pose an effective political threat to her, then she was unlikely to get the vigorous sort of foreign policy which she sought without, in effect, becoming her own foreign secretary. If, on the other hand, she appointed a strong person, then not only had she to surrender one of her own strong cards, but she also had to transfer it to a potential rival. Thatcher considered being and, in effect, on the big questions tried to be her own foreign secretary, but it did not work. There was just too much to do. As a consequence, the relationship between the political direction of British foreign policy and its diplomatic execution was never satisfactorily resolved under Thatcher's government and, indeed, over time it began to deteriorate, the victim of both political and personal differences.

Where the burden of guilt lay in the latter regard is not easy to say. According to Thatcher's opponents among those who had worked with her, and it must be said that an uncomfortably large number of the latter came to define themselves as the former, she was the problem. She became, according to Howe, impossible to work with on anything but her own terms, and these, he believed, were increasingly unacceptable. It is difficult to demonstrate with any precision, but it is also difficult to avoid the impression that Thatcher's sex played a part both in creating this opposition and explaining its intensity. There is circumstantial evidence to suggest that Thatcher either did not recognize or did not care about the particular codes of restraint for avoiding the public or peer humiliation of her colleagues which governed the way the men around her fought and argued their differences. And, there is circumstantial evidence to suggest that many of these men were extraordinarily sensitive to even acceptable forms of criticism and disagreement when their source was a woman. Highly speculative though these impressions might be, however, one is drawn, unavoidably, to the conclusion of the defence lawyer in *The Caine Mutiny* – with a little more help, the Captain might have done a better job.[20]

No matter who was primarily at fault and why, however, the disagreements at the centre of government had important consequences. The cause of imparting political direction to the Foreign Office was gravely weakened. That institution's reputation for being even worse than its fellows in believing that it knows better than its transient political masters is probably unfair. It does, as its defenders are quick to point out, respond to strong direction, but it also has a very strong set of institutionalized beliefs about the nature of the external constraints under which British foreign policy operates. When the call for it to revise its views about those constraints or to ignore them was not made by a unified executive, its prejudices about the transient nature of all politicians seemed confirmed. Then, it was so much easier for the Foreign Office to trust to its own instincts, especially as its own minister increasingly revealed himself as sharing them.

The disagreements also ensured that the Thatcher approach to foreign policy would not be maintained by her successors, at least in the short to medium term. This was because key elements of it, the emphasis on national independence and economic openness which resulted in her Euro-scepticism and atlanticism, had become closely identified with her defeat and with the most disagreeable renderings of her personality. There was even a suggestion from Thatcher, two days before she resigned, that implied that she might have devoted too much attention to international affairs. In a press interview, she called 1987–8 '. . . the two I lost,' because these were the years during which, in her view, Nigel Lawson, Howe's successor as Chancellor of the Exchequer, had pursued expansionary policies which permitted the revival of inflation.[21] It was during those two years, of course, that Thatcher's reputation as the leader of the potential third force in world affairs had reached its brief but impressive zenith. Not only was it impossible to preside over national economic policy and be an international statesman at the same time, therefore, perhaps her original instincts about the relative importance of the two had been right after all. Had she taken care of the former, then the rest would have fallen into place.

To judge by Thatcher's subsequent comments on foreign policy and world affairs, this was probably a transient sentiment at most. If it were not, however, then this is unfortunate, for the answer to Thatcher's problem, both then and now, could not be to neglect

foreign policy. Subsequent events quickly showed that the fundamental principles upon which she based her own statecraft were
broadly right. Within two years of her resignation, the EU, and
Britain in particular, had demonstrated the sort of economic and
political integration which Thatcher had opposed to be unsustain-
able. The monetary system collapsed and the ability of the EU to
perform as a single diplomatic actor on questions of international
peace and security had been exposed as non-existent by events in
the Balkans following the partition of Yugoslavia. The only country
which retained both the will and the capacity to try to act effectively
in terms of maintaining international order remained, as Thatcher
had always argued, the US.

Whether US policy in the Balkans and the Middle East will prove
successful remains difficult to determine as does, more importantly,
the extent of America's willingness and capacity to maintain its
present level of engagement in the wider world. Thatcher's confidence in the latter may be misplaced, but even if it is, this does not
invalidate her view that a special Anglo-American relationship
remains both a possible and beneficial objective of British policy.
To Britain's supreme good fortune, the US remains well-disposed
towards both Britain's view of the world and British interests in it. It
may not be the last superpower, a hegemon capable of maintaining
global order, but it remains the wealthiest and most powerful country in the world, and there is no evidence that any other country or
coalition of countries is in a position to replace it. Thus an alliance
with the US remains a central objective of British foreign policy for,
paradoxically, the more pessimistic the assessment of America's
ability to maintain its present level of international engagement is,
the more important that alliance becomes. Ideally, the US would
retain an interest in maintaining the European balance of power. If
this becomes more difficult, however, and the US decides to cut its
international commitments, then Britain must do what it can to
ensure that it is not among those which are cut, for big and powerful friends are even more important in the absence of hegemony
than they are in a well-regulated world order. Unfortunately, such
an alliance remains beyond the means of British diplomacy to effect
unless the Americans are willing, and no future British prime minister can count on having the sort of relationship which Thatcher
enjoyed with Reagan.

In an era when the USSR collapsed into its constituent nationalities, the EU purports to effect a triumph of institutions over

culture without the incentives and sanctions historically associated with the successful construction of political orders. Encouraged by the discipline of the Soviet threat and the rewards provided by the US, European elites formed in the midst of the catastrophe of European nationalism succeeded in keeping their countries engaged in practical collaboration. The Germans, in particular, cultivated and used their prosperity with admirable restraint, although the intensity with which even the postwar elite pursued unification and the new Germany's first *démarche* on the world stage – its Balkans policy – both had unfortunate and disturbing echoes. Leaving aside whether a common European identity is desirable, however, no progress has been made in creating one strong enough to sustain much beyond self-sustaining declaratory activity and a modest system of patronage for obtaining cooperation both inside and outside the Community.

Indeed, where the most impressive integration has been achieved, between Germany and France, it remains driven by fear of the past rather than inspired by a sense that the past has been transcended. Even the strongest enthusiasts for further integration are incapable of refraining from adding 'or else' to the end of their arguments. With the passing of the old external constraints and incentives, therefore, and the emergence of national elites who, rightly or wrongly, are not burdened by either a sense of fear of the past or a collective sense of guilt for the parts their parents and grandparents may have played in it, it is difficult to see how an international politics of nationally based great powers will not revive in Europe.

If it does, then the great powers will have enough disagreements among themselves which have to be managed without embarking on collaborative projects for which the political will does not exist and without exploiting the multiple opportunities which do for interfering in each other's internal affairs. If such disagreements and other problems are to be successfully managed, then they will be so by working with the real and successful political communities to hand, sovereign states, and not by attempting to work around or build over them. This was the argument on which Thatcher sought to base British foreign policy and called for others to base theirs. She may have made it too acerbically at times and, like her European opponents, she may have concentrated overly on the fear of what particular nations might do rather than on the enduring democratic and political fact of national identification and the positive consequences which flow from it.

Thatcher might also have been content to annunciate the broad principles of her country's foreign policy and then employed a foreign secretary who was capable of getting the Foreign Office to translate those principles into action. This is neither an original nor a novel observation, but it is one worth bearing in mind by anyone who aspires to succeed her. The Attlee–Bevin model of the relationship between prime minister and foreign secretary worked better than the Churchill–Eden or, it must be said, the Thatcher and anybody model in this regard. However, the argument that sovereign states would remain the basic pillars of stability and the principal vehicles of change in the post-Cold War international order, plus the judgement that this was a good thing, both belonged to her and virtually no one else among her contemporaries. So too, did her attempt to act accordingly, and for this, Thatcher deserves her mantle as the first post-Cold War statesman produced by a European great power.

Notes

INTRODUCTION

1. The term 'statesman' will be used throughout in preference to alternatives such as 'statesperson' or 'stateswoman', primarily because it conveys a meaning which the others do not. In addition, 'statesperson' is inelegant and 'stateswoman' is restrictive. Saying that Thatcher was a great stateswoman, for example, claims far less than saying she was a great statesman.

2. See, for example, Christopher Coker, *Who Only England Know*, Allied Publishers for The Institute of European Defence and Strategic Studies, London 1990, Peter Byrd (ed.), *British Foreign Policy Under Thatcher*, Philip Alan, Oxford, 1988 and Michael Smith, Steve Smith and Brian White (eds), *British Foreign Policy*, Unwin Hyman, London, 1988 for divergent interpretations of British foreign policy with similar assessments of Thatcher's limited impact upon it.

3. Margaret Thatcher, *The Downing Street Years*, Harper Collins, London, 1993, pp. 8–9. The Suez crisis came about after Nasser had nationalized the Suez Canal in 1956. After he refused to withdraw, Britain, France and Israel launched coordinated military attacks on Egypt. The British and French were operating with success in the Canal Zone for only some 48 hours when intense diplomatic and financial pressure, particularly from the US, persuaded the British that they ought to call the operation off and withdraw as quickly as possible.

4. Christopher Tugendhat and William Wallace, *Options for British Foreign Policy in the 1990s*, Royal Institute of International Affairs/Routledge, London, 1988, p. 119.

CHAPTER 1   THE PURSUIT OF INFLUENCE

1. For an excellent review of both the facts of Britain's decline and the literature which seeks to make sense of it see Colin Leys, *Politics in Britain*, University of Toronto Press, Toronto, 1983. See also Andrew Gamble, *Britain in Decline* (2nd edn), Macmillan, London, 1985.

2. For a review of these themes see Eric Hobsbawm, *Industry and Empire*, Penguin, Harmondsworth, 1969.

3. Correlli Barnett, *The Collapse of British Power*, Humanities Press International, Atlantic Highlands, NJ, 1986 and *The Audit of War*, Macmillan, London, 1986.

4. Anthony Verrier, *Through the Looking Glass: British Foreign Policy in an Age of Illusions*, Jonathan Cape, London, 1983.

5. The terminology here is from Paul Kennedy, *The Rise and Fall of the Great Powers*, Random House, New York, 1987.

6. David P. Calleo and Benjamin M. Rowland, 'Free Trade and the Atlantic Community' in Jeffrey A. Frieden and David A. Lake (eds), *International Political Economy: Perspectives on Global Power and Wealth*, Saint Martin's Press, New York, 1987.

7. Alan P. Dobson, *US Wartime Aid to Britain, 1940–1946*, Saint Martin's Press, New York, 1986.

8. For a strong statement of this thesis see Sir Nicholas Henderson's letter, when he was ambassador to Paris, to the Labour Foreign Secretary, David Owen, in which he speaks of '... the – in retrospect – almost unbelievable past failures [of British governments] to adapt to a rapidly changing world'. Cited in *The Daily Telegraph*, 2 June 1979.

9. David Reynolds, *Britannia Overruled*, Longman, Harlow, 1991, p. 157. For Bevan's comments see Richard Crossman, *The Diaries of a Cabinet Minister*, Vol. 2, Holt, Rinehart & Winston, New York, 1977, p. 182.

10. Robert Boardman and J.R. Groom (eds), *The Management of Britain's External Relations*, Macmillan, New York, 1973, p. 1.

11. Ritchie Ovendale (ed.), *The Foreign Policy of the British Labour Government, 1945–1951*, Leicester University Press, Leicester, 1984. Attlee's Foreign Secretary, Ernest Bevin, was convinced that a continuing world role for Britain was both necessary and possible. See Sir Frank Roberts, 'Ernest Bevin as Foreign Secretary', in Ovendale, p. 23.

12. See Anthony Adamthwaite, 'Introduction: The Foreign Office and Policy-Making', in John W. Young (ed.), *The Foreign Policy of Churchill's Peacetime Administration, 1951–55*, Leicester University Press, 1988, for the argument that Churchill tried to disrupt Eden's attempt to continue the orderly retreat to a more reduced world role begun by the previous government.

13. See Michael Howard, *The Continental Commitment*, Penguin, Harmondsworth, 1974 for a discussion of the significance of this commitment.

14. John W. Young, 'The Schuman Plan and British Association' in Young.

15. See, for example, Hugh Thomas, *The Suez Affair*, Penguin, Harmondsworth, 1967 and David Carlton, *Britain and the Suez Crisis*, Oxford University Press, Oxford, 1988.

16. *Thomas*, p. 46, and David Travers for the point about the problems of success.

17. F.S. Northedge, *British Foreign Policy*, George Allen & Unwin, London, 1962, pp. 132–67.

18. Cited in Geoffrey Goodwin, 'British Foreign Policy Since 1945', in Michael Leifer (ed.), *Constraints and Adjustments in British Foreign Policy*, George Allen & Unwin, London, 1972, p. 39.

19. Anthony Sampson, *Macmillan: A Study in Ambiguity*, Penguin, Harmondsworth, 1968, pp. 205–20. See also Harold Macmillan, *At the End of the Day*, Macmillan, London, 1973, pp. 22–3.

20. Harold Wilson, *The Labour Government, 1964–70*, Weidenfeld & Nicolson, London, 1971, p. 300.

21. Howard, p. 149 and *The Times*, 17 November 1964, cited in F.S. Northedge, 'Britain's place in a Changing World', in Leifer, p. 195.

22. George Brown, *In My Way*, Penguin, Harmondsworth, 1971, p. 221.

23. Edward Heath's theme was 'a Greater Britain in a Greater Europe', cited in D.C. Watt and J. Mayall (eds), *Current British Foreign Policy, 1971*, Temple Smith, London, 1973, pp. 585.

CHAPTER 2 FOREIGN POLICY AND THE 1979 ELECTION CAMPAIGN

1. See Fred Halliday, *The Making of the Second Cold War*, Verso, London, 1983, for a view of the end of *détente* in these terms.
2. See Mark Kesselman, Joel Krieger et al., *European Politics in Transition*, D.C. Heath, Lexington, Mass. 1992 for a discussion of British and European postwar politics in these terms.
3. Peter Jenkins, *Mrs Thatcher's Revolution*, Pan, London, 1989, p. 27.
4. Thatcher as reported in *The Daily Telegraph*, 14 April 1979, speaking in the House of Commons on the minor budget introduced by the government after its fall.
5. *The Daily Telegraph*, 23 February 1979.
6. *The Daily Telegraph*, 17 April 1979.
7. *The Daily Telegraph*, 9, 19 and 30 April 1979.
8. *The Daily Telegraph*, 12 April 1979.
9. *The Daily Telegraph*, 20 April 1979.
10. *The Daily Telegraph*, 5 April 1979 for Pym, 'Britain's Role In Europe'.
11. See *The Times* (International Weekly Edition), 30 April 1979 and *The Daily Telegraph*, 2 May 1979 for this section.
12. *The Daily Telegraph*, 7 April 1979.
13. See *The Times* (IWE), 30 April 1979.
14. *The Daily Telegraph*, 10 April 1979.
15. Pym's attack on the government's alienation of its European partners was delivered at a briefing to Conservative candidates, *The Daily Telegraph*, 26 February 1979.
16. Private interview, 30 May 1990.
17. Ibid.
18. See William Keegan, *Mrs Thatcher's Economic Experiment*, Penguin, Harmondsworth, 1985 for an account of what he regards as a dogmatic preoccupation with monetarism on the part of Thatcher, Sir Keith Joseph and Geoffrey Howe.
19. *The Daily Telegraph*, 30 April 1979.
20. Among the positions in Thatcher's first cabinet were: Geoffrey Howe, Chancellor of the Exchequer (with John Biffen as Treasury Secretary); Sir Keith Joseph, Secretary for Industry; John Nott, Trade Secretary; Lord Carrington, Foreign Secretary; and Francis Pym, Defence Minister.

CHAPTER 3 THE THATCHER-CARRINGTON PARTNERSHIP

1. See Margaret Thatcher, p. 27.

2. For the characterization of the partnership see *The Times*, 26 May 1980, and for Healey's comment, *The Times*, 8 May.

3. *The Times*, 18 April and 29 September 1981.

4. For David Watt's article, in which he placed Thatcher in the company of de Gaulle, Nixon and Begin, see *The Times*, 17 June 1982. For Thatcher's role in reassuring the US about EC and British policy on the Palestinian question see *The Times*, 9 and 10 November 1981.

5. *The Times*, 30 April 1980.

6. *The Times*, 5 January and 19 February 1980.

7. *The Times*, 28 March 1980.

8. *The Times*, 20 and 21 May 1980.

9. *The Times*, 26 May 1980.

10. *The Times*, 27 October 1980.

11. See *The Times*, 27 December 1979 and 29 January 1980 for the newspaper's and Thatcher's respective use of this term.

12. *The Times*, 11 October 1980.

13. More properly known as the Federation of Rhodesia and Nyasaland, this lasted until 1963 and consisted of the British protectorates of Nyasaland (Malawi since 1963) and Northern Rhodesia (Zambia since 1964), and the self-governing colony of Southern Rhodesia.

14. Donald Rothchild, 'US policy styles in Africa: from minimal engagement to liberal internationalism', in Kenneth A. Oye, Donald Rothchild and Robert Lieber (eds), *Eagle Entangled: US Foreign Policy in a Complex World*, Longman, New York, 1979.

15. Ibid.

16. *The Daily Telegraph*, 25 April 1979.

17. Rhodesia was landlocked and any force would have required airlifting to the colony. Rhodesia possessed an effective army and airforce.

18. *The Daily Telegraph*, 2 March and 6 December 1979.

19. *The Daily Telegraph*, 14 February 1979.

20. *The Daily Telegraph*, 26 April and 17 May 1979, respectively. Bishop Muzorewa's United African National Council (UANC) was declared the winner of the black part of the election by 24 April and formed a government at the end of May with five white ministers (including Ian Smith) out of a cabinet of 17.

21. *The Daily Telegraph*, 12 April 1979.

22. *The Daily Telegraph*, 7 May 1979. The 'six principles' referred to required any settlement to: guarantee majority rule; prevent retrogressive amendments of the constitution; provide immmediate improvements in the political status of the African population; make progress towards ending racial discrimination; satisfy the British that it was acceptable to the people of Rhodesia as a whole; prevent oppression of the majority by the minority and the reverse. Ibid., 23 May.

23. See *The Daily Telegraph*, 15–23 May 1979 for the following section.

24. *The Daily Telegraph*, editorial 18 June 1979.

25. *The Daily Telegraph*, 10 July 1979.

26. *The Daily Telegraph*, 11–23 July 1979 for this section.

27. *The Daily Telegraph*, 26 July 1979, and a private interview with a member of her first government with senior foreign policy responsibilities.

28. Lord Carrington, *Reflect on Things Past*, Fontana, Glasgow, 1989, p. 277.

29.   *The Daily Telegraph*, 2 and 4 August respectively, 1979.
30.   *The Daily Telegraph*, 6 and 7 August 1979.
31.   *The New York Times*, 23 September 1979.
32.   *The New York Times*, 23 and 24 September 1979. Counter-insurgency experts suggest a ten-to-one advantage is necessary in such conflicts.
33.   *The Daily Telegraph*, 7 and 10 August 1979, and *The New York Times*. 20 and 24 September 1979.
34.   *The New York Times*, 11 September 1979.
35.   *The Daily Telegraph*, 15 August 1979.
36.   *The New York Times*, 15 October 1979.
37.   *The New York Times*, 21 September 1979.
38.   *The Times*, 14 November 1979.
39.   *The Times*, 12 December 1979.
40.   *The Times*, 17 and 18 December 1979.
41.   *The Times*, 29 February 1980.
42.   *The Times*, 5 March 1980.
43.   *The Times*, 19 December 1979.
44.   *The Times*, 18 June 1981.
45.   *The Times*, 5 January and 19 February 1980.
46.   *The Times*, 1, 6, and 7 July 1981.
47.   *The Times*, 2 March 1981.
48.   *The Times*, 20 August 1981.
49.   *The Times*, 14 June 1980.
50.   *The Times*, 9 and 10 November 1981.
51.   *The Times*, 9 October 1981.
52.   *The Times*, 3 March 1981.
53.   Carrington interview while in Australia for the Commonwealth Heads of Government Meeting (CHOGM) cited in *The Times*, 6 October 1981.
54.   In public, Thatcher maintained that a Cuban withdrawal from Angola was desirable, but not a condition of a Namibian settlement, *The Times*, 6 October 1981. For her subsequent recollections and views see *Margaret Thatcher*, p. 158.
55.   *The Times*, 1 May 1980.
56.   *The Times*, 25 April 1981.
57.   *The Times*, 10 July 1981.
58.   *The Times*, 1 May 1980.

CHAPTER 4   THE DIPLOMACY OF DISASTER: LOSING THE FALKLANDS

1.   Thatcher, p. 186 and Lord Carrington, *Reflect on Things Past*, Fontana, Glasgow, 1989, p. 371. The question of blame has been extensively examined elsewhere, most notably in the official report, *Falkland Islands Review. Report of a Committee of Privy Counsellors*, Command 8787 (Chairman: The Rt Hon. The Lord Franks), (London: HMSO, January 1983). The Falkland Islands War resulted from the conflicting claims of Argentina and Britain. Argentina claimed that it had inherited all the possessions and rights of the

Spanish Empire in the area, including the Falkland Islands from which its garrison had been driven by the British in 1833. The British case rested primarily on the length of time it had occupied the Islands and latterly on the principle of self-determination. The inhabitants were of British 'stock' and wished to remain both British and on the Islands. The crisis began when Argentinian scrap-dealers contracted to dismantle a whaling station on South Georgia, a dependency of the Falkland Islands, arrived without British clearance, hoisted the Argentinian flag and received support from the Argentinian navy. Britain protested and sent troops to remove the scrap-dealers, and the crisis escalated, probably according to Argentinian intentions, from there.

2.   See *The Times*, 2 July, 8 July, 5 August and 11 September 1981.
3.   For details of the Bill see *The Times*, 15 January 1981. For Thatcher's own phrase uttered on television in 1978, see Hugo Young, *One Of Us*, Pan Books, London, 1989, p. 111.
4.   This account draws on *The Times* for 4, 7, 9, 12, 16, 17, 26–8 June, 1–5, 8, 9, 23–30 July, 4–6, 9, 12, 13, 18, 20, 22 August and 3 September 1980. The leader of the rebellion, Jimmy Stevens, was sentenced to 14 years in prison.
5.   *The Times*, 14 November 1980.
6.   *The Times*, 17 March 1981. According to *The Times*, 20 March 1981, the Cays were presently uninhabited and used only by fishermen drying their nets.
7.   *The Times*, 20 March 1981.
8.   *The Times*, 21 September 1981.
9.   *The Times*, 29 July, and 8, 12, 18, 21 and 22 September 1981.
10.   For the British declaration on leaving Belize and the subsequent reversal see *The Times*, 1 and 20 April 1982. For Guatemala's request that talks be reopened and the declaration that it no longer recognized Belize or the Heads of Agreement (although it seems as though it never did) see *The Times*, 9 June and 1 July 1982. These initiatives were handled through the special interests section of the Swiss embassy in Tegucigalpa from which, incidentally, the British representative had been withdrawn in May during the Falklands war. For the British response made by Cranley Onslow, Minister of State in the Foreign Office, on his visit to Belize and figures for the reinforced garrison see *The Times*, 21 September 1982. By 1981 the garrison consisted of some 1600 soldiers equipped with helicopters and surface-to-air missiles, supported by four Harrier jet aircraft at a total cost of around £25 million a year.
11.   Sir Anthony Parsons, interview. See also Paul Sharp, 'Thatcher's wholly British foreign policy', in *Orbis*, Vol. 35, No. 3, Summer 1991 for a discussion of these themes.
12.   Thatcher, p. 178 and Carrington, p. 368. This is not to suggest that his presence in London would have done anything to change the way in which events in the South Atlantic were unfolding.
13.   Carrington, p. 352–5.
14.   In March 1981, The Argentinian government offered 'special status' to the Falkland Islands and promised treatment as its 'most pampered region' should it join Argentina. *The Times*, 3 March 1981.
15.   Carrington, p. 355.
16.   For details of the Defence White Paper, *The Way Forward*, see *The Times*, 26 June 1981. As the crisis built in March 1982, a reprieve for both assault

ships was announced: *The Times*, 5 March 1982. For discussion of previous attempts to cut HMS *Endurance* and the Foreign Office's efforts to save it see Max Hastings and Simon Jenkins, *The Battle for the Falklands*, Pan Books, 1983, pp. 58–9. Had the Argentinians waited, not only would Britain have been in a weaker position, but also Argentina would have obtained new military equipment, particularly submarines and aircraft which could launch anti-shipping missiles, which were on order.

17. See Hastings and Jenkins, p. 42 for previous Argentinian demonstrations.

18. See Hastings and Jenkins for a discussion of the Indian invasion of the Portuguese colony of Goa in 1961 and Argentinian consideration of that operation pp. 46 and 65.

19. *The Times*, 5 February 1982.

20. Carrington, pp. 354–5. In presenting his policy of patient education about the merits of leaseback as a preferable alternative to a 'Fortress Falklands' policy of securing the Islands, Carrington takes advantage of the extensive military commitment to the Islands made by Thatcher's government after the war to make the contrast in his favour. It is, of course, conceivable that a much smaller garrison could have performed this role prior to the war.

21. Carrington, pp. 354–5. Carrington stresses the special character of Britain's deterrence policy in the Falklands as a tripwire policy. The Royal Marine garrison was inadequate for defending the Islands against all but the weakest demonstrations, but was sufficient to kill and be killed, thus supposedly raising the stakes of attacking in the minds of the Argentinians (it would also raise the stakes in the minds of the British public, making it easier for the government to respond).

22. Carrington, p. 368 and Thatcher, p. 178. In a debate in the House of Commons on the modernization of Britain's nuclear weapons on 29 March, John Nott refused to discuss the Falkland Islands crisis. The matters under discussion, he said, were '...too important to be diverted': *The Times*, 30 March 1982. *The Times* of 1 April reported that Richard Luce, a deputy foreign minister, had cancelled a visit to Mexico and was answering questions in the House of Commons the previous day. However, these were on the government's Central American policy, not on the Falkland Islands.

23. In the House of Commons debate of 3 April Thatcher, Nott and Carrington were charged by the Labour party as being guilty of appeasement. See Anthony Barnett, *Iron Britannia*, Allison & Busby, London, 1982 for an extended discussion of this debate and its echoes of the debate which brought about Chamberlain's resignation in 1940.

CHAPTER 5   RECOVERING THE FALKLANDS: THE DIPLOMACY OF WAR

1. For the editorial see *The Times*, 3 April 1982.

2. *The Times*, 31 March 1982 and Thatcher, p. 174.

3. Thatcher, pp. 183–4 and *The Times*, 5 April 1982.

4. Thatcher, pp. 206–7, and Hastings and Jenkins, pp. 163–6. In her autobiography, Thatcher maintains she told the American Secretary

of State, Al Haig, that her own political survival was at stake: Thatcher, p. 197.

5.   *The Times*, 5 April 1982 and Barnett, p. 30.
6.   Thatcher, p. 173.
7.   *The Times*, 10 April 1982.
8.   *The Times*, 5 April 1982.
9.   Hastings and Jenkins, p. 158.
10. *The Guardian* 12 June 1982 and cited in Barnett, pp. 134–5.
11. *The Times*, 29 March 1982.
12. It is this conviction which provides the fuel for the critique of British diplomacy in G.M. Dillon's *The Falklands, Politics and War*, Saint Martin's Press, New York, 1989, for example.
13. See the poll data summarized in Michael Clarke, *British External Policy-Making in the 1990s*, Macmillan and Royal Institute of International Affairs, London, 1992.
14. *The Times*, 15 April 1982.
15. Thatcher, p. 210.
16. *The Times*, 23 April 1982.
17. See Dillon, Chapter 3 and Barnett, Chapter 7.
18. See Hastings and Jenkins, Chapter 1 for an account of this period.
19. Barnett, pp. 123–4.
20. *The Times*, 12 June 1982.
21. *The Times*, 15 April 1982.
22. *The Times*, 21 May and 28 May 1982.
23. *The Times*, 29 June 1982. Powell maintained that 'In fact, the American struggle to wrest the Islands from Britain has only commenced in earnest now the fighting is over.'
24. Thatcher, pp. 182–4.
25. Hastings and Jenkins, pp. 168. On one occasion a British helicopter made a forced landing in Chile and the event was widely publicized. Ibid., p. 190.
26. For Ireland's policy see Paul Sharp, *Irish Foreign Policy and the European Community*, Dartmouth, Aldershot, 1990.
27. Thatcher, p. 188.
28. *The Times*, 4 May 1982.
29. Thatcher, pp. 200 and 204.
30. Thatcher pp. 229 and 221.
31. President Reagan's words, *The Times*, 7 April 1982.
32. Thatcher, pp. 191–2.
33. *The Times*, 5 April 1982.
34. Thatcher, p. 210 and *The Times*, 19 May 1982. See Hastings and Jenkins pp. 161–2 for details of the Labour party's positions and estimates of the extent of the opposition to Thatcher's policy within the Civil Service.
35. Noel Dorr, Ireland's Permanent Representative to the UN, cited in a press release from his mission for 25 May 1982.
36. See Dillon, Chapter 6 for an excellent discussion of the constraints imposed by logistics, weather conditions and the onset of winter on the period during which the task force could hope to make a successful landing.
37. Thatcher, p. 187.
38. *The Times*, 6 April 1982.

39. *The Times*, 23 April 1982.
40. *The Times*, 27 April and 7 May 1982.
41. *The Times*, 30 April 1982.
42. *The Times*, 8 April 1982.
43. *The Times*, 30 April 1982.
44. See, for example, Irving Janis, *Victims of Groupthink*, Houghton Mifflin, Boston, 1972, and Robert Jervis, *Perception and Misperception in International Politics*, Princeton UP, Princeton, NJ, 1972.
45. *The Times*, 22 April 1982.
46. *The Times*, 1,3, and 5 May 1982.
47. *The Times*, 21 and 26 May 1982.
48. *The Times*, 12 April 1982.
49. *The Times*, 22 April 1982.
50. *The Times*, 8 May 1982.
51. Thatcher, p. 222.
52. *The Times*, 28 May, 3 and 4 June 1982.
53. *The Times*, 11 June 1982.
54. *The Times*, 19 and 28 May and 10 June 1982.
55. *The Times*, 6 May 1982.
56. *The Times*, 16 May 1982.
57. Thatcher to the crowd outside the prime minister's residence at 10 Downing Street on receipt of the news of a ceasefire in the Falkland Islands: *The Times*, 15 June 1982.
58. *The Times*, 14 May 1982.
59. Conservative Central Office, New Service, 3 July 1982, cited in Barnett, pp. 149–53.
60. *The Times*, 29 April 1982.
61. In *Thatcher*, she notes the requests for reinforcements on pp. 189, 200 and 215. The initial force consisted of some 3000 troops lightly supported. Eventually nearly 100 ships and nearly 30 000 people were committed. See Hastings and Jenkins, p. 90 and pp. 393–403.
62. Thatcher, pp. 214 and 216.
63. Others have noted what they call Thatcher's attraction to and trust of 'men in uniform'. See, Hugo Young, p. 273. See also, Thatcher, p. 226.
64. Hastings and Jenkins, pp. 357–8. Argentina announced a provisional total 652 dead and missing.
65. Thatcher, pp. 195 and 232 and *The Times*, 15 June 1982.
66. See Kenneth Waltz, *Theory of International Politics*, Addison-Wesley, Reading, Mass. 1979, p. 111.
67. *The Times*, 16 June 1982.
68. Thatcher, p. 210.

CHAPTER 6   THATCHER'S US POLICY I: THE DIPLOMACY OF SUPPORT

1. Margaret Thatcher, *The Times*, 6 May 1984.
2. A. Wolfers, *Discord and Collaboration*, Johns Hopkins UP, Baltimore, Ind., 1962, p. 73.

3. The decision on new missiles for Europe was confirmed by a meeting of the Nato Nuclear Planning Group at Homestead Air Force Base in April 1979 a month before Thatcher was elected (see *The Daily Telegraph*, 26 April 1979).
4. *The Times*, 1 June 1984.
5. *The Times*, 19 December 1979.
6. *The Times*, 9 May 20–22, 1980.
7. *The Times*, 30 January and 24 July 1981 and 24 November 1982.
8. Denis Healy and Enoch Powell, *The Times*, 3 December 1982 and 17 September 1987 respectively.
9. This relationship has been examined extensively elsewhere; see, for example, Geoffrey Howe, *Conflict of Loyalty*, Macmillan, London, 1994 and Geoffrey Smith, *Reagan and Thatcher*, W.W. Norton, New York and London, 1991. The following paragraph makes extensive use of Smith.
10. Christopher Campbell, *Nuclear Weapons: Fact Book*, Hamlyn, Feltham, Middlesex in 1984.
11. Cited in *The Times*, 9 February 1981.
12. See *The Times*, 21 October and 5 November 1981 for Reagan and Haig respectively.
13. See *The Times*, 2 and 6 January 1982 for Thatcher and William Waldegrave respectively.
14. *The Times*, 2 January 1982.
15. *The Times*, 9 September 982. Reagan estimated $12 billion a year, *The Times*, 24 July 1982.
16. Hugo Young, pp. 256–7 and Smith, pp. 99–102.
17. *The Times*, 21 October 1982.
18. *The Times*, 1 July and 3 August 1982.
19. *The Times*, 23 September 1982.
20. *The Times*, 10 November 1982.
21. *The Times*, 22 August 1983.
22. *The Times*, 22 October 1983.
23. *The Times*, 30 July 1979, 22 June 1981, and 18 February 1982.
24. *The Times*, 13 March and 29 July 1982.
25. *The Times*, 14 March 1981 and 13 March 1982.
26. *The Times*, 27 October and 31 October 1983 for Howe and Thatcher respectively.
27. *The Times*, 28 October 1983.
28. *The Times*, 25 October 1983.
29. *The Times*, 24 October 1983.
30. *The Times*, 26 October 1983.
31. Norman St John Stevas, MP *The Times*, 26 October 1983.
32. *The Times*, 30 September and 7 October 1983.
33. *The Times*, 27 October 1983.

CHAPTER 7   THATCHER'S US POLICY II: THE DIPLOMACY OF INTERESTS

1. Blue Streak was liquid fuelled and, thus, required preparation before it was launched. The solid fuelled rockets which the US and the USSR were

developing could be launched almost instantaneously. This raised the possibility that Blue Streak missiles might be destroyed during their preparation time.

2. *The Times*, 9 July 1981. Chevaline had overrun its budget by £750 000 to cost £1 billion by the time it was ready: Campbell, p. 163.

3. P. Nailor and J. Alford, for example, argued that reconditioned Polaris missiles should be retained even if placed on new submarines: *The Times*, 1 March 1980. In 1982, the government announced that the life of Polaris would be extended by remotoring the missiles and improving the submarines' guidance systems. David Greenwood argued that the costs of Trident II, the missile and system with which the Thatcher government decided to replace Polaris, would absorb so much of the equipment budget that other missions would be affected; for example, securing the Western Approaches would be hurt by the resulting delays in warship construction and replacement: *The Times*, 9 February 1983.

4. *The Times*, 16 June 1980. Four submarines were to be built in Britain with an option for a fifth. Together with the warheads, these would cost some £4 billion. The Trident I missiles, also called C4s, would be provided by the US at a cost £1 billion. The deal was linked to an American agreement to purchase British Rapier surface-to-air-missiles to defend American airbases in Britain.

5. *The Times*, 4 March 1981. He repeated the argument about '... a second area of decision-making' later in the month also: 18 March 1981.

6. *The Times*, 9 March 1983 and 10 October 1985.

7. *The Times*, 17 March 1981. The precise capabilities of these weapons is supposed to be a secret and some variations exist in public estimates. Paradoxically, in this debate, opponents of the systems generally suggested higher capabilities for them than did their supporters.

8. *The Times*, 4 April 1981. The Pentagon also told visiting British MPs that C4 would costs between £4.5 and £5 billion. The MOD estimate was expressed as £500 million to £700 million over 15 years.

9. *The Times*, 20 October 1981 for Nott's earlier estimates, 12 March 1982 for the government's announcement, and 30 March 1982 for his comments on the independence of the system and 'essential lunacy' comment.

10. *The Times*, 2 December 1986 and 27 May 1986.

11. *The Times*, 4 August 1980 for the Defence Council's Memorandum, *The Future United Kingdom Strategic Nuclear Deterrent Force*, cited by Lord Chalfont, 20 January 1982; for Thatcher's comments on Trident being a more powerful weapon, and 17 March for comments on negotiating from a position of strength; for Thatcher and Britain's reputation see 11 October 1980; for Thatcher's letter to Reagan see 12 March 1982; and for her comments at the start of the Falklands War see 2 April 1982.

12. Ronald Reagan, 'Address to the Nation on the Strategic Defence Initiative', cited in P. Edward Haley and Jack Merritt (eds), *Strategic Defense Initiative: Folly or Future?*, Westview Press, Boulder, Col., 1986.

13. Thatcher to the UN cited in Sir Geoffrey Howe, 'Defence and Security in the Nuclear Age', an address to the Royal United Services Institute, London, 15 March 1985. The other quotations are from Howe, in what has generally been viewed as a very hostile speech to SDI. Howe maintains that

his tone was to balance the prime minister's over-enthusiasm for the project in a recent address to the US Senate. Whatever the tone of either speech, however, Howe's does reflect accurately the basic principles of Britain's conditional support for SDI research.

14. *The Times*, 18 April, 11 September and 7 December 1985. See 28 January 1988, for a report of the biggest contract to date worth £12 million going to Ferranti. Contracts with others worth a total of £27 million were said to have been negotiated.

15. Thatcher press conference at Andrews Air Force Base, 22 December 1984, cited in Haley and Merritt, p. 183. The full text of the four principles is as follows (Thatcher's words): 'We agreed on four specific points: First, the United States and Western aim was not to achieve superiority, but to maintain a balance, taking account of Soviet developments; Second, that SDI-related deployment would, in view of treaty obligations, have to be a matter for negotiations; Third, the overall aim is to enhance, and not to undermine, deterrence; and fourth, East–West negotiations should aim to achieve security with reduced levels of offensive systems on both sides.' For an account of this meeting see Geoffrey Smith, pp. 152–3.

16. *The Times*, 16 January 1986 and Mikhail Gorbachev, *Perestroika: New Thinking for Our Country and the World*, Harper & Row, New York, 1987, p. 171. Gorbachev set a date, 2001, by which all nuclear weapons should be destroyed.

17. See *The Times*, 13 and 16 October 1986, for the slow reaction in Britain to the implications of the Reykjavik agreement. See October 17 for the Thatcher–Mitterrand joint declaration on nuclear deterrence, and Geoffrey Smith, pp. 222–3 for details of the Thatcher–Reagan meeting the following November. The lecture anecdote is from a confidential interview.

18. By the INF treaty both sides agreed to remove and destroy all their missiles in the 300 to 3400 mile range.

19. *The Times*, 6 May 1983 for Thatcher and 13 December 1984, for Richard Luce reiterating Howe's conditions for a review.

20. *The Times*, 5 December 1986.

21. *The Times*, 28 March 1986.

22. For Moscow, *The Times*, 1 April 1986, and for Thatcher's thoughts on a non-nuclear world, 29 May 1986.

23. *The Times*, 21 September 1987 for Thatcher on the British deterrent, and 23 September 1989 for her speech in Tokyo on the denuclearization of Europe.

24. *The Times*, 13 June 1990 for Gorbachev and 27 September 1990 for James Baker, Bush's Secretary of State.

25. See *The Times*, 5 January 1988 for David Mellor's outspoken comments on his visit to the occupied territories.

26. *The Times*, 12 March 1982.

CHAPTER 8   THATCHER'S EUROPEAN POLICY I: THE *DEMANDEUR*

1. *The Times*, 17 October 1988 and 6 August 1990.

2. These questions come from Charles Pentland, 'International Organizations and Their Roles', in James Rosenau, Kenneth W. Thompson and Gavin Boyd (eds), *World Politics*, Free Press, New York, 1976.

3. See Paul Taylor, *The Limits of European Integration*, Columbia University Press, New York, 1983 for an example of this perspective.

4. The proportion of British trade going to the Commonwealth fell from 47.7 per cent in 1950 through 40.2 per cent in 1960 to 24.4 per cent in 1970: Reynolds, p. 222. In 1980, according to Thatcher, the EC had accounted for 40 per cent of British trade. Two years later, Cecil Parkinson maintained that Britain's trade with the Community had increased by 10 per cent. See *The Times*, 21 November 1979 and 14 February 1981 respectively.

5. Brown, p. 202. His riposte to Acheson's comment about Britain's role was: 'We have a role, our role is to lead Europe.'

6. The Luxembourg Compromise, by which any member could block proposals by claiming that their implementation would impinge on important national interests.

7. *The Daily Telegraph*, 2 April 1979, and 20 June 1979, *The Times*, 22 March 1980.

8. Brian Lenihan, *Dáil Debates*, Vol. 323, Col. 1263, 30 October 1980.

9. *The Daily Telegraph*, 19 May, 12 May and 11 May 1979.

10. *The Daily Telegraph*, 23 June 979. At the 1974 Paris summit it was agreed that heads of government should meet at least three times a year to discuss the business of the Council of Ministers or cooperation on matters external to the Community. Meeting as such they would be called the European Council, the chair of this Council (known as the President) rotating among members every six months.

11. *The Daily Telegraph*, 22 November 1979.

12. *The Daily Telegraph*, 1 November and 13, 1 December 1979.

13. Former Chancellor Schmidt on arguments within the EC, *The Times*, 13 June 1984.

14. *The Daily Telegraph*, 3 December 1979.

15. *The Daily Telegraph*, 4 December 1979.

16. *The Times*, 16 January and 11 March 1980.

17. *The Times*, 26 January 1982.

18. *The Times*, 11, 12, 14 and 19 May 1982.

19. *The Times*, 18 June for Hurd and 21 and 22 June 1982 for the Luxembourg Compromise.

20. *The Times*, 15 December 1982 on the freezing of the rebate, 17 December 1982 for Howe's consideration of withholding, and 27 February 1980 for the view of withholding as less disruptive.

21. *The Times*, 18 and 20 June 1983.

22. *The Times*, 2 December 1983.

23. *The Times*, 21 October 1983 and 16 December for Thatcher.

24. *The Times*, 17, 20, 21 March and for Thatcher's comment, 22 March 1984.

25. *The Times*, 4 May and 28 July 1984.

26. *The Times*, 29 March 1984.

27. *The Times*, 20–7 June 1984 for Fontainebleau and 2, 3 and 10 October 1984 for Lawson and the European Parliament.

28. *The Times*, 27 and 28 June 1984.

29.　*The Times*, 29 June 1984 for Rifkind and 27 June 1984 for French claims.

30.　*The Times*, 31 January and 30 April 1980 for its own editorial viewpoint, and 26 May and 22 July 1980 for Carrington's comments.

31.　*The Times*, 3 June and 7 July 1981.

32.　*The Times*, 5 June and 4 June 1981.

33.　*The Times*, 3 December 1979. For Mitterrand see *The Times*, 21 March and 25 May 1984.

34.　See, for example, Thatcher in *The Times*, 4 December 1979, 18 November 1980, 31 December 1982 and 24 June 1983.

CHAPTER 9　THATCHER'S EUROPEAN POLICY II: SOVEREIGNTY AND NATIONALISM

1.　*European Unification*, Office for Official Publications of the European Communities, 1987, p. 67 and Derek W. Urwin, *The Community of Europe*, Longman, London, 1991, p. 222.

2.　*The Times*, 1 December 1981.

3.　*The Times*, 18 October for Howe and 1 December 1984, for Thatcher.

4.　*The Times*, 10 June and 29 June 1985, and Urwin, p. 227.

5.　*The Times*, 23 May and 29 June and Howe, p. 409.

6.　*The Times*, 1 June 1985.

7.　*The Times*, 4 October 1985.

8.　*Unwin*, p. 231. A third senior minister, Michael Heseltine, was shortly to pursue a course of action on the government's reluctance to prefer a European to an American takeover of Westland, a failing British helicopter manufacturer, which would lead to his resignation the following month.

9.　*The Times*, 20 June 1985 for Rifkind and 3 July 1985 for Thatcher on harmonization. 30 November 1985, for British officials on the IGC and 1–2 and 6 December 1985, for Thatcher on the Luxembourg summit.

10.　*The Times*, 16 June 1986 for Cash and 9 October and 3 November 1986 for Lord Denning.

11.　*The Times*, 8, 17 and 18 December 1986.

12.　*The Times*, 6 June 1987 for Binyon, 30 June 1987 for Thatcher, and 1 July 1987 for Chirac.

13.　*The Times*, 7 July 1988 and Urwin, p. 240.

14.　*The Times*, 21 September 1988 for all the extracts from the Bruges speech.

15.　*The Times*, 23 September 1988.

16.　*European Unification*, p. 45.

17.　*The Times*, 7 May 1986 for Thatcher and 3 November 1990 for Nicholas Ridley, a former minister who resigned after expressing unacceptably anti-German views in a public setting.

18.　*The Times*, 19 November 1990.

19.　*The Times*, 26 June 1989.

20.　*The Times*, May 14, 1988.

21.　*The Times*, 21 June 1988 for Hannover, 19 September 1988 for Spanish television, and 26 October 1988 for Thatcher's comments on the responsibilities of a central bank.

22. *The Times*, 13 May and 16 June 1989, and 31 October 1990. Thatcher had given earlier intimations of the economic implications of her political nationalism. See, for example, *The Times*, 21 April 1981, for the following: 'Gradually, one has come to see that there are times when the battle is not necessarily between company and company but also between country and country.'

23. *The Times*, 17 January, 26 March, 20 April, 30 April 30 and 29 October 1990.

24. *The Times*, 21, April 1989.

25. *The Times*, 17, May 1989 for Plumb, 6 November 1989 for Wallace and 10 May 1989 for Cockfield.

26. *The Times*, 30 October 1990 for Howe and Geoffrey Howe, 'Sovereignty and Independence: Britain's place in the world', *International Affairs*, Vol. 66, No. 4, 1990, *The Times*, 29 October 1990 for Andreotti, 16 June 1989, for Thatcher, and 12 June 1990 for Douglas Hurd.

27. *The Times*, 6 November 1989.

28. *The Times*, 3 September 1990.

CHAPTER 10 THATCHER'S SOVIET POLICY: DIPLOMACY AT THE SUMMIT

1. George Walden, *The Times*, 5 October 1983.

2. *The Times*, 21 July 1979.

3. *The Times*, 9 February 1981.

4. *The Times*, 30 October 1982 and 28 May 1983.

5. *The Times*, 30 September and 14 October 1983. To be fair to Thatcher, she had also talked of planet-sharing in the Washington speech: see Smith, p. 117. For Callaghan, see *The Times*, 17 October 1983.

6. *The Times*, 6 October 1981.

7. Carrington's Alistair Buchan Memorial Lecture at the Institute of Strategic Studies cited in *The Times*, 22 April 1983, and in the *Nato Review*, cited in *The Times*, 29 August 1983.

8. *The Times*, 26 March and 16 January 1984.

9. *The Times*, 5 October 1983 and 15 December 1984.

10. *The Times*, 28 August 1982 and 13 February 1984.

11. *The Times*, 26 March 1984 for Thatcher, 2 July 1984 for Gromyko and Howe, and 5 November 1984, for Rifkind.

12. *The Times*, 10 December 1987.

13. For Howe, see *The Times*, 16 March 1985. For Thatcher in Moscow, see 18 March 1985, and for the American response see 21 March 1985.

14. *The Times*, 12 October and 22 July 1985.

15. *The Times*, 3 June and 4 June 1986.

16. *The Times*, 14 October and 14 November 1986, and 12 January 1987.

17. *The Times*, 17 December 1986.

18. In 1905, Kaiser Wilhelm negotiated a treaty of alliance with his cousin Tsar Nicholas on the Russian Imperial yacht at Bjorkoe in Finland, but their foreign minsters refused to endorse the agreement. See Harold Nicolson, *Diplomacy*, OUP, p. 33.

19. *The Times*, 10 December 1986 and 12 January 1987.
20. *The Times*, 4 and 12 February 1987.
21. *The Times*, 23 March 1987.
22. *The Times*, 25 March 1987.
23. *The Times*, 6 and 11 March 1987.
24. *The Times*, 2 and 3 April 1987 for Thatcher in Moscow, 30 April for her message to Bessmertnykh, and 27 November and 5, 8 and 10 December 1987, for Gorbachev's visit to Brize Norton.

CHAPTER 11 THATCHER'S GERMAN POLICY: THE 'UNAMBIGUOUS FAILURE'

1. Thatcher, p. 813: 'If there is one instance in which a foreign policy I pursued met with unambiguous failure, it was my policy on German reunification.'
2. *The Times*, 11 and 17 December 1987.
3. *The Times*, 8, 15 and 18 February 1988.
4. *The Times*, 1 March and 29 October 1988, and 12 January 1989.
5. *The Times*, 19, 24, 25, 27 April and 1 May 1989.
6. Thatcher, pp. 788–9.
7. *The Times*, 30 May 1989, 10 May and 3 July 1990.
8. *The Times*, 24 January, 2 June and 6 December 1989.
9. For Shevardnadze see *The Times*, 27 January 1988, 20 January and 7 March 1989. For Gerasimov see *The Times*, 14 June 1989. The final comments are those of Vitaly Churkin, head of the European Department of the Soviet Academy of Science, *The Times*, 12 June 1989.
10. For Thatcher see *The Times*, 12 July and 15 December 1988. For Uspensky see *The Times*, 15 February 1989.
11. *The Times*, 25 September 1989 and *Thatcher*, p. 792.
12. Ralf Dahrendorf observed that in the demonstrations which began in the GDR in the late spring of 1989, the chant of 'Wir sind das Volk' (we are the people) had changed in the course of the summer to 'Wir sind ein Volk' (we are one people). The latter, no doubt, reflected the prospect of German unification which was drawing nearer but, as Dahrendorf points out, it also represents a shift of emphasis '... not just from democracy to nationalism. It also uses people in two very different ways: as a society of citizens first, and as a somewhat mystical community second.'
13. *The Times*, 17 June 1985 for Kohl, 25 October 1988 for Kohl and Gorbachev's response, and 19 January 1989 for Fischer and Shevardnadze.
14. *The Times*, 3 May 1989, for the Hungarian decision and 1 June 1989 for Bush and Kohl.
15. *The Times*, 13 June 1989 for the FRG diplomat on self-determination, 20 July 1989 for Vagel, leader of the Bavarian Christian Social Union, on the lost territories and Kohl on the German question, and 11 and 12 September 1989 for Hungary's border opening and Kohl meeting GDR citizens.
16. *The Times*, 8 November 1989 for Brittan, a former minister in Thatcher's

government, who was now an EC Commissioner. *The Times*, 14, 20, and 25 November for Thatcher's position.

17. Thatcher, p. 792, and *The Times*, 20 November and 5 December 1989.
18. *The Times*, 7, 28 October and 2 November 1989.
19. *The Times*, 4, 14, 15 November and 20 December 1989.
20. *The Times*, 4 December 1989.
21. Hans Modrow of the GDR in *The Times*, 2 February 1990.
22. *The Times*, 17 July 1990.
23. *The Times*, 17 February 1990 and 19 February for Thatcher.
24. *The Times*, 26 January, 12 and 22 February 1990.
25. *The Times*, 28 February, 2 March and 6 March 1990.
26. *The Times*, 7 March 1990 for Gorbachev and Ferguson, 14 and 19 February 1990 for Thatcher and 9 March 1990 for Mitterrand.
27. *The Times*, 24, 29 and 30 March 1990.
28. *The Times*, 13 and 16 July 1990.
29. *The Times*, 9 June 1990.

CHAPTER 12 THATCHER'S STATESMANSHIP

1. From Shintaro Ishihara's book, *The Japan That Can Say No*, Simon & Schuster, New York, 1991 (English translation)
2. See, for example, *The Times*, 11 November 1985. See also *The Times*, 30 October 1985. For Mandela see *The Times*, 4 July 1990.
3. *The Times*, 6 June 1984 and 26 March 1985.
4. *The Times*, 24 October and 5 October 1990.
5. *The Times*, 20 May 1986.
6. *The Times*, 20 June and 2 July 1986, and 8 January 1988.
7. *The Times*, 14 June 1986 for AAM figures. See 25 June for the Department of Trade and Industry's figures on investment flows. See 7 June 1985, 15 October 1985 and 14 June 1986 (Thatcher) for estimates of jobs affected ('affected' is an opaque term which does not necessarily mean lost). See 16 June 1986 for claims about who could come to Britain.
8. *The Times*, 18 June 1986.
9. *The Times*, 30 June 1986.
10. *The Times*, 17 and 15 October 1985, 25 July 1986 and 19 October 1987.
11. *The Times*, 30 October 1985, 19 October 1987 and 4 August 1988.
12. *The Times*, 23 October 1990.
13. *The Times*, 14 November 1987 for Stanbrook, 31 July and 16 September 1986 for Howe.
14. *The Times*, 7 March 1989 and 3 February 1990.
15. *The Times*, 7 August 1990.
16. Howe, pp. 398–409.
17. Howe, p. 646.
18. *The Times*, 7 November 1988.
19. *The Times*, 1 July 1982.
20. Herman Wouk, *The Caine Mutiny*, Doubleday, New York, 1951.
21. *The Times*, 19 November 1990.

Select Bibliography

Anthony Barnett, *Iron Britannia*, Allison & Busby, London, 1982.

Correlli Barnett, *The Collapse of British Power*, Humanities Press International, Atlantic Highlands, NJ, 1986.

Correlli Barnett, *The Audit of War*, Macmillan, London, 1986.

Robert Boardman and J.R. Groom (eds), *The Management of Britain's External Relations*, Macmillan, New York, 1973.

George Brown, *In My Way*, Penguin, Harmondsworth, 1971.

Peter Byrd (ed.), *British Foreign Policy Under Thatcher*, Philip Alan, Oxford, 1988.

Christopher Campbell, *Nuclear Weapons: Fact Book*, Hamlyn, Feltham, Middlesex, 1984.

David Carlton, *Britain and the Suez Crisis*, Oxford University Press, Oxford, 1988.

Peter Carrington, *Reflect on Things Past*, Fontana, Glasgow, 1989.

Michael Clarke, *British External Policy-Making in the 1990s*, Macmillan and Royal Institute of International Affairs, London, 1992.

Christopher Coker, *Who Only England Know*, Allied Publishers for The Institute of European Defence and Strategic Studies, London, 1990.

Richard Crossman, *The Diaries of a Cabinet Minister*, Vol. 2, Holt, Rinehart & Winston, New York, 1977.

Alan P. Dobson, *US Wartime Aid to Britain, 1940–1946*, Saint Martin's Press, New York, 1986.

Jeffrey A. Frieden and David A. Lake (eds), *International Political Economy: Perspectives on Global Power and Wealth*, Saint Martin's Press, New York, 1987.

Andrew Gamble, *Britain in Decline* (2nd edn), Macmillan, London, 1985.

Mikhail Gorbachev, *Perestroika: New Thinking for Our Country and the World*, Harper & Row, New York, 1987.

P. Edward Haley and Jack Merritt (eds), *Strategic Defense Initiative: Folly or Future?*, Westview Press, Boulder, Col., 1986.

Fred Halliday, *The Making of the Second Cold War*, Verso, London, 1983.

Max Hastings and Simon Jenkins, *The Battle for the Falklands*, Pan Books, London, 1983.

Eric Hobsbawm, *Industry and Empire*, Penguin, Harmondsworth, 1969.

Michael Howard, *The Continental Commitment*, Penguin, Harmondsworth, 1974.

Geoffrey Howe, *Conflict of Loyalty*, Macmillan, London, 1994.

Shintaro Ishihara, *The Japan That Can Say No*, Simon & Shuster, New York, 1991.

Irving Janis, *Victims of Groupthink*, Houghton Mifflin, Boston, Mass., 1972.

Peter Jenkins, *Mrs Thatcher's Revolution*, Pan, London, 1989.

Robert Jervis, *Perception and Misperception in International Politics*, Princeton UP, Princeton, NJ, 1972.

William Keegan, *Mrs Thatcher's Economic Experiment*, Penguin, Harmondsworth, 1985.

Paul Kennedy, *The Rise and Fall of the Great Powers*, Random House, New York, 1987.

Mark Kesselman, Joel Krieger et al., *European Politics in Transition*, D.C. Heath, Lexington, Mass., 1992.

Michael Leifer (ed.), *Constraints and Adjustments in British Foreign Policy*, George Allen & Unwin, London, 1972.

Colin Leys, *Politics in Britain*, University of Toronto Press, Toronto, 1983.

Harold Macmillan, *At the End of the Day*, Macmillan, London, 1973.

Harold Nicolson, *Diplomacy*, Oxford University Press, 1969.

F.S. Northedge, *British Foreign Policy*, George Allen & Unwin, London, 1962.

Ritchie Ovendale (ed.), *The Foreign Policy of British Labour Government, 1945–1951*, Leicester University Press, Leicester, 1984.

Kenneth A. Oye, Donald Rothchild and Robert Lieber (eds), *Eagle Entangled: US Foreign Policy in a Complex World*, Longman, New York, 1979.

David Reynolds, *Britannia Overruled*, Longman, London, 1991.

James Rosenau, Kenneth W. Thompson and Gavin Boyd (eds), *World Politics*, Free Press, New York, 1976.

Anthony Sampson, *Macmillan: A Study in Ambiguity*, Penguin, Harmondsworth, 1968, pp. 205–20.

Paul Sharp, *Irish Foreign Policy and the European Community*, Dartmouth, Aldershot, 1990.

Geoffrey Smith, *Reagan and Thatcher*, W.W. Norton, New York and London, 1991.

Michael Smith, Steve Smith and Brian White (eds), *British Foreign Policy*, Unwin Hyman, London, 1988.

Paul Taylor, *The Limits of European Integration*, Columbia University Press, New York, 1983. Derek W. Urwin, *The Community of Europe*, Longman, London, 1991.

Margaret Thatcher, *The Downing Street Years*, Harper Collins, London, 1993.

Hugh Thomas, *The Suez Affair*, Penguin, Harmondsworth, 1967.

Christopher Tugendhat and William Wallace, *Options for British Foreign Policy in the 1990s*, Royal Institute of International Affairs/Routledge, London, 1988.

Anthony Verrier, *Through the Looking Glass: British Foreign Policy in an Age of Illusions*, Jonathan Cape, London, 1983.

Kenneth Waltz, *Theory of International Politics*, Addison-Wesley, Reading, Mass., 1979.

Harold Wilson, *The Labour Government, 1964–70*, Weidenfeld & Nicolson, London, 1971.

A. Wolfers, *Discord and Collaboration*, Johns Hopkins University Press, Baltimore, Md., 1962.

Herman Wouk, *The Caine Mutiny*, Doubleday, New York, 1951.

Hugo Young, *One Of US*, Pan Books, London, 1989.

John W. Young (ed.), *The Foreign Policy of Churchill's Peacetime Administration, 1951–55*, Leicester University Press, Leicester, 1988.

Index